THE UNITED STATES
AND THE PHILIPPINES

The American Assembly, *Columbia University*

THE UNITED STATES
AND THE PHILIPPINES

Prentice-Hall, Inc., *Englewood Cliffs, N.J.*

A SPECTRUM BOOK

301.2973
A512w

Current printing (last number):
10 9 8 7 6 5 4 3 2

Preface

The present edition of *The United States and the Philippines* is intended primarily for the general reading public, for colleges and universities, and for participants in American Assembly sessions everywhere on this subject. Edited by Dr. Frank H. Golay of Cornell University, the volume was first published in a limited edition as background reading for the participants in the Philippine-American Assembly at Davao, Mindanao, Republic of the Philippines, February 23-26, 1966. On that occasion Filipinos and Americans discussed political, social, economic, and military issues of the binational relationship and approved a final report of findings and recommendations, which may be obtained in a separate booklet from The American Assembly.

In the entire program on Philippine-American relations The American Assembly has had the advantage of the encouragement and support of the America-Philippines Society. The generous cooperation of the Society is gratefully acknowledged.

Neither The American Assembly nor the America-Philippines Society is responsible for any of the opinions found herein; they are the authors' own.

Clifford C. Nelson
President
The American Assembly

Table of Contents

7 *David Wurfel*
   Problems of Decolonization   149

Frank H. Golay

Introduction:

Restless Partners

This book was organized to provide a background of information helpful to understanding of the complex forces which have moulded the "special relationship" between the United States and the Philippines in the past and which will transform it in the future. Geography, history, self-interest, the Cold War, disparities in size, and in the maturity of nationalism, are realities not to be transformed in our time merely by more understanding; but they aggregate to a reality which cannot be comprehended without understanding. The understanding we seek to promote is not to be realized vicariously by reading these essays, but is indivisible from involvement in which members of both societies challenge their myths and prejudices by seeking further knowledge and fresh ideas.

Americans and Filipinos alike acknowledge that the relationship between their countries is a special one. Further generalizations about the relationship and its "specialness' are more-or-less true, depending upon the validity of the context of explicit and implicit assumptions from which they are derived. Images of the relationship are peculiarly Filipino

FRANK H. GOLAY, *Professor of Economics and Asian Studies and Associate Director, Cornell Southeast Asia Program, Cornell University, received his Ph.D. (Economics) from the University of Chicago. During 1955-56, he was in the Philippines as a postdoctoral Fulbright research scholar, returning in 1960 as a Guggenheim Foundation fellow, and in 1965 as a consultant to the Administration for International Development. Professor Golay is Chairman of the Philippines Council of the Asia Society, a member of the Southeast Asia Committee of the Association for Asian Studies, and during 1965-66, served as visiting lecturer, School of Oriental and African Studies, University of London. He is the author of* The Philippines: Public Policy and Economic Development *and editor of* Santo Tomas Story.

1

and peculiarly American, and, to be precise, are peculiar to the individual concerned. Obviously, the relationship is special to different individuals for different reasons and the satisfaction or restlessness with which the relationship is viewed varies widely in intensity.

Although for both societies the "special relationship" is an integrated whole which adds up to more than the sum of its parts, the day-to-day interactions of Filipinos and Americans—statesmen, tourists, students, Peace Corps volunteers, aid administrators, military personnel, business-men, diplomats, and others—concern parts and not the whole of Philip-pine-American affairs. These parts are exceedingly diverse; they serve many purposes and involve complex interests, they are valued or resented for many reasons, and they have different life spans. Within the whole, we can identify features which are stable because they serve interests recognized by both societies as of vital or major importance, or because they are compensating concessions to which the parties have agreed. At the central core stands the American commitment to defend the Philip-pines, which is presently stable and little challenged in either society. Within the framework of the defense commitment, however, we find that although the basic American access to military bases in the Philippines is stable, the conditions governing that access are undergoing rapid change as Philippine sovereignty is aggressively asserted. Relatively stable and noncontroversial at present are the military assistance arrangements and the Philippine sugar quota in the American market. Currently unstable are the economic aid relationship, the residual of mutual trade conces-sions, and the conditions under which American investors have access to Philippine resources and markets.

Americans, generally, look upon the relationship as special because they believe, rightly or wrongly, that the willingness of Filipinos to stand and be counted alongside Americans in resisting Japanese aggression was unique in the history of colonialism. Believing this confirms them in their confidence that there exists a congruence of interests forged in mutual trust and confidence which for both societies distinguishes the mutual re-lationship from any that might exist with third countries. This image also confirms for Americans their confidence in the enlightenment of American policy toward the Philippines. It was such self-confidence which led American policy makers two decades ago to seek to dictate the es-sential nature as well as the details of future Philippine-American rela-tions in constitutional and treaty arrangements which transferred power.

Filipinos, on the other hand, tend to see themselves as members of a society, subject for over three centuries, which was the first among Asian societies to coalesce in a nationalist movement and, after a prolonged struggle, achieve independence. This independence was compromised, however, by arrangements accepted in the environment of uncertainty which attended the transfer of power after World War II, or which were accepted under duress as the emergence of Communist China promised a hostile international environment. An increasing number of Filipinos recognize the relationship as special because it is the one they are challenged to reshape to conform to the emerging requirements of independence and sovereignty demanded by their nationalist struggle, which they see as incompletely fulfilled.

That history has overtaken their image of the "special relationship" is painfully evident to informed Americans. The detachment of the Filipino society in the face of the American plight in South Vietnam today contrasts vividly with the Philippine response to the crisis in South Korea a decade and a half ago. At that time the two societies were engaged in fruitful economic and political collaboration in carrying out major fiscal, monetary, and social reforms recommended by the Bell Mission of 1950. Today, American aid has dwindled to a fraction of earlier levels and its administrators search for new techniques to recover some part of the past effectiveness of this institution. Although we would be naïve to exaggerate the breadth and permanence of the coalition of nationalist forces which produced the demonstrations before the American Embassy in the winter of 1964-65, the latter are symptomatic of an undeniable decline in American political influence. Similarly, the scope for the participation of American capital and enterprise in Philippine economic development has been drastically curtailed by the vigilant and powerful forces of Philippine economic nationalism.

Once the vicissitudes which characterized the early postwar period of Philippine rehabilitation had been overcome and the United States had dictated various "ground rules" which were expected to regulate affairs with the independent Philippines, she lapsed into a passive role. Subsequently, mutual relations were shaped, for the most part, by Philippine initiative to which the American response, with few exceptions, ranged from passive acquiesence to legalistic resistance, followed by hesitant agreement in the face of Philippine insistence. Such a process ensured that the "special relationship" would be transformed piecemeal and that basic American policies would be nibbled away with insufficient concern for the national goals which initially prompted them.

Americans—the general public as well as those more directly involved—have become aware of the renewed vigor and restlessness of Philippine nationalism. On the other hand, our adaptation to the relentless pressures generated by this force all too frequently has betrayed little understanding of it. In some cases—the jurisdiction issue in the bases agreement is an unambiguous example—doctrinaire resistance to reasonable Philippine demands has been allowed to exacerbate relations and waste the potential gains from inevitable American concessions. In other cases—the "parity amendment" is illustrative—the passive role of the United States has permitted spurious issues and slogans to torment the relationship when they might readily have been removed.

So long as the issue of Philippine independence was unsettled, American policy toward the Philippines reflected an informed national concern manifested through party politics, as the two parties were sharply divided on the question. Once independence was scheduled in 1934, there ceased to exist any widely held, detached public opinion which would serve to ensure the promotion of the national interest. The Philippines is periph-eral to the consciousness of most Americans precisely because it is mar-ginal to any interest which Americans generally recognize as vital. Be-cause this is a fact of life, American policy toward the Philippines for three decades has been dominated by American economic interests in the Philippines and by security considerations identified and assessed by the military. It would be an unlikely coincidence if the national interest should be accurately identified by such a process.

Although the Philippines, by bold unilateral action and determined bargaining, has enjoyed persistent success in redressing the initial imbal-ance the United States sought to impose in mutual relations, this success has not been entirely satisfying. Filipinos are prone to complain that they "are taken for granted" in their affairs with the United States. It seems clear that they are articulating a restlessness with their dependency role. The reaction of the society to this dissatisfaction has been to espouse a vigorous nationalist position in seeking to change the form and substance of the relationship with the United States. Although they experienced al-most unprecedented success in this endeavor, it is not entirely satisfying to many Filipinos because they are tormented by the knowledge that the relationship can never carry for the American society the same relative im-portance that it does for their society. They are frustrated by the suspicion that their diplomatic triumphs may have resulted as much from pater-nalistic indulgence on the part of the United States as from aggressive and astute bargaining and diplomacy on their part.

This record of success also generates a frustrating response among the newly independent states of Asia and Africa within which the Philippines seeks stature and influence. Members of this peer group find the pecul-iarly pragmatic nationalism displayed by the Philippines in the "spe-cial relationship" unrecognizable as nationalism and instead of respect-ing the substantial diplomatic accomplishments, they are dismissed as a denial of Philippine independence and sovereignty. It is this response that Filipinos find puzzling and humiliating and which goads them to renewed efforts to establish the authenticity of their nationalism.

Four Filipinos and four Americans, qualified by diverse research, ad-ministrative, and diplomatic experiences and representing a range of academic disciplines, responded to the challenge to distill from their study and understanding of the two societies the information and insights which each felt would serve the overall goal of this book. In addition to his expertness, each of the contributors has at one time or another had a prolonged exposure to the other country and society. The book has not been dominated by any prescribed point of view, except that the authors were asked to approach their assignments both as scholars and nationals. Although there was no concern for consensus, a pattern of emphasis builds up as the successive essays come to grips with the new Philippine nationalism, which insists on exploring new loyalties and assuming new obligations as Filipinos grope for an Asian identity.

Informed Filipinos and Americans alike will be aware that this survey of relations between our two countries emerged in growing concern for the future of a collaboration—part myth and part substance—which Americans and Filipinos generally have professed to value. The implications of the persistent turbulence and frictions in Philippine-American affairs can no longer be ignored and they are not to be swept away by turgid professions of confidence and trust which are belied by recent history. Mutual interests and obligations are spelled out in the formal compacts between our countries, but they promise to become meaningless if political, intellectual, and social developments continue to erode values and purposes which must be held in common if the "special relationship" is to be more than an illusion.

To assert that affairs between our countries are turbulent is to say that further changes will take place. It behooves Filipinos and Americans, and their policy makers, to understand the forces that are rapidly changing Philippine-American relations in the hope that unnecessary frictions attending this process are minimized. It seems clear that the process of arriving at a relationship which will best serve the two societies is not one of hard bargaining, the results of which can only mirror disparities in strategic power and economic strength, nor does paternalistic acquiescence by the United States promise to be fruitful. At the same time, there is need to sweep away the sterile slogans and clichés which have lost their power to convince—if such power ever existed. Clearly also, the process needs to be protected from special pleading by the variety of interests which in the past have shown little capability of discerning the national interest of their respective countries, let alone the mutual interest. More important, however, is the need for both societies to face honestly the question of the extent and the nature of common interests. Recent history affirms the cogency of this inquiry.

Salvador P. Lopez

1

The Colonial Relationship

In April 1963, during an interview with the Voice of America in the chancery of the Philippine Embassy in Washington, D.C., I was asked if it was true that I had proposed in a speech in Manila that the Philippines abandon its special ties with the United States in favor of closer relations with its neighbors in Asia. What struck me at the time was not so much the question itself as the tone of disbelief, as if to say: "How can any Filipino, least of all a Filipino Secretary of Foreign Affairs, dare even to say such a thing, let alone think it?" Two years later, during a press conference in Detroit, a reporter asked me to explain how it was possible that there should be anti-American demonstrations in Manila, and this also in a tone of pained surprise which seemed to say, *"Et tu, Brute?"*

No Filipino of any sensibility can fail to be touched by these spontaneous reactions of Americans to recent events in the Philippines. If these attitudes were merely patronizing, they could perhaps be dismissed as the product of ignorance. However, they are more likely expressions of injured innocence rebounding from the long-held assumption that the Philippine-American relationship is without parallel in the history of colonization and that nothing can adversely affect that relationship in the predictable future. Such reactions are of a piece with the attitude

AMBASSADOR SALVADOR P. LOPEZ, *Permanent Representative of the Philippines to the United Nations, has served as Under Secretary and Secretary of Foreign Affairs and as Ambassador to France for his country. He received his M.A. (Philosophy) from the University of the Philippines and was a prominent journalist and literary critic before being called to serve in his country's foreign service. In 1941 he received his country's highest literary award for his volume of essays,* Literature and Society. *Long active as the Philippines' representative to the UNESCO, he most recently served as Chairman of the Commission on Human Rights in 1965-66.*

of a member of the American delegation to the United Nations who, having heard me refer to the Philippines during a meeting as a "former colony" of the United States, remonstrated with me afterward to say that the Philippines could more properly be described as a "dependency," since the United States was never a "colonial" power and never, in fact, treated the Philippines as a colony.

The ingenuousness of this view springs from a combination of innocence and ignorance that is not without a certain charm. The Filipino can understand it only by recalling the reverse manifestations of the "colonial mentality" amongst his own countrymen. Both attitudes have long been nourished on the comfortable assumptions that have grown around the relations between the Philippines and the United States—assumptions based partly on the fact that those relations were "special" and partly on the belief that they were "unique." In the context of such attitudes the term colonial when applied to Philippine-American relations, whether before independence or since, would have a pejorative connotation arising from the universal opprobrium which colonialism and imperialism have acquired in fairly recent times.

The "Style" of American Colonialism

The Philippine-American relationship, however, was "special" mainly in the sense that it conformed to no pre-existing pattern of colonial administration by the Old World imperialist powers. The special character of the relationship is best seen in the term "unincorporated territory," which the United States Supreme Court used to describe the Philippines in the so-called Insular Cases. This was meant to indicate not only that the status of the Philippines was different from that of a state of the Union, but also that it was different from that of an incorporated territory like Alaska after purchase or Hawaii after annexation. Although the Philippines was a part of the United States and subject to its jurisdiction, the Constitution did not follow the flag to the Philippines. The Filipino was not an American citizen but a citizen of the Philippines owing allegiance to, and under the protection of the United States. Most aptly was it said that the Philippines was foreign to the United States for domestic purposes, but domestic for foreign purposes.

COLONIZATION BY IMPROVISATION

The consequences of existing in this kind of political limbo were to be felt in all aspects of Philippine life for the duration of American rule. This twilight zone encouraged political and administrative improvisation, which magnified the risks of error even though committed in good faith. Moreover, the imprecise definition of the legal and constitutional safeguards of Filipino rights may have permitted motives of calculated self-interest and deliberate exploitation to influence American policy and conduct in the Philippines. Yet precisely the reverse is usually claimed under the heading of "special relations," to which the quality of uniqueness is often added to emphasize the notion that nothing in the entire history of colonialism quite compares with the generous and high-minded altruism of the American rule in the Philippines. As a first requirement of objectivity, any study of the colonial relationship between the United States and the Philippines is bound to reject such a facile generalization. It must abandon the time-worn clichés and view the relationship, together with its unique or special characteristics, as an integral part of the history of colonialism and imperialism.

Indeed, the basic drives behind the coming of the United States to the Philippines are hardly distinguishable from those that impelled the older imperialist powers of the period. Any observable differences were those of emphasis, not substance. The conquest of the Philippines was the second act in the American drama of the Pacific, of which the first was the opening of Japan by Commodore Perry, and the third, the policy of the Open Door in China. The acquisition of the Philippines resulted from the same impulse that brought about the purchase of Alaska and the annexation of Hawaii—a desire to share in the opening up of trade opportunities in the vast and populous continent of Asia. This created a consequential need for naval bases or stations in the Pacific to help ensure such participation in the face of the established British and Dutch influence and the more recent incursions of the French, Germans, and Russians. Having achieved the conquest of a continent in a little more than two hundred years of expansion, Americans could not be indifferent to the siren voices which urged the United States to have and to hold its share of the political and economic benefits flowing from the exploitation of Asia. Their government, having preempted further European intervention in the affairs of the New World by proclaiming the Monroe Doctrine, now undertook to do two things. First, it proceeded to make the Caribbean an American "lake" where the interests and power of the United States would be paramount. And secondly, it endeavored to make certain that as a Pacific power the United States would not be excluded from the competition for the wealth and markets of Asia as it had previously been excluded from the carving up of Africa. Theodore Roosevelt was the most unabashed advocate of the latter doctrine in the political field, as Alfred T. Mahan was its leading exponent in the strategic field.

In brief, this doctrine rested upon a belief in the so-called "manifest destiny" of the United States as a rising power requiring the commerce of the world to sustain its growing industries, and as the new bearer of freedom and democracy to "benighted peoples" outside the pale of Western civilization. One may choose to emphasize the selfish commercial interests or the benevolent civilizing aims, but in either case, the American capacity to achieve either or both objectives depended, in the end, on the sinews of naval and military power. This fact inevitably provided encouragement to the blatant jingoism which helped to plunge the United States into the war with Spain in 1898.

THE INITIAL ENCOUNTER

The liquidation of the Spanish Empire, which began in 1829 with the liberation movement in South America led by Simon Bolivar, concluded with the liberation of the remaining Spanish colonies—Cuba and Puerto Rico in the Caribbean, and the Philippines and the Marianas in the Western Pacific. But this was not achieved without a certain duplicity in high places which did not scruple to use falsehood and half-truth to arouse popular sentiment against Spain. Another aspect of American policy at this time was the strange indecision regarding the ultimate fate of the Philippines, which was first evident in the attitude of Admiral Dewey toward General Emilio Aguinaldo and which never ceased to cast doubt on American intentions until the approval of the Independence Act in 1934, and even beyond.

The relations between Dewey and Aguinaldo are germane in this context because of the light they throw on the subsequent course of Philippine-American relations. Whether or not Admiral Dewey, or Consul-General Pratt in Singapore, or Consul-General Wildman in Hongkong, did assure General Aguinaldo that the United States had come to help the Filipinos throw off the Spanish yoke and would recognize their independence, is less important than the fact that this vacillation in motives and aims would become a characteristic feature of American policy toward the Philippines almost to the very end of the colonial regime. It is not necessary to accept wholly either Dewey's or Aguinaldo's version of this matter, and thus implicitly brand the other a lie. It is reasonable, however, to believe that there existed no clear-cut understanding between the two men. Being fighting men, each with a job to do, they naturally concentrated their attention on the most speedy means of defeating the common enemy. Dewey's original instruction was to destroy the Spanish fleet in Manila Bay. After winning a major naval victory ten thousand miles from home, he recognized the value of Filipino cooperation in order to hold Manila. He also understood the usefulness and convenience of a naval base in the Philippines. At the same time, he knew that the political decisions were not his to make. Dewey recorded his judgment that the Filipinos were better prepared to govern themselves than the Cubans and he may therefore have believed that the Philippines would not be forcibly annexed but would be set free, like Cuba. However that may be, he acted quite correctly in seeking Aguinaldo's help in defeating the Spanish forces in Manila and in providing him with guns and ammunition for this purpose. This cooperation, however, did not necessarily imply endorsement of Aguinaldo's long-range revolutionary objectives. This was also the attitude of the generals who subsequently commanded the American forces and directed the military government of the Philippines after the occupation of Manila.

For his part, General Aguinaldo felt greatly encouraged by the support of the American military and consular officers. Yet Aguinaldo would have known better than to accept the assurances of these officers as binding commitments on behalf of the United States government. A reasonable interpretation of Aguinaldo's conduct in this affair is that while he received no such commitments from any American in responsible authority, he trusted that, after defeating Spain, witnessing the valor of Filipino troops, and ascertaining the capacity of the Filipinos for self-government, the United States would decide to withdraw its forces and recognize the independence of the Philippines.

In short, there is no warrant for believing Dewey to have been the author and Aguinaldo the victim of a deliberate deception. Both took a gamble on future developments that they could only vaguely foresee and never fully control. They tried, in effect, to "use" each other for their own ends.

INDECISION AND DRIFT

Dewey and his successors were in no position to give any definite commitment for the simple reason that, at that time, they could not have known the intentions of the United States government. There was a profound division of opinion at home. On one side were those who, like Senator Lodge, advocated outright annexation of the islands for the unambiguous purpose of "civilizing the natives" and incidentally extending the frontiers of American power and influence. On the other were those who, like Senator Hoar, opposed the acquisition of an oriental empire by military force as incompatible with American traditions. President McKinley may or may not have gone down on his knees to pray for divine guidance in formulating a Philippine policy, but it is certain that for a long time he was groping for such a policy and did not quite know what to do with the Philippines.

President McKinley's indecision reflected the state of public sentiment. The acquisition of an overseas territory on the other side of the globe was without precedent in American experience. To a great many Americans, the very notion of colonizing a faraway country inhabited by a people of a different race and culture was repugnant. Moreover, there existed no administrative machinery in Washington with trained personnel to direct the affairs of the new dependencies, and many thoughtful Americans were deeply concerned over the unforeseeable consequences of their involvement in the affairs of a nation so far away from home.

In December 1897, referring specifically to the acquisition of Hawaii, President McKinley had said: "I speak not of forcible annexation because that is not to be thought of, and under our code of morality that would be criminal aggression." It is neither just nor necessary to impute hypocrisy to him as within a year events in the Philippines forced him to make vital policy decisions contrary to principles he had avowed. His vacillation in regard to the Philippines was wholly appropriate to the head of a civilized Christian state, but his scruples were soon to disappear in the face of developments beyond his control. In August 1899, he told troops departing for the Philippines: "The Philippines are ours as much as Louisiana by purchase or Texas or Alaska." Nothing succeeds like success, and the swift victory of American arms confirmed the faith of Americans in their "manifest destiny" and the clamor grew for the extension of American power and influence in the Pacific.

Meanwhile, Aguinaldo, with the blessings of Dewey, who gave him arms, was consolidating his leadership of the revolutionary forces, winning battle after battle against the Spanish troops until he laid seige to Manila itself. On June 12, 1898, he proclaimed the independence of the Philippines, and on June 23 the Constitution of the Provisional Government, of which he became the head.

Although some of the more sophisticated Filipino leaders probably mistrusted Dewey's intentions from the beginning, most of them sincerely believed that the Americans had come to aid the Filipinos in their struggle for independence and would sail away as soon as this goal was achieved. Numerous incidents in rapid succession, however, had the effect of heightening mutual suspicion and hostility between Americans and Filipinos. However well disposed the Filipino leaders might have been toward the Americans as allies and liberators, the latter's conduct during the fighting before Manila in August convinced them that they had misjudged American intentions. While welcoming Filipino cooperation in taking Manila, the Americans made it clear that they would not allow Filipino troops to enter the city. Worse still, the latter were told to move back from positions around the city which they had helped to capture.

THE DECISION MADE

The annexationist trend of American policy became more clearly evident during the negotiations (from which the Filipinos were pointedly excluded) for the Peace Treaty, signed in Paris on December 10, 1898, by which Spain ceded the Philippines to the United States for $20 million. On January 4, 1899, President McKinley issued the so-called "Benevolent Assimilation Proclamation" which made it clear that the United States intended to retain the Philippines unconditionally. This was followed by the appointment on January 20, upon the advice of Admiral Dewey, of the Schurman Commission to investigate conditions in the Philippines and to recommend steps "to facilitate the most humane, pacific, and effective extension of [American] authority throughout the islands."

The Philippine response to these actions consisted of a series of moves by General Aguinaldo to strengthen the political basis of his authority while maintaining at the same time an impressive revolutionary force in being. During the negotiations for the peace treaty, he sent Felipe Agoncillo to Washington and Paris in a vain effort to obtain a hearing for the Filipinos. Forced out of Manila, Aguinaldo, on September 15, 1898, called a meeting of the Revolutionary Congress in Malolos and organized a cabinet which included some of the ablest and most distinguished Filipinos of the time. On January 5, 1899, he issued a proclamation protesting President McKinley's proclamation of the previous day as constituting an "intrusion by the United States Government in the administration of these islands." This policy of defiance was mainly the work of Apolinario Mabini, political philosopher and strategist of the Revolution.

By the time the Schurman Commission was appointed two weeks later and before it could reach the Philippines, the lines were drawn and conflict became inevitable. Significantly, the Philippine-American war broke out the night of February 4 and the news was received in Washington barely a day before the Senate ratified the Treaty of Paris, by only one vote more than the required two-thirds majority. Without reviving the pointless debate about who started the war, the sequence of the two events and the closeness of the vote clearly suggest that the timing of the outbreak of hostilities may have been calculated to influence the vote in the Senate. No less significant was the tie vote in the Senate three weeks earlier, on January 11, on a resolution presented by Senator Bacon disclaiming any intention on the part of the United States to exercise sovereignty over the islands and asserting instead its determination, upon the establishment of an independent government, "to leave the government and control of the islands to the people." The deciding negative vote was cast by Vice President Garret. These two close votes showed that there was substantial and broadly based opposition within the United States to the conquest and annexation of the Philippines. After the outbreak of hostilities, this popular movement centered around the Anti-Imperialist League.

REVOLUTION RESUMED

But neither were the Filipinos unanimous as regards the future of their country. While the revolutionary leadership was committed to the struggle for an independent republic, there were elements that favored outright annexation leading to ultimate statehood, or a protectorate status under the United States. Still more interesting is the fact that some of the leaders of the Revolution, if not Aguinaldo himself, actually entertained these as alternative relationships on which to fall back in case the United States should refuse to leave voluntarily or could not be pushed out by force.

There was bound to be a hardening of positions, however, as the day of decision approached. In the end, President McKinley, despite his well known misgivings and doubtless influenced by the enthusiastic public response to the emergence of the United States as a world power, accepted and propagated the notion that it was "only the Tagalogs, one of eighty tribes inhabiting the islands," who were opposing American rule, and that the forcible extension of American sovereignty over the archipelago was "in accordance with the wishes and aspirations of the great masses of the Filipino people." For his part, Aguinaldo, whatever else he might have been willing to consider as an acceptable compromise, had reached a point where he had no option but to fight for the survival and recognition of the Malolos Republic.

Thus, the initial encounter between Aguinaldo and Dewey that initiated the "special relationship" so auspiciously in May 1898, degenerated in less than ten months into a major armed conflict between two presumed allies. The superior power and resources of the United States foredoomed Filipino resistance to defeat, but not in shame. The determination of the Filipinos had been grossly underestimated and by their valor they won the grudging respect of their adversaries. Nor was their sacrifice wholly in vain. It would stand as a constant reminder, which the Americans would never be allowed to forget, that independence was the only just and proper destiny for the Philippines.

The struggle lasted more than two years, in some areas long after the capture of General Aguinaldo on March 23, 1901, and became one of the most bitter and bloody wars in the history of colonization. Admiral Dewey later wrote in his autobiography: "The growing anger of the natives had broken into flame. Now, after paying twenty million for the islands, we must establish our authority by force against the very wishes of the people whom we sought to benefit."

Toward Self-Government

The American colonial rule may be divided into four distinct periods: 1899 to 1913, between the ratification of the Treaty of Paris and the end of the Republican Party control in Washington; 1913 to 1921, the period of the Democratic Party tenure; 1921 to 1934, between the appointment of Governor-General Leonard Wood and approval of the Tydings-McDuffie Independence Act; and from 1935 to 1946, comprising the Commonwealth regime, the Japanese occupation, and terminating with the inauguration of the Republic.

Under the American party system, colonial policy inevitably became an issue in the struggle between the two major parties. As regards the Philippines, a conservative Republican tradition emerged which contrasted sharply with the opposing liberal Democratic tradition. The Republican tradition, rooted in the McKinley policy of annexation and "benevolent assimilation," found its best expression in the Taft slogan of "the Philippines for the Filipinos" and in the declared intention "gradually to extend to them, as they show themselves fit to exercise it, a greater and greater measure of self-government." The absence of any reference to independence was deliberate, and the word did not occur in official Republican policy statements until many years later, and then only in vague or equivocal contexts. On the other hand, the Democratic tradition grew out of the presidential campaign of 1900 in which the Democratic candidate, William Jennings Bryan, was nominated on a platform which explicitly condemned imperialism and called for the recognition of the sovereignty and independence of the Philippines. The Democratic policy achieved its highest expression in the preamble of the Jones Law of 1916 which proclaimed "the intention of the people of the United States to withdraw their sovereignty over the Philippine Islands and to recognize their sovereignty as soon as a stable government can be established."

Nevertheless, the genius for improvisation and the pragmatic spirit of American politics permitted these two policies, which apparently were contradictory, to direct and propel the political development of the Filipinos without nullifying each other. After immediate independence and statehood, the two extreme solutions, were foreclosed at the beginning of the American occupation, the preparation of the Filipinos for popular self-government over a shorter or a longer period of time became a commitment of Republicans and Democrats alike. During the forty years that followed, there would always be a perceptible difference in emphasis and style between a Republican and a Democratic regime in the Philippines, but it would never become such as to arrest or permanently divert the progress of self-government. The generous idealism of Governor Taft, the friendly complaisance of Governor Harrison, and the heavy-handed authoritarianism of Governor Wood provided interesting contrasts in the unfolding pattern of development, but the broad meaning of the pattern was never really in doubt. In the end, the two policies converged in the approval by the United States Congress of the Tydings-McDuffie Independence Act of 1934 which, like its predecessor, the Hare-Hawes-Cutting Act of 1933, enjoyed bipartisan support in both houses.

LEARNING BY STRUGGLE

It would not be correct to infer from the foregoing that progress toward Filipino self-government was the exclusive result of benevolence on the part of the colonial power. The three-year Philippine-American war had demonstrated the existence of a strong Filipino desire for independence which sporadic acts of altruism and periodic grants of political autonomy would not quench. Aguinaldo's successors, Manuel L. Quezon, Sergio Osmeña, and Manuel A. Roxas, were to pursue in peacetime the goal of the revolution against Spain and of the war against the United States —Philippine independence. In effect, the Philippine insurgency had meant simply that the Filipinos bitterly dissented from the McKinley thesis that they were incapable of self-government and needed to be trained by the Americans even against their will. After the Filipino revolutionary leaders were finally defeated in the battlefield, the colonial regime sought to mollify Filipino aspirations by appointing to the Taft Commission three distinguished Filipinos, all of them known "Americanistas" who favored permanent annexation in one form or another. But these men clearly stood outside the mainstream of Filipino political aspirations, and their pretensions to leadership were quickly rejected by the people. In 1907, when the elective Philippine Assembly was established, it was not they but the younger nationalist politicians who won control of the chamber and thus became the acknowledged leaders of the Filipino people. Nor would the idea of permanent political ties with the United States be revived, except briefly during the campaign for the Independence Acts of 1933 and 1934 and during the first years of the Commonwealth regime when dominion status was proposed and promptly discarded as an alternative to independence.

Despite clashing personalities and conflicting ambitions, which caused power to seesaw between Osmeña and Quezon during the next thirty years, these two men would become inseparable allies in the sustained Filipino struggle to terminate American rule. Alternately or together they would use every argument or stratagem to win concession after concession from the colonial power, to expand Filipino autonomy in all fields, and to maintain at a high pitch the popular clamor for independence. By tactics of non-cooperation and obstruction, or of ingratiation and cajolery, as the situation required, they advanced the national cause steadily. Meanwhile, even as they acquired increasing skill in the continual skirmishing with the colonial administration, they were also hastening the political training of their own people through the organization of an effective party system as an essential element of representative government.

STYLES OF COLONIAL ADMINISTRATION

The contrasting administrations of the Wilsonian appointee, Governor-General Francis B. Harrison, and of his successor Leonard Wood, who extended the Republican "return to normalcy" to the Philippines in 1921, represented, in different ways, notable deviations from the normal course and rhythm of Philippine political development. It is hardly surprising that American political historians generally consider Wood to have been the best of the Governors-General after Taft, while the Filipinos confer that honor on Harrison. A good case can be made for the idea that the two administrations, in fact, complemented each other and that the Filipinos profited from the bipolarization of colonial policy which they represented. There are those who believe that Governor Harrison Filipinized the government too fast and aroused the appetite of the

Filipinos for autonomy somewhat beyond their capacity to digest properly each new concession. It is nonetheless true that shortcuts and a certain amount of "cramming" are not necessarily undesirable in the political development of nations, since they sometimes provide a challenge to responsibility and act as a goad to effort. Governor Wood, in his turn, tightened the laxities in administrative discipline that had developed under his popular predecessor, and if he had kept to this laudable purpose he would have received broad support on both sides of the ocean. Unfortunately, he made the mistake of trying to halt the inexorable progress of Filipino autonomy, basing his actions on the letter of the very law which made a stable government the necessary prerequisite of independence. The Filipino leaders saw clearly that to freeze autonomy meant, in effect, to postpone independence indefinitely. Quezon, therefore, fought Wood with the passion of a man who saw the latter's campaign for good government as something more than an implied reflection on Filipino capacity for self-government, and that it could be invoked to invent an excuse to renege on the solemn promise of the Jones Law.

The steady advance toward Filipino autonomy and independence thus resulted from the confrontation between an American colonial administration which desired to achieve good government through self-government, and a Filipino leadership for whom self-government was a good in itself. The broad spectrum of the colonial relationship may be seen in the contrast between the classical Quezonian statement of nationalist defiance: "I prefer a government run like hell by Filipinos to a government run like heaven by Americans," and the other revealing statement attributed to the same source but made in private: "The trouble with the Americans is that they do not oppress us nearly enough!"

STEPS TOWARD AUTONOMY

Despite policy improvisations and basic differences between the two parties in "styles" of colonialism, the progress of Filipino autonomy runs along a fairly straight course from the beginning to the end of the colonial regime. The Philippine Commission, initially headed by William Howard Taft, which in 1901 had made the first gesture toward Filipino aspirations by including a minority of Filipinos in its membership, began in 1907 to share legislative powers with the popularly elected Philippine Assembly. This arrangement, however, led to frequent deadlock and consequent paralysis in government, faults which were not to be cured by a subsequent decision to appoint a majority of Filipinos to the Commission. In 1916 the Jones Law replaced this system with a legislature of two chambers, both elected by the people. In addition, the executive authority of the American Governor-General was exercised through department secretaries all of whom, with the exception of the Secretary of Public Instruction, were Filipinos. Upon the establishment of the Commonwealth government under the Independence Act of 1934, the last step toward complete self-government was taken, with a unicameral National Assembly (replaced in 1940 by a bicameral Congress), a popularly elected Filipino President, and a High Commissioner exercising on behalf of the United States government certain residual powers over foreign affairs, defense, and currency.

There is a certain symmetry in the evolution of Filipino self-government. The Jones Law of 1916 stands at the exact midpoint between the Schurman Commission of 1899 and the Tydings-McDuffie Independence Act of 1934; in other words, it took two equal periods of seventeen years each, first, to lay the groundwork for internal autonomy, and secondly, to lay the foundations for a stable government in preparation for independence. It was a long period by the standards of the postwar United Nations theory and practice of instant decolonization, but a short one by the standards of nineteenth and early twentieth century imperialism.

WHAT MIGHT HAVE BEEN

It is tempting to dwell on what might have happened if any one of the various moves in the United States Congress to free the Philippines before 1946 had succeeded; for example, if the Treaty of Paris in 1899 had been rejected, if the Bacon amendment had been approved, or if the tie vote on the Clarke amendment to the Jones Law of 1916, which provided for Philippine independence in not less than two years nor more than four years, had gone the other way. Filipino historians are prone to point out that the Malolos Constitution compared favorably with the Constitutions of the United States and the Latin American republics, and to draw the inference that the Filipinos, left to themselves, would have succeeded in establishing and maintaining a free and united republic on sound democratic foundations. But, however excellent it may be on paper, the Malolos Constitution can hardly be said to reflect faithfully the degree of political consciousness and maturity of the masses of the people at the time nor to have grown directly out of their experience and aspirations.

The Revolution and the revolutionary government were led by a small elite of politically conscious intellectuals, most of them members of the learned professions, who were able to articulate the grievances of an oppressed nation without necessarily bespeaking its traditions and ideals. Philippine society at the time, in common with Asian society in general and with Malay society in particular, had an essentially oligarchic base, and three centuries of Spanish rule had given it an even more distinctly authoritarian cast. Almost inevitably, the Malolos Republic would have reflected these traditional premises of Philippine society. It is reasonable to suppose that the Philippines would have developed a political system resembling, on the one hand, the self-perpetuating oligarchies of Latin America and, on the other, the "guided democracy" of Indonesia. In addition, the young Republic would have been confronted almost immediately by regional challenges to its authority, in particular, by serious separatist movements in the Visayas and in Moslem Mindanao and Sulu. The American colonial rule had the effect of moderating the impact of these internal pressures, thus permitting the new Philippine society to develop along more democratic lines and to acquire a more lively sense of national identity.

SHORT COURSE ON DEMOCRACY

Ralston Hayden wrote in 1926 that the Filipinos "utilized the political powers which they were granted to obtain an ever greater control over their own affairs," and that "many of their measures bear a striking resemblance to those by which Anglo-Saxons have always resisted political authority imposed upon them without their consent." In other words, the political struggle became of itself an important element of the political education of the Filipinos, particularly since few if any of the essential elements of representative democratic government can be said to be inherent in the Asian or the Spanish tradition. They learned by struggle, kept what they won, and valued what they learned. In a sense, the Filipinos had to telescope into forty years the lessons of the English Magna Carta, the American Declaration of Independence, and the American Constitution.

The achievements of the American colonial administration in health, education, and public works are generally acknowledged to have few if any parallels in the history of colonization. These stand out even more graphically against the meagre Spanish record in these fields. But no less important are the principles and practices which the American colonial regime sought to graft upon the Filipino political tradition: observance of civil liberties, especially freedom of speech and of the press; respect for the independence of the courts; separation of church and state; preservation of a civil service based on the merit system; maintenance of fiscal responsibility; establishment of a representative government based on the popular will; and adherence to the rule of law.

Lacking these principles and institutions, democracy in the Philippines would be inconceivable, and none of them except, perhaps, for the civil service which reached a high stage of development in Imperial China, is indigenous to Asia or to the Philippines. In forty years of colonial tutelage and twenty years of independence, the Filipinos have succeeded in making these a vital part of their heritage. While it is perhaps possible that they would have accomplished this by their own unaided efforts in an equivalent period of time, the experience of other countries that have recently made the sudden leap from colonialism to freedom and independence without preparation militates against this assumption. In many countries of Asia and Africa, the tendency following the sudden withdrawal of the colonial power has been for the peoples to revert to their tribal patterns of political, economic, and social organization. The shorter their contact with Western ways and traditions, the greater has been their inclination to abandon these in favor of their own traditional ways. The question remains whether the principles and institutions of Western democracy and representative government, whatever their merit, are necessarily adaptable to the experience, character, and aspirations of the great majority of the peoples of Asia and Africa. Amongst many of them, Western political forms have become little more than a transparent mask for authoritarian regimes of one type or another. Amongst others, even such an outward pretense has been discarded, and the reversion to absolute despotism has been complete.

THE PHILIPPINE PATTERN

So far as the Philippines is concerned, however, such a regression to pre-Spanish or even to Spanish patterns of political, economic, and social organization would be inconceivable. It would be repugnant to the great majority of Filipinos, who have come to regard the principles and institutions of democracy as an essential element of their political existence. However, they have no cause for complacency. Although apparently sound and sturdy, these principles and institutions are constantly exposed to attack, erosion, and decay. The ancient traditions of oligarchy and authoritarianism lie very close to the surface of Philippine life. The prevailing economic and social system remains hospitable to a recrudescence of these traditions. At the same time, the Constitution of the Republic, like the Malolos Constitution, sets up one of the most powerful executives of any democratic government in the world. While this may be a valid response to the need for national discipline and for a strongly centralized, unitary system of government, it also offers a standing invitation to dictatorship.

The Western-style democracy of the Filipinos, like their Catholic religion, has acquired certain qualities of the race and the native soil. Just as their Catholicism has struck adventitious roots in the animistic traditions of their forebears, so their democracy has developed a special patina as a result of exposure to the tropical air and sun. Their politics display a certain frenetic quality that partakes of the exuberance of their town fiestas, and partisan feeling is as bitter as party loyalty is fickle. Political principles and institutions patterned on American models, such as the principle of individual rights and the conduct of political party conventions, have assumed an exaggerated, larger-than-life reality. The lenient application by the courts of the laws on libel and slander has helped to give the widest possible berth to freedom of speech and of the press, justifying the claim that the Philippine press is one of the most uninhibited (if sometimes irresponsible) in the world. On the other hand, the familiar phenomenon of the "cultural lag" is manifested in the tendency for the Philippines to adopt and maintain policies—"free enterprise," for example—in their pristine form, long after these have either been abandoned or radically transformed in the United States.

The American Record

One of the more glaring failures of the American colonial regime was the absence of any conscious effort to develop self-government and self-reliance at the level of the *barrio* and the town. Contrary to its own traditions, the colonial power chose instead to make the small local units almost totally dependent on the insular government for projects and undertakings of all kinds. At the same time, suffrage was for a long time so narrowly restricted to a small group of educated Filipinos or wealthy property owners that the orientation of the regime was bound to be conservative, if not reactionary. By its tacit alliance with the Filipino economic elite, the American colonial regime acted as a damper on the Filipino revolutionary spirit, and postponed to a much later day all important initiatives for the transformation of Philippine society.

Given the character of American society itself after the turn of the century, the United States could hardly have been expected to carry out in the Philippines a radical program of economic and social reform. It would have been illogical for the burgeoning capitalist society of the McKinley-Roosevelt-Taft era to initiate any action likely to encourage revolutionary economic and social changes in the former Spanish colony. Under American as under Spanish rule, the liberal elements in the colonizing power had little or no power to influence colonial policy. Indeed, even where policy reflected the enlightened will of the metropolitan government, there frequently was an attempt—at best misguided and too often sinister—on the part of the colonial administration to thwart the magnanimous purpose of the sovereign power. Those who held the reins of economic power both at home and in the islands ultimately dictated, through their allies in the political and military establishments, the nature and direction of colonial policy.

Nowhere was this link more clearly evident than in the economic policies of the colonial administration. This fact explains why the American record in promoting the economic progress of the Philippines does not match the American performance in the political field. This contrast is heightened by the comparatively meagre results achieved in the two important areas of agrarian reform and economic development. In the end, this failure tended to negate the substantial achievements in self-government, since an economic system shaped from abroad by the requirements of the metropolitan power and dominated at home by a conservative landowning class could hardly have provided an appropriate foundation for sound and stable political institutions.

THE NEGLECTED PROBLEM: AGRARIAN REFORM

The timidity with which the colonial regime confronted the agrarian problem arose mainly from its inability to provide informed leadership in initiating and carrying out necessary reforms. Having no relevant experience, the colonial administrators in Washington and Manila were little inclined to apply the necessary pressure on the Philippine government to engage the entrenched power of the *cacique* landowners. They were overawed by the sacrosanct principle of the right of private property, and tended to support the landowners' summary view of all tenant protests and uprisings as acts of communist radicalism and violence or of sheer banditry, which needed to be suppressed in the name of public order.

In a legal sense, the root of the difficulty lay in the provision of the Treaty of Paris by which the United States undertook to respect the property rights of private persons and of civil and ecclesiastical bodies in the ceded territories, including the Spanish royal grants and friar lands. There was a good case for refusing this undertaking and leaving the matter to future determination within the framework of the economic and social progress of the islands. The interruption of the Philippine Revolution had forestalled the certain confiscation of these lands by any revolutionary government that would have been set up. Rather than yield to pressure by Catholic and other vested interests on both sides of the Pacific, the United States could have declared these vast landed estates reverted to the public domain after three centuries of exploitation. The alternative was to perpetuate a system rooted in injustice and greed.

The Filipino participation in the government, however, must bear its share of the responsibility for this failure. A legislature dominated by landlords and their allies blocked from the beginning the passage and enforcement of measures of land reform initiated by progressive elements among the Filipinos and in the American administration. Thus, the Rice Share Tenancy Act of 1933, which sought to protect the tenant farmers from the abuses of the landlords, was first emasculated by the latter's legislative allies and then effectively nullified by them through tactics of evasion and obstruction.

The United States can claim one achievement of lasting value, although essentially negative in character; through the limitation of individual homesteads to 144 hectares and of land purchase by corporations to 1024 hectares, the public domain was protected from exploitative large-scale alienation and the land was thus preserved for future generations of Filipinos. The Philippines was spared the dubious advantage of agricultural development achieved under the plantation system prevalent in some neighboring countries, which called for massive infusions of foreign capital and alien labor. The Filipinos benefited from this policy, ostensibly motivated to protect the patrimony of the Filipinos but at the same time serving the interests of the American beet sugar industry which traditionally sought to prevent the growth of a highly competitive sugar industry in the Philippines.

COLONIAL TRADE POLICY

The American failure to encourage a balanced and diversified Philippine economy was due to a short-sighted policy of pressing for immediate commercial advantage—a policy that would persist through the period preparatory to independence and beyond. This required the riveting of the Philippine economy to the American economy through free trade arrangements between the two countries. These arrangements originated in one of the goals outlined by the Taft Commission in 1901, namely, the opening of the islands to commercial development by American capital. Although the United States, under the Treaty of Paris, was obligated to admit Spanish merchandise into the Philippines on the same terms as merchandise of the United States for a period of ten years, ways were found to favor American manufactured goods. This policy was implicit in the provisions of the first Tariff Act adopted by the Philippine Commission in 1901, confirmed by the Philippine Tariff Act adopted by the United States Congress in 1902, and firmly entrenched in the so-called free trade relations established between the two countries in 1909 over strong Filipino opposition.

These free trade preferences inevitably encouraged the production of major cash crops—sugar, copra, abaca, tobacco—to the detriment of the rice industry, tradition-bound and landlord-ridden, until today the Philippines is a chronic food-deficit area. At the same time, the heavy influx of American manufactured goods led to the decline of native handicrafts and developed in Filipino consumers a predilection for imported, and especially American goods. The result was a colonial economy of the classical type which made the country an important source of raw materials and a heavy importer of manufactured goods. Emphasis was laid almost exclusively upon the raw material and extractive industries, while light consumer goods industries and power production received minimal encouragement. The free trade arrangement, which called for a combination of free tariff and fixed quotas, had the further adverse effect of discouraging efforts to diversify and increase agricultural production. In the end, this colonial-type economy developed a certain mystique of its own, including an entire system of conservative values based on the certitudes of land ownership, the non-risk mentality of the pawnshop owner, and the closed family enterprise system, which combined to postpone industrial development.

American economic policy in the Philippines was essentially inspired by short-term considerations. Once the political decision was taken to grant independence to the Philippines, the United States government and American business enterprises seemed to be absorbed almost entirely in an effort to protect or promote American interests rather than to ensure conditions which would enable both countries to pursue their common ideals and interests. The negotiations attending the grant of independence became a complicated and none-too-subtle interplay of selfish motives and magnanimous intentions, so that it was hard to say when the Tydings-McDuffie Independence Act was finally approved in 1934 whether it represented the triumph of American idealism or of the American dairy and beet sugar interests.

CULTURAL AND SOCIAL PROGRESS

Outside the domain of political activity and self-government, the outstanding American achievements in the Philippines lay in public health and education. The control or eradication of the deadly epidemic diseases of the tropics—smallpox, cholera, leprosy, bubonic plague, beriberi, malaria, rinderpest—was made possible by the dedicated leadership of great American public health administrators like Dr. Victor G. Heiser. As a result of their work, the life expectancy of the Filipino rose steeply from 14 years in 1900 to 40 in 1940, and is today one of the highest in Asia.

In education the achievement was equally outstanding. In 1903, at the inception of the American occupation, the literacy rate was 44 per cent of the population ten years of age and over; in 1918, it rose to 49 per cent; and in 1948, two years after independence, it was almost 60 per cent—again, one of the highest in Asia, although the ratio of those functionally literate clearly is substantially smaller than the measure of formal literacy. It is worth noting that this progress was achieved despite the fact that the problems of education were rendered even more difficult and complicated by the decision to use English as the medium of instruction in the public schools.

THE LANGUAGE ISSUE

Filipinos who had their entire schooling during the American regime and learned their three R's in English may be startled by the thought that there could have been any other possible medium of instruction at the time, considering the multiplicity of Filipino languages. But there was. Filipino children could have been taught to read and write in their own native language during the first four years of school, reserving the teaching of Tagalog and English to the fifth grade and beyond. In this way, there would have been the possibility at least of making every child permanently literate in his own tongue, even if he later dropped out of school, while ensuring that Tagalog would eventually become the national language, and English the medium of communication with the international community and of contact with the best that has been thought and said in the world.

The debate on the language question is not new. It began during the early years of the American regime when colonial administrators like N. M. Saleeby questioned the wisdom of imposing on the Filipinos a language that was totally alien to them, and with which their own tongues had no affinity. Dr. Saleeby explained the decision to use English as the result of an instinctive and irresistible impulse on the part of the thousands of American officers and teachers who felt a deep moral obligation at the end of the Philippine-American war to help in the reconstruction and progress of the country and for whom the use of a tongue other than their own would have been impossible. He considered this to be a mistake, however, holding that the principal Philippine languages are in fact sister languages, as closely related to each other as are the Romance languages. He saw clearly that the choice at the beginning of the colonial regime of one of these—Tagalog, for instance—as the national language would have resulted in a more rapid increase in functional literacy, a more efficient educational system, and a stronger sense of national unity, while accelerating the development and enrichment of the national language itself.

The choice of English would have been justified if it were possible to ensure the employment of a sufficient number of American teachers in Philippine schools for an indefinite period of time, and if it were probable that the Philippine languages would eventually be supplanted by English as the common language of daily life among the people. Both conditions were impossible of fulfillment. The result of the mixture of English, Tagalog, native vernacular, and now Spanish as well, in Philippine schools has been the conversion of our educational system into a Babel of tongues. By enormously complicating the learning process, this policy has doomed the majority of Filipino students to be hardly literate in the national language based on Tagalog, as well as in his own vernacular, if other than Tagalog, virtually illiterate in English, and almost totally illiterate in Spanish.

This is not to question the undoubted value of English as a great and useful language and as the instrument by which the Filipinos have come to know and imbibe the enlightened libertarian traditions of the Anglo-Saxon peoples. The values inherent in English have left their mark on the intellectual and cultural life of the Filipinos. They have developed a vigorous journalism and a literature of some distinction in English, and the native genius of the Filipino will continue to find in this language a responsive instrument for creative thought and imagination. Nevertheless, this limited achievement of the few, however valuable to itself, hardly compensates for the maleducation of the many.

Beyond the use of English in the schools, there seems to have been a none-too-subtle intention to make the Filipino the "little brown American of Asia"—as avid a consumer of American ideas and ideals as he would be of American goods and services. It seems strange that a progressive and industrial America should have omitted to emphasize in the

Philippines the vocational, technical, and scientific skills which it knew from its own experience to be required by a developing industrial economy. Today, somewhat tardily, the Peace Corps volunteers are trying to make good the omission of the "Thomasites," who came at the very beginning of the American regime, by bringing to the rural areas some of the vocational and technical skills so badly needed by a developing country with a fast-growing population and an economy at the take-off stage of industrialization. Ironically, the quality of English being taught and learned in the Philippines today has so badly deteriorated that we could profitably use in our schools some of the old Thomasite emphasis on good English, oral and written.

APPETITE FOR EDUCATION

Education remains the Philippines' greatest hope and the people's appetite for education, especially for general academic education as distinguished from technical or vocational education, remains insatiable. Although it is the most important single activity of people and government, standards have seriously deteriorated, and technical training remains inadequate. While Filipinos are solely to blame for allowing this situation to develop and continue, the American colonial administration must accept its share of responsibility for the initial policies that determined from the start the general character of education in the Philippines.

One of the most salutary influences of the American educational system in the Philippines lies in a wholly different field. The avidity of the Filipino for education was proverbial even during Spanish times. The more the Spanish rulers kept education from him, the more deeply he thirsted for it. His desire for education is matched only by his respect for learning. The best-loved Filipino heroes were writers, journalists, poets, and the greatest of them all, José Rizal, was a physician, poet, novelist, and linguist. It is this great hunger for education which, in the end, will prove to be the salvation of the Filipino. From it has come his rejection of obscurantism and his acceptance of the rational and scientific spirit. This is the Filipino's best credential for effective participation in the life of the modern world, and Americans have a right to take credit for having helped him to receive and treasure this priceless boon.

Out of the Past . . .

Contrary to the spirit of its own tradition, lacking any experience in colonial administration, and in disregard of the expressed wishes and resolute heroism of the Filipino people, the United States embarked in 1898 upon an unprecedented colonial adventure that would alter the course of its own history. The Civil War, by preserving the Union, had ensured that the United States would continue to prosper upon a solid foundation of federal authority, while the steady expansion of the Republic until it spanned the vast continent from ocean to ocean foreshadowed its emergence as a formidable power of the modern world. But it was the conquest and acquisition of the Philippines which first planted and then nourished in the American soul the evangelical zeal for good works and the taste for power. The American presence in the Philippines, lasting nearly fifty years, foreshadowed the constructive goals of the American occupation of Japan, the generous American aid program to underdeveloped countries, and the resolute American defense of South Korea and South Vietnam.

The colonial relationship between the two countries was given its special character by the fact that at the time of their encounter, the United States differed as much in historical background and experience from the European colonial powers as the Philippines differed from the neighboring colonial territories in Asia. Spain, Portugal, Britain, France, and Holland each had more than three centuries of colonial rule behind them. With practically no rules of law to inhibit them, these powers had pursued the classical goals of imperialism, namely, to occupy and hold territories inhabited by "backward races" for the purpose of material profit, political domination, or to gain merit in heaven. By the end of the nineteenth century, the practice of naked imperialism had begun to fall under the influence of more benign principles. Without abandoning the belief that the advanced Western nations had a mission to organize the world politically and to diffuse as widely as possible their laws, customs, and institutions, the European political philosophers had begun to advance the idea that the government of backward peoples was a "sacred trust" which imposed on the colonial powers a dual obligation to the native peoples and to the world at large. The phrase later passed into current usage and is used in the Charter of the United Nations.

By the time of America's entry into the circle of imperialist powers, therefore, the era of uninhibited imperialism had come to an end. Humanitarian considerations had begun to moderate the policies of the colonial powers. In the case of the United States, its approach to the task of administering dependencies was further conditioned by its own experience as a former colony that had been driven by oppression and misrule to fight for its independence.

The Philippines, the other party to the encounter, was equally unique among its neighbors. It had undergone three hundred and thirty-three years of Spanish rule, and in the process had emerged as a Christian community with a national identity forged, ironically enough, by the self-same highly centralized and oppressive colonial rule which the Philippine revolution sought to overthrow. The British in India, the Dutch in Java, and the French in Indochina had generally followed a common policy of leaving intact the system of government, the cultural institutions, and the social customs and usages of the native inhabitants. Thus, they permitted the kings and princes to keep their titles, ranks, and ceremonial prerogatives, while the real power of government was in the hands of the colonial administrators. By disturbing as little as possible the existing patterns of social organization among the indigenous peoples, these colonial powers hoped to keep them docile and hence easier to dominate and exploit.

Spain, on the other hand, followed an entirely different policy. Earnestly believing that they had evolved a better system of government and a better social organization than any other people, and that they possessed the only true religion in the world, the Spaniards proceeded to abolish the titles and privileges of the royal families and the nobility, establishing in their place a system of local government based on limited suffrage, similar to that which existed in Spain. They converted the people, eventually gave them Spanish names, replaced the native script with the Roman alphabet, destroyed the vessels of the ancient native culture. Like Mexico in the Americas, the Philippines was to be a New Spain established on the soil of Asia.

When the Americans came to the Philippines more than three hundred years later, they found a relatively homogeneous people, with a developed sense of national consciousness, professing for the most part the Roman Catholic faith, recognizing the authority of a central government, and regulating their individual and social conduct under established legal codes.

With extraordinary prescience José Rizal in his masterly historical treatise, *The Philippines a Century Hence,* foresaw in 1889 the possibility that the "great American Republic, whose interests lie in the Pacific and which has no hand in the spoliation of Africa, may someday dream of foreign possession," and attempt to wrest the Philippines from Spain. Rizal correctly predicted that the United States would be a formidable rival should it join in competition with the colonial powers aggressively extending their empires in the last half of the nineteenth century, but he rejected this prospect on the ground that to do so would be "contrary to its traditions." Aguinaldo and Mabini shared this belief but, unlike Rizal who was martyred by the Spanish, they lived to see it disproved.

This remarkable study, written nearly a decade before Dewey sailed for Manila Bay, should have been prescribed reading for President McKinley and Senator Lodge, as well as for the American generals and colonial administrators. They might have been enlightened and even chastened by Rizal's forthright prediction that if America ever attempted to supplant Spain in the Philippines, the Filipinos "will defend with inexpressible vigor their liberty secured at the cost of so much blood and sacrifice." Equally instructive was his blunt affirmation that "colonies established to subserve the policy and the commerce of the sovereign country eventually become independent," and that "history does not record in its annals any lasting domination exercised by one people over another of different race, of diverse ways and customs, of opposite and divergent ideals."

Toward the Future

To recall the elements of the historic encounter is to understand the origins of most of the current problems between the Philippines and the United States. These problems have their roots in the failure to recognize the symptoms of the long trauma inflicted by foreign rule on the Filipino mind and soul. The Filipino, the most Westernized man of Asia, usually succeeds in giving the impression that he is quite proud and happy to wear the political and cultural finery of his former masters. But this son of Asia is never really at home in the West, and now that he is free of foreign rule, he is often driven by nostalgia to revisit the ancestral home of the spirit and to rediscover his national identity. Although he is grateful for the illumination which Western thought and science have brought into his life, and while he recognizes his dependence on American power for his security, he feels a need to belong to Asia, to be accepted in Asia. The ambivalence of the Filipino is one of the significant facts of life in Southeast Asia.

Behind the ambivalence lie the surviving remnants of the colonial relationship. It is unfortunate that, on the eve of independence in 1946 as during the early years of the colonial regime, American policy appeared to emphasize, not the rehabilitation of the Philippine economy so as to strengthen the foundations of an important ally in Southeast Asia, but rather the protection and promotion of American strategic and economic interests. American policy makers led by Paul V. McNutt, the last American High Commissioner and first American Ambassador to the Philippines, seemed to be more interested in securing parity rights for Americans and ensuring American control of the greatest possible number of military bases in exchange for minimal payments of war damage and Filipino war veterans' claims than in assisting a war-ravaged nation to rebuild its educational and cultural institutions and to rehabilitate its economy. Although the situations in conquered Japan and the liberated Philippines were hardly identical, it is noteworthy that the reform of Japanese political and economic institutions was undertaken with comparatively more sympathetic consideration and vigorous assistance during the brief American military occupation of that former enemy country.

The tragedy of the spotty American record during the pre-independence negotiations with the Philippines was that the questions of parity rights, the status and extent of military bases and criminal jurisdiction within the bases, Filipino veterans' rights, and war damage payments, would prove to be deep and persistent irritants in relations between the two countries. The Filipinos, motivated by sentiments growing out of their wartime comradeship with the Americans, expected their views and claims to be accorded utmost generosity. In this they misjudged the temper of the American negotiators, who approached the question of mutual relations in the postwar period on the basis of a cool assessment of the national interest and accordingly made few if any concessions to sentiment.

No one was more keenly aware of the disparity in the approaches of the two countries than Vice President Elpidio Quirino, who conducted the negotiations on behalf of the Philippines. He spoke for a nation dazed, torn, and bleeding from enemy occupation, and he was hopeful that the powerful feelings of comradeship aroused in the common re-sistance to Japanese invasion and in the subsequent liberation would carry the negotiations safely across the shoals of conflicting national in-terest. On the other hand, his counterpart, High Commissioner McNutt, spoke for a country that had emerged from the war the richest and most powerful in the world, with expanded global interests and responsi-bilities. The disparity in power between the two countries could only have been bridged by deep understanding nourished by a spirit of magnanimity. The failure to build such a bridge in 1945-46 was to inspire in later years the nationalistic fervor—mislabeled "anti-American"—with which Senator Claro M. Recto denounced the patent inequities in Philippine-American relations. Still later, it would generate the power-ful clamor—including the unprecedented demonstrations before the American Embassy in Manila—for revision of the Military Bases Agree-ment.

Filipinos must accept and adapt to the fact that they are involved with Americans in an unequal partnership. Although it may be true that a genuine partnership can exist only between equals, it is nevertheless pos-sible to establish a relationship between unequals that does not require mendicant subservience as the inevitable complement of overwhelming power. The unequal partnership becomes tolerable to Filipinos only if a deliberate emphasis on partnership serves to redress—and obscure—the basic inequality.

This is the only kind of "special relations" to which Filipinos and Americans should aspire. In the context of contemporary Southeast Asia, it is perhaps the only kind which they can meaningfully develop. It is not for Filipinos to say what America's role in Asia, particularly in South-east Asia, should be, but they would be derelict as partners if they failed to express the hope that it will be a role compatible with the traditions that have made America great, as well as with the just aspirations of Asian peoples to dignity, freedom, and well being.

Filipinos must fulfill their destiny by finding themselves and by being themselves. Having regard to the vicissitudes of their history, this is bound to be a difficult task. It will involve loyal acceptance of their responsibilities as Asians and active participation in the life, work, and destiny of Asia. It will require them to abandon the habit of regarding the Western elements of their heritage as things that set them, not merely apart from their neighbors, but above them as well. They should not be expected to flaunt in the face of their neighbors the ideals, principles, and ways of life which they share with the West, but quietly to live by them and to cherish them for as long as they derive sustenance from them.

Americans and Filipinos should abandon the fatuous idea that the Philippines is the "show window of American democracy in Asia." This is not merely pretentious and, at best, only partly true, but it creates an unflattering image of the Philippines as an American political super-market in Asia, constantly risking ignoble failure if customers, who may suspect a neo-colonialist snare of some kind, do not queue up at the door. The related notion that the Philippines serves as a "bridge between Asia and the West" also places a heavy strain on the capabilities and resources of the Filipino nation which may have little desire to take on this role, being content to be itself, at peace with its neighbors and in fruitful co-operation with them. Filipinos can best serve the principles and purposes they share with Americans by avoiding a self-conscious and deliberate intent to promote them amongst their neighbors. The true merit of these principles and purposes will be made manifest only through good works and worthwhile achievements.

This, then, is the only kind of partnership possible between the United States, heavily saddled with responsibilities for the freedom, security, and prosperity of the free world, and the Philippine Republic, determined to rediscover its national identity within the framework of a free, secure, and prosperous Asia. The disparity in power and influence between the two countries cannot be made to vanish by any kind of emotional leger-demain, but it may be held within manageable proportions by a reasoned understanding of their common interests and purposes. The essential in-gredient in such a relationship is mutual respect, which has nothing to do with the arrogance of the strong or the insolence of the weak, but with the honest recognition of the true interests of each and of the various ways in which these interests fall together and coincide.

Thomas R. McHale

2

The Philippine Society in Transition

Internal development—encompassing social, political, and economic changes—has played a critical role in shaping the pattern of Philippine relations with the United States. The interaction of internal development with external affairs, particularly with the United States, has reflected the accelerated erosion in traditional institutions and values and the emergence of new ideas, organizational forms, and national goals, many of which are subsumed under the term "nationalism."

This essay will not attempt to analyze all facets of Philippine modernization which impinge directly or indirectly on Philippine-American affairs; rather, it will sketch the broad outlines of those specific social and cultural trends—many of which are common to all developing countries—which have fundamental political ramifications. Three more-or-less self-evident propositions establish an appropriate point of departure. First, significant changes in social, economic, or cultural spheres are rarely isolated from political changes. Second, although purposely sought objectives motivate major changes in any nation, autonomously generated forces of change frequently have been of even greater importance. Third, of all factors leading to change in the Philippines, none has been more fundamental than the growing need to restructure an increasingly large segment of the society, economy, and polity on a base other than agriculture.

THOMAS R. MCHALE, *Executive Vice President, Victorias Milling Company, Negros Occidental, Philippines, received his Ph.D. (Political Economy) from Harvard University. He was first in the Philippines with the Naval Air Corps during World War II and subsequently returned for various periods as graduate student, research scholar, economic consultant, and corporation executive. He is the author of numerous articles on Philippine social and economic problems and history.*

The Interwining Complexities

Analysis of the matrix of cultural values, social roles, and technical skills underlying any modern political system emphasizes the complexity of the political development process. Typically, and almost by definition, substantial gaps exist in developing societies between the "requirements" of social, cultural, and technical resources embodied in the human factor which are necessary for optimum internal development, and the "availability" of such resources. It is abundantly clear that formal constitutions, enlightened reform legislation, access to massive foreign aid, and the "paper exercises" of development planners can have little impact when organizational and technical skills, as well as the cultural acceptance of an appropriate role for government, are lacking. Modern governments can exist and mature only where attitudes and behavior patterns provide at least minimal support to the institutionalized political process. To look at political development in isolation from the broad changes that permeate all aspects of the social environment, therefore, is unrealistic. Neither the "economic man" nor the "political man," of Western literature, exist as basic building blocks for the political economy in newly developing countries, and thus the valid image of political development can emerge only in understanding the complex of social changes peculiar to the society under scrutiny. In the context of Philippine political development, resources and attitudes necessary to ensure a political structure functionally specific to government responsibilities remain inadequate, despite rapid changes that have been initiated over the past three decades.

The influence of cultural and psychological constraints is manifested clearly in the elements common to political and economic development. In terms of organizational theory, it is apparent that modern political parties with functional roles unrelated to particular individuals, and large-scale business enterprises geared to a market economy, require a cultural base with organizational forms and values extending beyond those kith and kindred ties that circumscribe most traditional activities. Despite the obvious differences in roles and functions, modern politicians, administrative bureaucrats, and large-scale entrepreneurs are cut from a common socio-psychological cloth. Moreover, the same factors which limit the growth of open-stock corporations, modern labor unions, and large-scale cooperative credit instrumentalities also restrict the development of modern political parties, effective governmental administration, and successful economic planning.

PURPOSEFULNESS IN DEVELOPMENT

Although political development is never wholly and is rarely, in large measure, the result of purposefully sought political objectives, the process always involves the emergence of goals, the pursuit of which relates to control over political institutions and the uses of "legitimate" power in the society. In most developing areas, the purposefully sought goals are generated in a narrowly based segment of the population, but as development goes on they usually involve an increasing proportion of the population.

Obviously, in any concrete situation, political objectives and autonomous transitional pressures continuously interact. Obvious also, no two developing countries share the same set of circumstances bearing on modernization, nor do they follow identical detailed or sequential paths. Nevertheless, similarities appear which warrant general analysis of development. The Philippines is groping for progress toward broad "purposefully" sought political development goals which tend to be universal in developing societies. For example, persistent efforts are made to shift attention from "local" to national problems and their solutions, and to absorb many small and highly personalized power loci into a larger national polity. Similarly, uninterrupted initiative confirms the longing of the society for government not confined, as at present, to minimum provision of social services and such custodial functions as maintenance of law and order, but performing a promotional role which explores and develops the potential contributions of communal consumption and services, social overhead capital, and direct government participation in production. Self-evident is the goal of economic development, with major dimensions of expanding welfare, power, and prestige for all or part of the nation. It should surprise no one that industrialization is frequently used by Filipinos as a synonym for economic development. Directly related is the priority for economic diversification, often stated in terms of the transformation of the "colonial-type" export economy to a more diversified economic base. Still another essential ingredient of national economic development is the redistribution of the capacity to generate wealth and income, usually away from foreigners and resident aliens and their enterprises, in favor of Filipinos. Finally, the observer is struck by the energy and ingenuity which is applied to creating and legitimizing new instrumentalities on both the political and administrative levels for resolving conflicts and proposing goals.

The dichotomy between the "means" and the "ends" of political development is not a simple one. In many situations the "means" of political decision making become an end of the development process; and the pursuit of "ends" necessitates continuous adaptation of the "means." For example, changing the patterns and organizational loci of power in the pursuit of political development usually involves broadening the base of power while narrowing the instrumentalities through which power is exercised. Similarly, it is rarely relevant to distinguish industrialization, as the means to economic development, from the universal goals of social organization—welfare, power, and prestige.

THE UNWILLED CHANGE: THE RATIO OF MAN TO LAND

Fundamental structural change is underway in most developing areas in the size and organization matrices of populations and the relationship of these to an agricultural land base. Agricultural peasant societies, in many cases, have reached limits to the historic pattern of mitotic, "more of the same," expansion in which population growth has merely increased the number of small face-to-face kin groupings within which almost all significant social, economic, and political relationships are maintained. As a result, among the changes which accompany development is a shift away from the omni-functional role of kin groups and a comprehensive restructuring of society within organizational forms that functionally are more discrete, flexible in size, and increasingly independent of the heretofore dominant kin-ordered forms.

A close look indicates that Philippine development is accompanied by, and geared substantially to a steadily increasing population and the growing incapacity of existing agricultural land resources to support it. Support in this context involves two overlapping dimensions; the utilization of available labor, in the sense of providing a socio-economic niche for individuals in agricultural production, and which, at the same time, offers assurance of economic returns sufficient to meet existing, but inevitably expanding, consumption levels. The term does not imply a physiological dimension, despite the alarming references found in both the popular and pseudo-scientific literature on the subject. The limits to the capacity of the Philippine resource endowment to "feed" an expanding population cannot be identified so long as technological advance is unpredictable. Such an inquiry would be irrelevant, moreover, as the previously specified dimensions of the concept of "support" establish prior limits to the land resources required for orderly economic development and social stability.

Because most Filipinos exist psychologically, as well as physiologically, close to a subsistence level, land has become a unique social, political, and economic factor around which other aspects of rural life tend to orbit. Land is the key factor of production and source of wealth, and basic social relationships, the status hierarchy, and the ethos of the culture are closely linked to the control and use of the land. This is in direct contrast to industrial countries where land is a minor component of aggregate wealth and is considered only one of several important variable input factors of production, all monetarily measured and allocated by market processes. Agricultural land is the base for an all-embracing way of life for the peasants, who comprise the great majority of Filipinos. Within the peasant culture few relationships are structured on monetary considerations; and limited specialization, almost no alternative employment possibilities, and a cultural attitude toward time that can best be described as "sometime" oriented are prominent and stable features.

Upon leaving the rural peasant milieu, however, the Filipino becomes involved with specific monetary relationships, development of technical skills, increasing functional specialization, possibilities of social mobility, impersonal markets, and "time" as an important dimension of economic activities. Those who leave the rural areas—whether attracted away or forced out—usually forsake the security of a traditional, ascribed role in the peasant culture for a life that requires constant adaptation of behavior to new people and situations. For such Filipinos, family and kindred cease to be the sole legitimate locus of social, economic, and political activities, the unchallenged source of values, and the focus of loyalties. New, multiple, and diverse values and loyalties emerge as the individual's role and status become more dependent on his function and income in the market place.

While a small but steady stream of Filipinos has been attracted to the urban areas in this century, a growing number are now being forced to seek their future outside of the agricultural sector. Circumstances, rather than design, produced this exodus, but the result has the same effect as the pull of population to the towns and cities by the promise of better things. Political development in both direction and speed is closely tied to the resulting erosion of the Philippine peasant culture.

Population: Quantitative and Qualitative Changes

Population growth by itself and in relationship to agricultural resources, appears to be the most basic and important factor of change. The estimated population of the Philippines in 1965 of 32,300,000 is more than quadruple that of 1896 and over double the 1939 population. Today, Filipinos outnumber the combined populations of Canada, Sweden, and Norway.

The growth of population has been accompanied by the almost complete disappearance of unoccupied frontier agricultural lands in the Philippine lowlands. Until the 1930s, population growth could be absorbed with little economic and political impact. Structurally, the society consisted of a small, largely urbanized, power-holding and power-wielding group on top and, on the bottom, a highly fragmented and apathetic peasantry that could be either manipulated or ignored. The peasant culture expanded mitotically; as increases in population led to cell-like growth in which the traditional centripetally structured social, economic, and political relationships were constantly reduplicated in the newly opened land areas in the form of new peasant family units. This pattern of land settlement is confirmed by the relatively constant modal size of Philippine lowland farms, the unchanging agricultural technology, and the assimilation of such frontier areas as Nueva Ecija, the Cagayan Valley in Luzon, and the Cotabato Valley in Mindanao to a pattern of cultural typicalness, including extensive tenancy, small farm units, social fragmentation, and class bipolarization.

The inexorable arithmetic of the man-land ratio cannot be denied. No official estimate of the labor force in 1965 is available, but projections of reliable estimates for 1963 suggest that it totaled approximately 11.5 million persons. Land that can be cultivated totals, probably at the very most, 10,000,000 hectares. Approximately 7,500,000 hectares, including practically all the arable lowland areas, are now being utilized. The arable man-land ratio, using cultivated plus potentially cultivatable land, works out less than one hectare per labor force member for 1965.

The low availability of land relative to labor, alarming enough in the aggregate, also must be related to the fact that the average Filipino farmer, using traditional tools, techniques, and a single *carabao* (water buffalo), can handle about 2.5 hectares of lowland rice land, the most important of the labor intensive agricultural activities in the Philippines. With two *carabaos* he can almost double this figure.

Currently, there is no significant tendency—or clear opportunity—to shift to more labor-intensive techniques or crops in the Philippines. If such a move developed, it could hardly be expected to do more than absorb the high level of underemployment in rural areas rather than open up new employment opportunities. Finally, the bleakness of any objective assessment is compounded by the fact that most of the potentially arable, although still uncultivated, land remaining in the Philippines is unsuitable for such a labor-intensive crop as lowland rice, and is usually devoted to crops with far lower labor input requirements.

Under no system of cultivation now practiced in the Philippines is the economic return from less than several hectares sufficient to provide a laborer with an "adequate" level of earnings comparable to that established as a legal minimum industrial wage. Increasing material aspiration levels can be met by the average Filipino farmer only by a substantial increase in productivity. Conceptually, such an increase might result from new, land-saving technology; but presently such a tendency does not exist. Alternatively, it might result from increasing the amount of land the peasant has under cultivation, but this clearly cannot result from the settlement of the remaining unoccupied land.

In the absence of a substantial increase in non-agricultural employment, it will be difficult to maintain, let alone improve, the existing man-land proportions. It is also obvious that farm mechanization, rationalization of current traditional agricultural practices, or the introduction of labor-saving technology is likely to intensify rather than mitigate the problem of the unfavorable man-land ratio. Unemployment and underemployment—the very terms were practically unknown in the pre-World War II Philippines—have rapidly emerged as critical social and economic and, ultimately, political problems of the nation. There can be no concealing the fact that a large and rapidly growing segment of the population is faced with increasing poverty on the land and without alternative opportunities off the land.

URBANIZATION

Corollary to the large and rapid increase in population, and its impact on the labor picture, has been a movement from outlying rural areas to Manila and other urban centers. Part of the urban growth has resulted from population growth, but the increasing proportion of the urban population is explained by internal migration. Recent sample surveys in Manila indicate that approximately half of the city's residents were born elsewhere, with a far higher percentage of the adult working-age population born in the provinces. This same pattern appears to hold for all the urban or semi-urban areas.

By far the most important urban area is metropolitan Manila, with a population growth substantially above that of the Philippines as a whole, and over twice that of the rural villages or *barrios*. In addition to the increasing proportion of Filipinos living in metropolitan Manila, there has been a somewhat less rapid, but still significant movement of Filipinos into the chartered cities, provincial capitals, and municipalities or *poblaciones*. Over the fifty-seven years between the first reliable census of 1903 and the recent census of 1960, the average annual population growth of metropolitan Manila was 4.34%, of the chartered cities and provincial capitals, 3.98%, for the *barrios*, 1.77%, and for the entire country, 2.16%.

The increasing importance of Manila as the nation's primate city has been both a cause and result of its relatively more rapid absolute and percentile growth. Less than 250,000, or just over 3 per cent of the total Philippine population, lived in Manila and its suburbs in 1903. By 1960, the total metropolitan population of Manila was 2,100,000, or 7.7 per cent of the nation's population.

In addition to its substantial growth, both absolute and relative, Manila has continued to be the dominant entry point for new ideas, people, products, and services. It has also become the hub of widely enlarged governmental power, the center from which mass media are dominated, and the only significant industrial area. The primacy of Manila is so complete that intellectual and ideological movements in the Philippines rarely exist for any prolonged period independent of the city; and political influence is increasingly associated with bases in the power syndrome of the city. The tendency for provincial governors and municipal mayors either to maintain a residence in Manila or to spend a good deal of their time in the city, is but one manifestation of this fact of political life.

Manila's urban ferment contrasts sharply with the timelessness of the *barrio*, although adaptations have prevented a complete erosion of traditional values and attitudes in the city. Traditional means of structuring interpersonal relationships in the rural Philippines, however, are clearly inadequate for growth, or even survival in the city. While new patterns of individual behaviour and a new set of organizational forms are emerging in the city, the lag in the emergence of new institutions and in the process of human adaptation prolongs the estrangement of the members of the urban proletariat, who can be described most accurately as proto-urban rather than urban.

In the rural areas of the Philippines, as has been noted, it is not only possible but highly probable that almost all of an individual's significant social and economic interaction takes place within a relatively small group. Typically, this small in-group consists of individuals related by blood or ritualistic kinship, all well known to each other; performing roles and deriving status, in large part, in accordance with an inherited, stable, formal ordering of social relationships. Urban living, on the contrary, requires interaction with a constantly changing and ever-widening number of individuals, many of whom are external to an individual's area of primary trust. In such interaction, individuals typically have no recognizable status, as such, but are mutually related only through functionally specific roles.

SOCIOLOGY OF URBANIZATION

Growing urbanization has forced an increasing number of Filipinos to adapt themselves to diverse functional relationships, frequently of a transient nature, rather than permanent relationships within a small kin group encompassing most aspects of life; it has thus opened up new opportunities for many, as well as creating new problems. Urbanization usually is associated with a sharp increase in organized crime; juvenile delinquency; social problems concerning the aged, the indigent, and the physically handicapped; and rapidly growing problems of mental health. Recent preliminary studies suggest that the last problem is now far more acute in Manila than in most urban centers in the West.

Operating in an urban milieu calls for the growing acceptance of specific rights and obligations, and an increasing emphasis on contractual rather than emotional or customary ties. It also involves a change in organizational forms, whether social, economic, or political, and increasing detachment of political activities and goals from the more general and diffuse goals of the household or kindred unit. Most Filipinos moving into Manila and other cities require prolonged periods of time to fit into an urban culture and, in the meantime, remain largely alienated from city life and needs. They are gradually conditioned, however, by the monetary rather than social nature of most activities in the market place and begin to think, organize, and act in new ways.

Rural mores are constantly reinforced by the face-to-face contacts which effectively maintain social sanctions against transgressions of the established "morality." Within a typical lowland Christian rural *barrio*, for example, crimes of passion have been the only important criminal problem; and organized crime, *per se,* is conspicuously absent. The city, however, with its depersonalizing impact and its lack of an effective means to reinforce private morality, has yet to develop alternative means or even an awareness of the need for an effective public morality. Graft in government, for example, is impersonal and therefore frequently is condoned. Since no immediate social sanctions are available to reinforce a public morality, both a grafter and his accusers tend to be opportunistic in their attitudes.

Changing Educational Pattern

Changes in the institutions, coverage, standards, and content of Philippine education have also been significant in the process of political development. Most noteworthy has been the influence of the public school system, staffed, financed, and controlled by the national government, as an agency of political socialization. There are indications that the high positive correlation which has traditionally prevailed between the rural father's political values and attitudes and those displayed by his children, breaks down substantially when children go to school from a household that has no background of formal schooling. This decreasing correlation is most frequently found in urban areas where the average number of years of formal education increases. The explanation is obvious. Kith and kin now compete with the school, where centrally controlled curriculum content and teachers with high status act as carriers of new values and attitudes. The most dramatic indication of this form of political socialization is found in the attitudes and values of many politicians who came from humble backgrounds and were educated primarily under the "Americanized" system.

In addition to the direct role of the school and the professional teacher in political socialization, the effect of increasing literacy should be noted. An illiterate or preliterate society must educate itself largely through oral traditions. The limitations of this means of "education" are clear. Family members monopolize verbal contacts with the typical rural Filipino child and young adult in their formative years. Without functional literacy they must rely on verbal communication for their awareness of their place in history and the means by which they should adapt themselves to their physical, social, and political environment. The kith and kin group had little or no competition in the formation of attitudes and values and in communicating awareness of technological possibilities and the range of alternative political and economic choices, until education and literacy opened non-verbal avenues of information and ideas.

Education and literacy also have had a significant impact on class attitudes, aspirations, and mobility. A comprehensive analysis of these phenomena is lacking, but there are convincing indications of the relative rigidity of a large sector of Philippine rural society. Studies in the 1930s indicated that over half of the tenants in a large selected sample of rice farmers married within their native towns, and over 90 per cent within their native provinces. Marriage patterns indicated that the children of landless tenants invariably married tenants or landless farmers, and less than 5 per cent of the children of peasant smallholders married into the landed proprietor class. More recent studies have indicated increasing geographic and social mobility in areas where education levels and literacy have increased, although such increases are limited.

DIMENSIONS OF GROWTH

The dramatic growth in the number of students is the most important dimension of this major process of change. In 1903 the census reported a total enrollment in all Philippine schools of over 356,000; in 1960, school enrollment totaled more than 5 million. In 1903 less than 14 per cent of the 7 to 17 age group was in school; the figure for 1960 was approximately 35 per cent. Admittedly, a wide gap exists between the theory of legal, compulsory, free primary education and the observance of the law. Nevertheless, there has been a tremendous increase in both the number of the students and the percentage of the school-age population actually participating in the educational process.

Of still greater significance in the educational picture is the increase in the number of students at the secondary level and in higher education. In 1903, less than 19,000 students were in secondary school; and only 436 were at the level of so-called "superior" schools. On a percentage basis, this represented only a minor fraction of 1 per cent of those in the secondary school and higher education age group. In 1960, over 650,000 students were in Philippine secondary schools; and over 250,000 were in university or collegiate level institutions. An additional 50,000 were in various kinds of special vocational schools. This represents about 10 per cent of the respective age groups. A good percentage of the students in the upper levels of education are working for qualifications that are academically worthless and vocationally useless. Nevertheless, this education has the important effect of expanding material aspirations on the one hand and status aspirations on the other. Education, by providing a new symbol of individual prestige, has eroded the existing foundations of social status and authority. It also serves as one of the most important vehicles of political socialization for potential recruits to the power elite.

Expanding Communications

Another important change that has taken place in the Philippines is the growing diversity in the means and speed of communications. A consequence of this is the increasing influence wielded through mass media techniques and the growing importance of control over such media for political manipulation. Increasing literacy is partly responsible for this development. For example, somewhat less than 20 per cent of the Philippine population in 1903 was even theoretically capable of verbal communication in a mutually intelligible language and a far smaller proportion was capable of communication through a mutually intelligible written medium. In absolute numbers, probably less than 10,000 Filipinos were involved at the turn of the century in any serious way with "national" politics at the literate level of awareness.

The number and circulation of newspapers and periodical literature is a good indication of functional literacy. In 1902, the islands had only 12 publications printed in English (which were read almost exclusively by the American community), 24 in Spanish, and 4 in Tagalog. Total circulation for all daily, weekly, and monthly periodicals was 68,236, of which only 3,422 was in Tagalog or other native languages. Not only was there no national press, but there was nothing approaching a national communication system on a technical level. Before the establishment of a telegraph network in the early part of the twentieth century, the dissemination of news took weeks in most areas and months or years in the more remote localities.

THE QUALITY OF LITERACY

According to the 1960 census, over-all literacy has increased to 72 per cent of the population over ten years of age, with approximately two-fifths of the population literate in English or Tagalog, which is the basis of the official "national language." These figures probably exaggerate, to a considerable degree, the extent of functional literacy. Nevertheless, they give an indication of the substantial increase in the number of Filipinos who potentially, at least, are capable of effective participation in democratic policy formation. In absolute figures it seems safe to say that there are 10-12 million Filipinos who have some degree of literacy and probably 3-4 million who are functionally literate either in English or in the national language.

Increased literacy has been accompanied by an increase in publications. In 1960, newspapers registered with the Post Office Department had a combined circulation of six million, over half of which was in English or English combined with some other language. Over 500,000 of the total circulation was on a daily basis. The ten English-language daily newspapers in Manila had a combined circulation of 289,580; Tagalog daily newspapers had a combined circulation of 42,678. The circulation of the weekly *Philippines Free Press,* the most widely read and quoted, and perhaps most influential publication in the Philippines, exceeded 100,000 by 1961. On weekends the total circulation of Manila news and interpretive organs, including Sunday editions of the major English language newspapers, was over 400,000.

The constant exposure of many Filipinos to the influence of the written word is changing the national political process. Today it is possible to ideologically communicate with a significant percentage of the population. The increasing knowledge of political ideas and awareness of policies has produced a wider response throughout society. Political functionaries are increasingly forced to adapt ideas, actions, and reactions to the demands of the national press. Control of press organs has become critically important for those intent upon gaining or maintaining political power.

NEW MEDIA

Other media are also playing an expanding role in the political socialization process. In 1939, there were less than 10,000 dwellings with radios. In 1960, 516,826 dwelling units reported at least one radio in working condition. In 1965, the Philippines had an estimated 1 million radio receiving sets, served by approximately 50 radio broadcasting stations throughout the islands. The increase in the number of radios has been rapid since the transistor radio eliminated the need for access to an electric grid or possession of heavy and expensive batteries. This growth—over fifty-fold since 1939—has enlarged the radio audience to approximately 15 million. The audience, however, is still largely concentrated in the cities and nearby areas. In 1960, almost two-thirds of all Manila households were reported to have radios, but less than 5 per cent of the rural households possessed them.

The use of television has been expanding rapidly since its introduction in 1952. In 1965, the Philippines had eight television stations, six of which were in Manila. Most of the approximately 100,000 sets are concentrated in the Manila area, but a steady expansion of the audience in other areas has now begun. The potential television audience in 1965 was estimated to be around 1 million.

Both radio and television have great potential importance as means of exposing Filipinos to news, ideas, and new value orientations. Several studies made in recent years, however, suggest that radio and television still tend to "entertain" the typical Filipino rather than to inform or orient him. This pattern is changing, however, and all major political factions now seek to control radio and television stations in addition to newspapers.

Movies are also an important medium of communication—but of a different type. The American movies in particular have been a key vehicle of cultural transfer, although the impact has been concentrated in material aspects of culture. Movies produced in the United States and by the domestic Philippine film industry have outlets extending from the Sulu Archipelago to the Batanes Islands. Total annual movie attendance figures are not known, but with some 750 movie theaters it is probably in excess of 50 million.

The fact that the written and spoken word reaches ever-widening audiences cutting across all the traditional barriers of class, kinship, ethno-linguistic identities, and island geography has introduced a new dimension to Philippine political life. The growing capacity to disseminate news and political dialogue widely has meant that appeals of a class or ideological nature have begun to acquire importance. Contemporary Filipino politicians have become aware of the effect of the increasing range and variety of communications. Those seeking national office have felt obliged to develop a national image unrelated to a traditional family-oriented base of power. They are aware, furthermore, that this development which permits the modern advertiser to seek out and develop mass tastes, markets, and response mechanisms, offers the politician a new means of gaining and maintaining power. To an increasing degree, politicians are depending upon public relations techniques and seeking to "capture" mass media to ensure continuation of their political power.

Monetization and the Market Process

The role of money and the market mechanism in the allocation of goods and services, and in the provision of incentives and rewards for Filipinos, has expanded steadily during the twentieth century. The processes of the monetized market economy sustain the individual in his pursuit of welfare and status and serve as the most important means of mobility in the society. The relationships of the traditional society are no longer very important outside the rural Philippines, and money can now buy status and security.

Although statistical evidence is inadequate for precise intertemporal comparisons, the rapid growth in the money supply establishes the outlines of the expanding role of money in the Philippine economy. At the beginning of the twentieth century, the total money supply was approximately ₱35 million. By 1950, the supply had increased to approximately ₱1,300 million. By 1965, it was more than ₱2,800 million, or eighty times the estimated level at the turn of the century. If this figure is adjusted for population growth alone, the per capita money supply has increased more than sixteen-fold. Deflated for the upward shift in prices, perhaps 350 per cent, the per capita money supply, adjusted, is four to five times what it was at the turn of the century.

In addition to the money supply *per se,* there has been a rapid expansion in the diversity and amounts of "near money" in the Philippines and a substantial increase in the velocity of money circulation. Increasing monetization has been accompanied by a rapid proliferation of banks and other financial intermediaries, such as insurance companies and factoring houses. Total assets of the Philippine banking system in 1965, other than those of the Central Bank, were ₱5,000 million. These assets were held by over 1,600 banking facilities scattered throughout the Archipelago. At the turn of the century, in comparison, total banking assets were probably less than ₱20 million, and they were held by 12 banking establishments.

THE POLITICAL IMPACT

Traditional Philippine relationships do not depend on either legal rights or specific contractual conditions for the usual income-flow relationships. Invariably, claims on income are based on the kinship tie and on close personal relationships, and a large part of income is produced in kind and services. Increasing monetization, however, has caused shifts toward a society in which the right to receive wages, or income in the form of rent, interest, or dividends, emerges from expressed or implied promises of individuals or groups to pay money, subject to carefully defined and agreed upon conditions. Such "market" contracts, expressed or implied, do not concern themselves with the contracting parties as such and, therefore, have depersonalized an increasing number of relationships formerly structured by tradition.

Monetization has permitted a greater degree of identification with class and industrial interests. It has given the wage laborer and his employer, for example, an objective means of structuring relationships on the basis of wage payment, which is time-restricted and free from the traditional, diffuse web of social obligations that characterizes the typical pre-money economy. Increasing monetization has also promoted the recognition of new economic relationships in the larger society which form the basis for identification of the individual with special "industrial" interests. Recent decades have seen the emergence of Filipino importer, exporter, and manufacturing interests further subdivided into groups identified with particular commodities or services, such as sugar, lumber, mining, textiles, shipping, and electric power. Such groupings exist to organize and exert political power in support of objectives that benefit groups without a common kincentric identity. Thus, increasing monetization has introduced a new fluidity to society and shifting loci of power.

Monetization has not been evenly accomplished and its effects have stopped short of the *barrio* economy. This has led to the persistence of economic, social, and political pluralism. In Manila, and to some degree in other urban areas, there is a dynamic, market-oriented economy that is responsive to changes in monetary and fiscal policies and composed of elements tending to organize politically on non-kin lines. The *barrio*, on the other hand, comprises a sluggish, non-monetized, production-consumption complex on which national monetary and fiscal policy have little impact, and the social organization remains traditional and kin centered.

Implications for the Special Relationship

The general direction and the rough dimensions of major changes taking place in the Philippine society have been drawn in this essay—but what is the relevance of such changes to Philippine-American, affairs? The answer, at best, can be only a qualified one. Many American and Filipino policy makers, despite increasing knowledge and statistical confirmation of the rapid transition underway, neither recognize nor accept the implications of growth and change. Others recognize change, but are confused by a Philippines which, increasingly, speaks with many voices rather than few; aspires toward a variety of goals that, not infrequently, are inconsistent with one another; and seeks rather than projects an identity derived from a distinctive national self-image.

Central to understanding is awareness of the consequences of the rapid transition in both the nature and extent of communications, which is concomitant to the growth in the Philippine population and its cultural and social transformation. The power elite of the Philippines formerly communicated on the basis of face-to-face contact; and effective control and manipulation of significant changes in the society and polity were largely the product of personal contacts within a numerically restricted circle.

The situation is no longer the same. The vast majority of Filipinos might remain peasants in a social, economic, and cultural sense, and might remain largely unaware or indifferent to the potential for national development. They might continue not to seek to participate in the process through which national decisions are made; and the Philippine nation, *per se,* might rarely involve most Filipinos to any significant degree. Such possibilities are denied, however, by the significant and growing number of Filipinos discontented with their role and their function in a "peasant" syndrome. The stability of the past and the role of the manipulated has no appeal when their new aspirations cannot be realized within the confines of the traditional social and economic structure. Population growth, urbanization, literacy, and education all combine to expand aspirations at a compounded rate. Such changes generate imperative pressures for a body politic structured on an ever-widening population base with a proliferation of competing groups, special interests, and seekers of political power.

American relations with the Philippines have become increasingly complex as more and more Filipinos share power. In the not too distant past, all issues were highly personalized and uncomplicated. The ideas of a few individual political figures like Quezon, Osmeña, Recto, and Laurel defined the alternatives of importance. Steadily, the relative power and influence of specific personalities has dwindled. For example, no postwar president has even approached Quezon's power. More and more, abstract concepts, such as those of nationalism, and policy issues central to the pursuit of material aspirations have become important; and access to radio, the printed word, and television has become a basic prerequisite to effective national political power.

Industrialization, urbanization, and the communications "explosion" have a corollary in the erosion of the traditional Filipino social system. Such a system is dysfunctional in the urban and industrial context, which requires *stateways* rather than *folkways* for survival, and the role of impersonal markets gains importance at the expense of traditional face-to-face relationships.

Industrial development in the Philippines, as elsewhere, requires large-scale organizational forms and a heavy concentration of capital; it also requires a high degree of flexibility, functional specialization, and a heavy measure of contractual order. The traditional Filipino social structure does not provide the base from which these requirements can be secured. It was for this reason that Americans and other foreign residents provided the significant "corporate" activities in the Philippine economy until recent decades. Gradually, however, as Filipinos accumulated capital or gained access to credit, they have entered the industrial field. An increasing number of Filipino corporations have been established and equity transfers have given Filipinos control over foreign enterprises. The result has been the rapid expansion of the Filipino corporate sector, and the clear tendency for such expansion to be promoted and protected by legislation and the administration of economic policies. The resulting appearance of Filipino interests competing at the corporate level has provided a completely new dimension to the Philippine economy and polity.

There is no doubt that in the future the economy will be more and more dependent upon the development of the Filipino corporation. Moreover, the Filipino, as his counterpart in other societies, is bound to make use of his national political position in competitive situations where such an appeal might provide him with an advantage. This has particular relevance to Philippine-American relationships since corporate activities of the past, dominated by Americans, involved the latter in few situations directly competitive with Filipinos, which were delineated by distinctions of nationality.

Corollary to government promotion of the Filipino corporation is the clear rejection of the "logic" of comparative advantage which underlay the colonial economic relationship with the United States. Within this construct, it was assumed that Filipinos were economically better off exchanging the products of their agricultural sector and their labor services in such extractive industries as mining and forestry for the products of industrialized countries. The post-independence spurt of industrialization has involved the rejection of comparative advantage and substitutes the assumption that industrialization, is a more desirable goal for the Philippines. With new tools and new organizational forms, the Philippine society seeks an increasing level of Philippine and Filipino industrial productivity. The pursuit of these goals tends to penalize the import-export segment of the economy in favor of the domestic industrial producer, and to curtail the opportunities of foreign investors.

Insofar as Philippine nationalism rejects extensive foreign control over its growing industrial complex, it must accept and promote a drastically reordered Filipino society. Such a society must take over both the goals and structure of an industrial order. In doing so, it can rely primarily on the private organization of resources, or it must devise institutions of government capable of efficiently organizing, controlling, and operating industry.

One of the great ironies of the evolving situation in the Philippines—and perhaps one of its most confusing aspects—is that Filipinos appear, at least superficially, to become politically more alienated from Americans as they increasingly acculturate to the material and the organizational aspects of things American. American businessmen in the Philippines in the past dealt primarily with Chinese merchant buyers and sellers and a few Filipino officials. Now they not only must accommodate themselves to the Philippine polity but they are forced to compete with Filipinos and their organizations seeking the same material goals as American corporations. Increasingly, these Filipinos are conditioned and organized on the basis of Dale Carnegie courses, the Harvard Business School orientation, and the leverage of chambers of commerce. As corporately oriented Filipino industrial and commercial activities have grown, political power in the Philippines has shifted from the segment of the population whose wealth and income flows are tied to agricultural land, to new elements emerging in the fields of industry, banking, and commerce. Essentially, power has shifted away from those who have historically accommodated themselves and their interests to a set of relationships and attitudes associated with American colonial policy. More and more, power and influence is going to individuals and groups who exploit "Filipino First" or other nationalistic appeals as weapons in the competitive struggle between Filipino and non-Filipino industrial and financial interests.

Concomitant to industrial development is the emergence of Filipino professional managers and technicians who assimilate to their functionally specific roles as the economy diversifies and the polity expands. In all societies—and the Philippines does not appear to be an exception—"managers" gain power over productive and distributive functions as production becomes more complex and industrial units become larger. The emergence of professional Filipino managers and technicians also hastens the erosion of the racial and economic specialization that heretofore has tended to channel Filipino energies into agriculture, Chinese and Chinese-mestizo energies into trade and commerce, and Western energies into large-scale public utilities and industrial processing activities.

In summary, Filipino-American relationships are closely—and increasingly—intertwined with social transition in the Philippines. Filipinos and Americans cannot expect to continue to structure mutual relations on the basis of the interaction of a few individuals and a few vested interests. The size, aspiration levels, and economic bases of the Filipino elite are changing rapidly—and the past offers few guidelines to the future.

Onofre D. Corpuz

3

Realities of Philippine Foreign Policy

If our world were one of self-evident certainties; and if men possessed full knowledge of events, and acted upon that knowledge with reason and objectivity; then the policies and affairs of nations would be wondrously simple things.

But we live in a world of intricate probabilities, and men act upon partial knowledge, as much with will and passion as with reason. Thus, there is seldom a clear and straightforward relationship between the foreign policies of a nation and the reality of objective circumstances and events.

The Limits to Reality

It is tempting to presume that a country's foreign policy is always a response to, or a consequence of, the reality in which the country finds itself. But such a presumption is bound to result in gross oversimplification. Reality itself is subjective as well as objective—there are realities and realities. For one nation, fear is the greatest reality; for another, power; for many, it is cherished myths and alluring causes; for others, it is an aspiration for material well being in some remote future. For all of them, the facts of reality are colored by perspectives and interpretations that themselves are predetermined by subjective visions of national purposes and interests.

ONOFRE D. CORPUZ, *Under Secretary of Education and Professor, Department of Political Science, University of the Philippines, received his Ph.D. (Political Economy and Government) from Harvard University. He has served as his university's Vice President for Administration and Secretary and as consultant to various departments and agencies of the Philippine government. Professor Corpuz is the author of* Bureaucracy in the Philippines *and* The Philippines, *plus numerous articles.*

Not all purposes are achievable, and some are dangerously irresponsible. Moreover, the mustering of national resources and energies in the pursuit of national purposes frequently leads to a reordering of the reality in which a nation finds itself. And societies that discover that reality can be changed, often come to feel that it *must* be changed. No nation, indeed, passively submits to reality. Men and nations view their relations as they regard their relations with nature; the former, like the latter, ought to be constantly improved for the benefit and advantage of men.

What, then, are the realities of Philippine foreign policy? These realities are not to be sought in the immediate and particular situations that exist when the specific foreign policy decisions are made. Rather, they are found in certain circumstances whose influence upon Philippine foreign policy extends beyond the problem at hand and transcends the moment of decision.

Geography Versus History

Among the fundamental and most enduring realities which circumscribe Philippine foreign policy is a kind of indecisive tension between the country's ethnic and physical geography on the one hand, and its modern historical connections on the other. The former pulls us toward the world of Southeast Asia; the latter draws us toward the Western, United States-dominated world. In order to understand the nature of this tension, we must go back all the way to the early sixteenth century, prior to the thrust of the West into Southeast Asia.

By this time, cultural forces from India and Arabia to the west, and from China to the north, had penetrated deeply the Indo-Chinese and Malay peninsulas, and had spread across the Indonesian archipelago. The great religious traditions from the west—Hinduism, Buddhism, Islam—had captured the imaginations of Southeast Asians. Extensive trading and tributary relations had developed with the expansive empires to the west and north, and populations moved restlessly in response to pressures arising in ambition for empire and the opportunities to colonize more hospitable lands. Such factors contributed to the emergence of a "Southeast Asian culture," more or less uniform, within the geographically fragmented regions of the area.

One area—the Philippine archipelago—was largely by-passed by this process of cultural diffusion. The Philippines lay at the extreme end of the overland and offshore routes from India and China, and received, relatively later, and with diminished intensity, a small share of the cultural influences that had transformed other societies in Southeast Asia. In the Philippines, at the end of the fifteenth century, there were no royal or imperial capitals, no seats of great civilizations comparable to those of Angkor, Borobudur, and Pagan.

But if the archipelago was on the periphery of Southeast Asia relative to India and China, it was, in the sixteenth century, the gateway for the penetration of Southeast Asia from the east across the Pacific Ocean. The forces behind the initial penetration were imperial ambition and Christianity, and the vehicle, Spain. The Asian cultural tradition—dominated by Islamic and Buddhist influences—established in the rest of Southeast Asia, including central and southwestern Mindanao, served as a bulwark against the extension of Hispanic influences beyond the Philippines. After three and a third centuries of relative isolation and assimilation to things Spanish, the archipelago was lost by Spain to a contrasting and vigorous branch of the European tradition—the United States.

This history goes far in explaining the ambivalence or dualism—often uncomfortable—in Philippine culture and in the Filipino national outlook. It is inevitably reflected in contemporary foreign policy. For almost four hundred years as a colony, first of Spain and then of the United States, the Philippines faced outward and away from Southeast Asia. It is this reality of the Philippine experience that has been searchingly examined by Filipinos in recent years. The divergent directions given to Philippine aspirations by our Asian geography on the one hand, and by our historical associations with the West on the other, have caused the priorities in our foreign policy to undergo a pendulum-like oscillation.

CONTINUING EXAMINATION

Appropriately enough, the examination started in the 1930s, when independence and statehood could be foreseen. It was then that Filipinos —statesmen and laymen alike—reflected on the alternatives open to the society that was soon to become a nation. The possibility of Japanese expansion was a forceful reminder of the grave problems of independent statehood and emphasized the now conspicuous fact that the Philippines was of Asia. In part, in response to the menace of Japanese ambitions, the idea of a union of Indonesians, Malayans, and Filipinos emerged. In other words, pre-independence contemplation of the nation's future included considerations that may be characterized, with some validity, as "Asia-oriented." Similarly, the wartime anti-United States propaganda from Japan undoubtedly impressed some Filipinos; and its effects upon Philippine foreign policy, although diminished and postponed by Japanese arrogance and brutality, supported new emphasis upon Asia.

The collapse of the United States' presence, and its absence for more than two years, also emphasized the need for the Philippines to find a place in Asia. This was more than offset, however, by the joint Filipino-American resistance on Bataan and Corregidor, the return of the United States forces in 1944, and the postwar dependence of the Philippines upon United States assistance in rehabilitation, which renewed and then sustained the American presence—tangible and intangible.

The "close and special ties" in our relations flourished after independence and were most intense during 1950-57, the period when Magsaysay served, first as Secretary of Defense and then as President. But the omnipresent, although not unsolicited, American influence in virtually all aspects of Philippine policy provoked a logical reaction—which has proved more permanent than a mechanical swing of the pendulum.

Although the Philippines had been independent for more than a decade, the wide-ranging system of political, economic, and military agreements with the United States greatly reduced the range of alternatives and choices that were expected with independent nationhood. Furthermore, the great events of world affairs and international diplomacy during this period opened up new perspectives. Postwar nationalism led to the liquidation of European colonialism in Southeast Asia; Communist China emerged as an ominous new world power; and the American presence in Asia was challenged in Korea and Indochina. The reordering of the postwar world inevitably drew our attention to Asia.

NEW PERSPECTIVES

Our new-found awareness of Asia, reinforced by our suddenly increased contacts with fellow Asians, was a profound experience. We discovered that while the Philippine archipelago was in Asia, our credentials as Asians were suspect. Many Filipinos, in the course of conversations with fellow Asians learned that the latter considered the Philippines to have no foreign policy of her own; that she was merely a puppet of the United States.

Soon after independence, many of us had hoped that the Philippines could make a constructive contribution toward understanding in a troubled world by undertaking the combined roles of representative of Asia to the West, and the interpreter of the West to Asia. Now we ruefully realized how presumptuous were our pretentions to the first role. We realized, with a jolt, that we could not represent Asia because we were not acceptable to our fellow Asians. We came to realize that we were unqualified to speak for Asia because we did not know the histories and cultures of our Asian neighbors. Above all, we came to believe that our alienation from Asia had arisen precisely from our long association with the West. And so, to a growing number of thoughtful Filipinos, escape from this estrangement became a problem which transcended, but strongly influenced, our foreign policy perspectives.

It is against this background that Filipino intellectuals, journalists, and university student leaders of the late 1950s called for a "return to Asia" in national perspectives and policies. "Asia for the Asians" was a familiar slogan for a time. Ultimately, this call could not fail to be reflected in official policy, and presidents Carlos P. Garcia and Diosdado Macapagal—from the two dominant and rival parties—led the country deep into Southeast Asian diplomacy. Garcia, in 1961, initiated the organization of the Association of Southeast Asia, with Thailand, Malaya, and the Philippines as members. Subsequently, in 1963, Macapagal became the chief architect of Maphilindo, in which the Philippines participated along with Malaya and Indonesia.

RETURN TO ASIA

For a time, indeed, the Philippines pursued a new and leading role in Southeast Asian diplomacy. Our claim to North Borneo, and our effort to serve as an honest broker in resolving the difficulties between our Maphilindo partners, promised to continue and augment the auspicious beginnings of Philippine leadership in regional affairs.

But our new initiatives could not be sustained. The Philippine claim to North Borneo led to the breaking of diplomatic relations with Malaysia, and our role as mediator in the conflict between Indonesia and Malaysia became untenable. We relinquished our ambition to exercise leadership in the diplomacy of Southeast Asia even before we had been able to assume such a role. Our relations with Indonesia deteriorated. We had no relations to speak of with Burma, Cambodia, and Laos; we had no ties with North Vietnam; our remaining diplomatic connections were limited to Thailand and beleaguered South Vietnam.

The slackening of our relations with Southeast Asia was succeeded, in 1964-65, by a period of renewed attention to our relations with the United States. These years were featured by controversy over the military bases and the parity rights issue. By the mid-1960s, the hovering shadow of the United States in Philippine foreign policy formulation became conspicuous as Philippine policy in Vietnam was discussed not as an aspect of Philippine policy in Southeast Asia, but as an issue arising from our relationship with the United States.

It is tempting to conclude, in retrospect, that once again our historical connections proved to be more decisive in our foreign affairs than our Asian geography. But this is so only momentarily and superficially. The apparent failure of the Philippine diplomatic initiatives in Southeast Asia was not due to the lesser validity of the realities of our Asian geography. In assessing the events of 1961-63, we must consider not merely the fact of the failure of our initiatives, but we must give due regard to the long-term trends that are discernible in the complex of realities that circumscribe Philippine foreign policy.

NECESSARY CONDITIONS

The failure of Maphilindo is not entirely explained by Sukarno's rigid *Konfrontasi* policy; and the dormant state of ASA was due not solely to the Philippine claim to North Borneo. More fundamentally, these failures were due to the present inadequacy of economic integration and the lack of cultural and political relations necessary to support *intra*-Southeast Asian relations on a continuing basis. The significance of Maphilindo and ASA in Philippine foreign policy lies in the fact that they were recognized as alternatives by a society that was beginning to find its "close and special ties" to the United States too close for comfort and too special for self-respect. It may be granted that economic assistance and the security umbrella provided by the United States are objectively necessary to the Philippines, but they may become ties that bind to the extent that elbow room to explore rewarding and psychologically fascinating foreign policy alternatives no longer exists. Freedom with all its uncertainties is, after all, as necessary as security—to nations as well as to men.

The failure of the return-to-Asia policy was primarily due to the fact that it was premature. Our relations with Southeast Asia, relative to those with the world of America-Europe, are more tenuous and are not sustained by as comprehensive a range of established channels and ongoing contacts. The movement between the Philippines and the West of teachers and students; of commodities and ideas; of credits and investment financing; and the comfortable familiarity of legal and political institutions, are not yet matched in relations between the Philippines and its geographical neighbors. This does not mean that the policy was mistaken, nor does it mean that our relations with Asia must first equal our relations with America-Europe in volume and intensity for the former to flourish. It only means that our relations with our geographical neighbors have to be stimulated beyond their present levels. And this is bound to take place.

PROMISE FOR THE FUTURE

Here we may be suspected of glossing over blunt and conspicuous difficulties. The countries of Southeast Asia are predominantly agricultural and raw materials producing; they therefore lack the complementary features of differentiated economies. But a decade can encompass basic changes in the economic environment. Above all, the recent establishment of the regional Asian Development Bank in Manila, surely to be followed by a regional common market, will contribute to the emergence of a regional economy. The Philippines is well situated to play a leading role in this process, and economic interests, therefore, promise to lead the nation's foreign policy closer to Southeast Asia. Barring a sudden deterioration which could result from escalation of hostilities in Vietnam, we are presently on the threshold of a period in which the necessary economic underpinnings of diplomatic projects, such as ASA and Maphilindo, will emerge.

What are the implications of closer Philippine relations with Southeast Asia for our relation with America-Europe? It is clear that the two are not necessarily incompatible. We long ago gave up the illusion of a self-flattering role as a "bridge of understanding" between Asia and the West. That optimistic vision derived from a self-image that was basically mistaken: an image of ourselves as neither Asian nor Western. We have come to realize how right we were in feeling that we were not Western, for all the overlay of Western elements in Filipino culture, just as we have come to realize how wrong we were in believing that we were not Asian. It is a paradox that our realization that we are Asians began, as it were, with the challenge to our Asian identity by Asians. In any event, it is absolutely necessary that the Philippines develop closer relations with Southeast Asia. We have to do so, not least, in order to develop a counterpoise to the closeness of our relations with the United States.

As for our relations with America-Europe as a whole, more and more Filipinos take them for granted as corollary to economic development, rather than as a threat to the national character. The cases of Japan and other Asian states, such as India, are taken, rightly or wrongly, as examples of successful and selective national adaptation of non-Asian political and cultural elements. These cases, and similar others, are taken as models by our policy makers. Thus, eventually, we can foresee that the tension between our Asian geography and our non-Asian history will cease. It will be resolved—not without friction and controversy—in favor of a basic Southeast Asian orientation accompanied, but not dominated as at present, by selective relations with America-Europe.

"Close and Special" Ties

If geography is a silent reality of Philippine foreign policy, the United States is a constant, conspicuous, and controversial presence. The facts of Philippine-United States relations are so well known and have been so extensively discussed that it will not be necessary to go into the details. In general, these relations are characterized by the now trite formula of "close and special ties."

It has often been suggested that it is in the mutual interest of both countries to maintain these ties. But this is not necessarily so. It might indeed be desirable from the American viewpoint to seek to keep relations with the Philippines close and special, that is, to maintain and consolidate its position on the basis of present arrangements. Certainly the United States maintains its missions and installations under conditions that confer upon American officials and officers in the Philippines greater freedom than they enjoy in other countries. There is a wide range of possible modifications in the terms of United States relations with the Philippines. Such modifications obviously could be carried to the point beyond which further changes would curtail the American position.

THE BASIS FOR POLICY

For the Philippines, on the other hand, the proper object of policy is not the maintenance of its present ties intact, but rather the negotiation of relations, whether close or distant, special or non-special, that confer net advantages upon us. It is in the interest of the Philippines to re-negotiate its ties with the United States for the sole purpose of maintaining present advantages and at the same time loosening and "de-specializing" those ties.

Assuming these considerations to be correct, and assuming furthermore that the present critical re-examination by Filipinos of our mutual relations will continue, future changes will likely be on the side of less close and less special ties. If this analysis is correct, the relationship in the near future is likely to maintain present ties, but with new concessions to the Philippines, meaning that the United States will have to pay a higher price for advantages presently enjoyed. Alternatively, the present ties may be continued intact.

Negotiations leading to either of these alternatives do not promise to be comfortable. With respect to the first variant, it is necessary to bear in mind that concessions are never a solution. Concessions have a way of convincing the recipient that he was right, and the giver wrong. And concessions, in the nature of this case, will always be regarded as long delayed and overdue. With respect to the second, we may safely assume that Filipinos will bring to their re-examination of ties with the United States confidence that changes will favor the Philippines. To them, the United States will appear as the defender of an obsolete status quo. We will tell ourselves that we are promoting a cause, and that the United States is preserving an interest.

CURRENT PRIORITIES

The question of close and special ties with the United States is brought into clear focus by the issues of "parity rights," under which Americans and their enterprises are extended national treatment in the exploitation of natural resources and the operation of public utilities, and also in arrangements for access by the United States to military bases in the Philippines. The terms of these relationships are now widely regarded in the Philippines as unwarranted and unjustifiable impositions. The net effect of "parity" has been, on the whole, an erosion of the Filipinos' belief in the United States' capacity for fair dealing toward her friends and allies. These special rights for Americans were required by the United States Congress in return for war damage payments and special treatment for Philippine agricultural exports to the United States—a fair exchange, except that the Philippines was thereby forced to amend her Constitution. It is now increasingly difficult for Filipinos to understand why the United States government should feel that American businessmen in the

Philippines cannot operate profitably like other foreign businessmen without the privileges of "parity." As for the military bases issue, thoughtful Filipinos who have friendly feelings for the United States are impatient with the United States for obstinately resisting changes in the jurisdictional provisions of the agreement, thereby permitting these provisions to generate unnecessary friction and irritation. The long denial of Philippine jurisdiction over off-base and some on-base offenses became more and more difficult to accept, considering that Philippine courts and patterns of justice are in the American image. Certainly, Philippine justice will compare favorably with recent samples of justice administered by Southern courts in civil rights cases.

The history of popular Filipino reaction to the growing criticism of these resented features of the relationship is instructive. From the postwar years to the mid-1950s, criticism was considered as anti-American and even pro-communist; there followed a period in which it was considered harmless, and tolerated, although critics were regarded warily; since the late 1950s it has achieved respectability and is now accepted as a concomitant of nationalism.

This persistent criticism was part of the prolonged "great debate" initiated by Senator Claro Recto in the Magsaysay administration, which has covered the whole range of issues in Philippines-United States relations. Its persistence suggests that the halo of fairness and rectitude that graced America's image in this country has been tarnished, in the same way that the Japanese victory in 1942, the stalemate in Korea, and events in Vietnam today have obscured the aura of United States invincibility.

THE IMPERATIVE NEED

Different times and changed circumstances demand reconsideration of the treaty provisions covering economic relations between our countries. If the need of the Philippines at the end of World War II was for preferential treatment in the American market and for the security promised by United States bases, even at the sacrifice of Philippine equality and pride, today there exists an imperative need to redeem that sacrifice. Increasingly, therefore, there will be popular pressure upon the Philippine government to demonstrate forthright assurance that Philippine relations with the United States are the result of decisions freely and honorably arrived at. That is to say, that the obligations we assume in consequence of those relations are obligations we assume from free choice, and not burdens imposed upon us by the inescapable circumstances of unequal power. We need this assurance from our government in order that we can fulfill our obligations willingly, and not indifferently or resentfully. More important, we need this kind of assurance in order that we can successfully pursue our foreign affairs where we can most constructively contribute to world peace—in Southeast Asia.

The larger interest of the Philippines in a resolution of current issues in relations with the United States therefore turns upon an essentially psychological need. Filipinos wish to evolve their policies in Southeast Asia without the haunting shadow of real or imagined American pressures on the Philippine government. They want to be able to feel that the military bases arrangements do not impair or violate Philippine sovereignty. As for the parity rights issues, there are economic considerations involved, but the economics of abrogation or termination is still an open question, and equally can mean difficulties as well as gain. On this issue, therefore, the material considerations are not decisive, and the fact that it is referred to as an "irritant" in the relationship between our countries indicates the psychological dimensions involved.

The psychological quality of the Philippine interest in the resolution of these and future irritant issues is sometimes overlooked. In a recent book manuscript this writer had occasion to refer to the fact that the unpaid balance of Philippine war damage claims was an important irritant to Filipinos. The American scholar to whom it was referred for comment inquired: "Since the balance was relatively small ($28 million) why should it be significant?" The answer, of course, was that the amount was important, but only incidental. Filipinos were concerned primarily because the United States had assumed the obligation to pay Philippine war damage claims, but had not discharged its obligation in full some twenty long years after the end of the war.

ILLUSIONS OF A COLLECTIVE PERSONALITY

The contrasting approaches exemplified by this case are seen by Americans—and even Filipinos—as a difference that operates across the entire array of mutual problems. This being so, it has become a phenomenon attracting attention and study by scholars in both societies. Unfortunately, such scholarship has been monopolized by the cultural anthropologists and the sociologists, and the results have been faulted by the parochialism—shared by the social sciences—of these disciplines. Their studies suggest that there is a United States outlook and a Filipino style in the approach to issues. They imply, furthermore, that the American view represents the normal, "rational," and objective way of looking at things, whereas the Filipino view represents a unique and idiosyncratic way of looking at the world.

These implications have been popularized through the scholarship of Americans who have specialized in Philippine studies and who have developed an important following among Filipinos. Their studies have focused attention on significant and esoteric aspects of Filipino behavior and psychology—and therefore interesting to foreign observers. There is nothing wrong in these studies, as such, and the information generated is reliable, but they have been used to support somewhat mischievous interpretations. Thus, the "lowland Filipino" has been pictured as viewing the universe of social relations in interpersonal terms, and as regarding

Philippine-American relations as a system of interpersonal obligations, where the United States is conceived to occupy a father-role.

To the extent that these notions have influenced the Filipino image in the minds of United States policy makers or officials, they have contributed to the discord and confusion which obscures the essential nature of our relationship. The view of the Filipino approach to Philippine-United States relations as unique is relevant only in the sense that the United States approach would also appear unique, if the latter were projected from knowledge of American child-rearing practices, patterns of courtship, marriage and divorce, or to the American value system in the context of race relations, factory mores, and psychoanalysis, to name only a few features of American culture that attract the attention of foreign scholars.

In any event, it is entirely possible that the American scholar's ascription of unique cultural traits to the Filipino is, in fact, a mechanism by which the former verbalizes *his* own image of the Filipino instead of a description of the Filipino image of Philippine-United States relations. This is to suggest that Philippine decisions on matters of common concern with the United States have been conditioned by realities, of which Filipino psychology and behavior are only a part, and that Americans do not realize the narrow limits to the influence of these determinants of Philippine policy.

PRESSURES FOR CHANGE

The nature of our relations with the United States, which have led to "close and special ties," derived from realities of which we were not unaware or unconscious. An obvious and transient reality was our inexperience in international diplomacy in the early post-independence years. More significant, but also unstable, was the credit of good will that the United States earned from the generation of Filipinos that had matured during the colonial years. A comparable reality was the dependence of the Philippine economy upon the United States immediately after independence. Finally, foreign policy has been confined by the lack of sustaining economic, cultural, and political relations with Southeast Asia relative to our close bonds with the United States.

Today, Filipinos have acquired diplomatic experience; a new generation is emerging as a force in national politics; our economy is no longer so dependent on the United States, and, more important, Filipino perceptions of the economic aspects of the relationship have changed; and the attractions of Southeast Asia, whether economic, racial, or romantic, are becoming more powerful each year. In the light of these developments of the last two decades, Philippine foreign policy, in the foreseeable future, will seek to promote deeper involvement of Filipinos in the life and diplomacy of Southeast Asia and a liquidation of the close and special ties with the United States.

The return to Asia will be in response to the forces of technological growth and of the entrepreneurial spirit that are building up in the Philippines; the challenging opportunities for Philippine diplomatic participation and leadership in the search for solutions to Southeast Asian problems, and to a call—which cannot be clarified by analysis, but which more and more Filipinos will be heeding—to live and belong in Southeast Asia. Filipinos can be expected, therefore, to seek psychological relief from every dissatisfaction, every irritant, in affairs with the United States by turning toward the other branch of our historic orientation. Such relief is additional, of course, to the fact that the leverage to be gained from diplomatic successes in Southeast Asia can prove helpful in the settlement of issues with the United States.

The formula "close and special ties," has lost its appeal to many Filipinos. On many occasions—and for diverse purposes—the formula today serves merely to evoke emotional protest by Filipinos; and although sentimental reactions are useful for their cathartic effect, they generally do not help in the resolution of issues. It is therefore noteworthy that in 1965, for the first time, the discussion on parity rights was not limited to the old and sterile demand for "re-examination" or abrogation but that a new approach was suggested, namely, that the Philippines begin taking the necessary measures to cushion her economy from the impact of the termination of preferential treatment of its exports to the United States in 1974. This suggestion is an earnest of the growing realism of the Philippine approach to the important problem of foreign trade, as well as an indication of the intensity of the felt need to terminate parity rights.

As for the issues arising from the jurisdictional provisions of the Military Bases Agreement, their settlement is less within the power of the Philippine government and more within that of the United States. This fact makes the United States in Manila the logical target of protest rallies and demonstrations each time an "incident" occurs. The rallies toward the end of 1965 were the largest and most thoroughly organized in the history of Philippine-United States relations. There is every reason to expect that the experience in organization gained by them will be applied in the future, and we can expect more organized anti-Americanism, as well as more organized pressure on the Philippine government.

In this connection, it is also noteworthy that the Filipino demonstrations so far have been organized in response to accidents involving the shooting of Filipinos by American military personnel. It is not improbable, however, that a future demonstration against the United States Embassy will be part of a deliberate anti-American campaign launched with a planned *incident*.

AN ALTERNATIVE RELATIONSHIP

What would be the picture of Philippine-United States relations with-out "close and special ties"? Provided that parity rights are terminated and that the jurisdiction of Philippine courts is extended to that now exercised by the courts of other countries in which the United States has bases, the scope and closeness of relations would depend on mutual agreements between the two countries. Liquidation of these ties would not mean the severance of relations. It is likely, of course, that there would be difficulties for Philippine export agriculture. These difficulties would increase if, as is equally likely, a Philippine decision to terminate parity rights in 1974 and a Philippine effort to amend her military agree-ments with the United States would be answered by reduction of Ameri-can assistance.

In this connection, it is noteworthy that United States Congressman Clement Zablocki, Chairman of the Far Eastern Affairs Subcommittee, issued a thinly veiled threat of suspension of American aid in early 1966, when the Philippine government was engaged in debate on the question of expanded Philippine efforts in Vietnam. Bald pressure of this sort can only accelerate the phasing out of the present era in Philippine-United States relations. The reality of the close and special ties between the two countries contains a considerable element of genuine friendship and affection on the part of Filipinos for America. Mr. Zablocki's threat has cleared the air for more and more Filipinos; they will support Presi-dent Marcos' call for the dispatch of a Filipino engineering unit with security troops to Vietnam, not out of sentimental friendship for the United States, but out of a hard and realistic assessment of the Philippine situation.

Countries that are not as well situated as the Philippines in terms of manpower quality and natural resources have sustained rapid economic development. The task of coping with the difficulties that must accom-pany liquidation of the close and special ties will give the Filipino people a jolt they have needed for some time, to tighten up their governmental institutions, to mobilize and develop their resources more efficiently, and to learn the lesson they have not yet learned—that self-interest is still the paramount motivation and overpowering purpose in the foreign relations of sovereign states.

Policy Formulation and Implementation

A third reality of Philippine foreign policy is a factor that is omni-present and flamboyant, but is often overlooked. This concerns Philippine politics—specifically, the process by which foreign policy is formulated and the organization through which it is implemented.

The conduct of the foreign affairs of the Philippines is vested in the president. He is elected for a four-year term by national suffrage. Presidential candidates are sponsored by political parties. The parties are essentially alliances or coalitions of the personal political machines of local leaders in the more than fifty provinces. Since the position of these leaders is secured by their local strength, they are rarely subject to the discipline of national party organizations. The national parties have not yet evolved into organized movements which support national causes generated in ideological commitment. As a result, political power is widely dispersed and the bases of power are fragmented. No Philippine president has ever been re-elected after a full presidential term of four years. There are no political institutions in the Philippines that have enabled a leader to stay in power as long as have Indonesia's Sukarno, India's Nehru, Burma's Ne Win, and Malaysia's Tungku Abdul Rahman.

THE NARROW BASE

Under these circumstances, the fragmented bases of political authority in the Philippines have tended to proliferate leaders whose orientations are primarily local. The ad hoc and non-institutionalized character of party organizations, moreover, has prevented them from developing the resources and competence necessary to support the president in policy planning and management. In practice, these matters tend to be almost entirely left by default to the president. The involvement of the party leadership in national governmental affairs is therefore narrowly limited. When the president decides to adopt a policy, such as the expansion of Philippine involvement in Vietnam, the party and its leadership are only a shade less ignorant than the general public about the calculations that went into his policy choice. Consequently, the president's own party colleagues have only two alternatives: to join the opposition in criticism or, as is more likely, to support the president with less than full enthusiasm and without full comprehension of the complicated issues involved. In policy matters, therefore, the role of the president's party generally tends to begin after the president has made a decision, and not during the decision-making process.

Foreign policy decisions reached in this manner are rarely assured of easy acceptance by independent minded party colleagues, in which the Philippine Congress abounds. Even after his policies are adopted, the president has to resort to more persuasion, and often, in the end, to naked power, to obtain the support necessary to give effect to these policies. This process, which dissipates executive leverage, will be prolonged where policies require implementing legislation and/or appropriations. Moreover, a third wave of presidential cooperation or coercion may be necessary for the serious administrative implementation of projects.

The president's dominance in policy making and management decision making is made palatable by the extraordinary participation of his party colleagues in the staffing of government positions. Such participation relieves the pressure on political leaders obligated to followers and constituents. In such a system, however, considerations of bureaucratic integrity and efficiency suffer in priority. These circumstances of the Philippine political and governmental system account for much of the wide gap that frequently divides executive policies and legislative support, and the discrepancy between legislation and administrative achievement.

BUREAUCRATIC QUALITY AND MORALE

The classified civil service in the Philippines has for some time now enjoyed a mythical reputation as a career service. There is no doubt that there is a large body of dedicated career employees, but the ranks of the classified service has been an admixture of career and non-career people since independence. Filipino legislators admit, sometimes ruefully, that their offices are primarily employment agencies or placement bureaus. This results from pressures generated by the large size of the unemployed labor force, pressures that are focused upon the security and status of bureaucratic employment. Political intervention in the civil service might be defensible if politicians were to "recommend" for employment only those persons who are qualified. In the politics of government hiring, however, transfers and promotions are usually initiated by the employee, who solicits an endorsement from the politician. Where this practice is widespread, as it is in the Philippines, the civil service ceases to be a professional and neutral bureaucracy.

CONSEQUENCES FOR FOREIGN POLICY

As a result, the employee does not owe his primary loyalty to the service, or to the chief executive, but to his political sponsor. Thus, we have a paradox in which a chief executive with vast constitutional authority and political power has lost practical control over the governmental bureaucracy. Such a situation undermines the capabilities of the Philippine government in foreign affairs negotiations. The president and his envoys abroad start from a position of weakness whenever they face negotiators who are familiar with the president's relatively tenuous control over his civil servants.

Were the Philippine foreign service truly a professional and career service, it would have attracted to its ranks a fair share of the finest minds in the nation. As it is, the outstanding men in the service have been a handful of ambassadors and department secretaries, almost all of them political appointees. The career area specialists and desk men of the department are not noted for ideas, nor for profound and authoritative knowledge of the history, language, culture, economy, demography, politics, etc., of the countries with which we have relations, as well as of those with whom we have no ties but whose activities in world or regional affairs affect our national interests. Consequently, the department is not noted for independent research, and it is doubtful if the department can produce the imaginative and competent foreign policy planning that is commensurate to the needs arising from our position in Southeast Asia.

In no other country, perhaps, must the chief executive be his own foreign policy planner. Should the president wish to be relieved of this task, in order to be able to devote more time to problems other than those of foreign affairs, he might consider a re-examination of the staffing procedures in the department. Without truly professional and intellectually creative men in her foreign service, the Philippines must expect limited success in efforts to attain a leadership role in Southeast Asian diplomacy, and we will continue to face frustration in our campaign to remove irritants in our relations with the United States.

Challenge and Promise

This essay on Philippine foreign policy discussed an order of reality different from that which circumscribes our perception of the day-to-day conduct of foreign affairs. Other realities such as, for instance, the presence of Communist China in the Asia to which the Philippines seeks to return, and the resurgence of Philippine nationalism since the late 1950s, have been analyzed frequently and in depth. The realities of our Southeast Asian geography, the ties to the United States, and Philippine politics have been selected for treatment because they will give direction to Philippine activities in the coming decade, and because they suggest the measure of the tasks that confront the Filipino national leadership.

The focus on problems should not lead us to ignore the constructive record of the Philippines in world affairs. Its apprenticeship in international diplomacy took place during the early postwar period, when world politics was featured by extraordinary tensions. Both inside and out of the United Nations, Philippine diplomats took positions for the welfare of non-self-governing peoples, for the recognition of the aspirations of colonial nations, and for the promotion and protection of the rights of workers, women, and minority groups. It was a leading voice in almost every effort to defend freedom and world order through law, thus committing itself irrevocably against international communism and giving valuable support to the United States.

It was possible for the Philippines to assume these positions largely because of the Filipinos' commitment to democracy and human rights and, in part, because of the generally progressive and benevolent character of its experience as a former colony, which enabled the Philippines to speak out with understanding and moderation on all questions involving colonialism, nationalism, and imperialism.

The Philippines' efforts to cope with the foreign policy challenges of the 1960s will continue to carry the spirit of its commitments to democracy and moderation. Supporting those commitments, and furnishing hope for rewarding achievements, are certain features of the Philippine social and political system: the essentially libertarian spirit of our laws; the freedom of the Philippine press; the permissiveness and openness with which we conduct our relations among ourselves and with other people; and a political maturity that understands the need for, and the mechanics by which political power is transferred. As for the economic challenges, the Philippines is still in a comfortable position with respect to natural resources, the development of which will be accelerated by the growing pool of quality manpower and Filipino entrepreneurial talents.

All things considered, the Philippines is more favorably situated than most other developing countries. Informed Filipinos therefore feel confident that their leaders will meet the tasks of domestic and foreign affairs with ultimate, if not undiluted, success. The earlier, and the higher the level attained in meeting domestic goals, the more promising will be the prospects of achievement as the Philippines continues to conduct its affairs with other nations on the basis of mutual benefits and understanding.

George E. Taylor

4

The Challenge of Mutual Security

Ever since independence there has been going on in the Philippines a continuing re-evaluation of the Philippine-American relationship. To a much lesser degree, the United States has undergone the same process. This is not surprising, in view of the changes in the Philippines and in the rest of Asia since World War II. In the Philippines, the generation that won independence is being replaced by men who have little or no memory of the American period and who take independence for granted. Their emotional and intellectual patterns are different, as is their view of the world. At the same time, Philippine relations with Asian countries have changed beyond recognition. Filipinos have had more contact with Asia in the two decades since independence than they had in three and a half centuries of Spanish and American occupation. They travel widely in Asia, take their place at international conferences, and behave as representatives of an independent power, even if they are not always regarded as such. Filipinos have held high positions with the United Nations and the Southeast Asia Treaty Organization. The diversification of their trade has been matched by the assimilation of cultural influences. The American cultural and economic monopoly is increasingly a thing of the past.

GEORGE E. TAYLOR, *Director, Far Eastern and Russian Institute, University of Washington, received his D. Litt. (History) from the University of Birmingham. He lived and studied in China throughout the 1930s and served in the U. S. Office of War Information and the State Department during and immediately after the war. Professor Taylor spent 1955-56 in the Philippines as a consultant to the Institute of Asian Studies of the University of the Philippines and has returned on several occasions to participate in official conferences and to engage in study and research.* The Philippines and the United States: Problems of Partnership, *which he authored for the Council on Foreign Relations, is the most recent of his several books.*

The present generation of Filipinos now has before it various examples of the behavior of ex-colonies toward their former masters, ranging all the way from Indonesia, which has defied the Dutch and ostentatiously flaunted its hostility to the West, to Malaysia, which stayed within the British Commonwealth and has sought to maintain and enlarge the British economic stake. There is apparently more than one way for a former colony to survive in the contemporary world. It is only natural that Filipinos should have been influenced by these events, and it is high time, therefore, that the United States review its relations with the Philippines, as it has, in very large measure, with other Asian states.

The American Commitment

The United States has two related sets of obligations to the Philippines. The earlier commitment, made in the period immediately following World War II, guarantees Philippine security and is defined in three military pacts: the Military Assistance Agreement of 1947, the Military Bases Agreement of the same year, and the Mutual Defense Treaty of 1951. The more recent commitment is the one shared with the Philippines as a member of the Southeast Asia Treaty Organization, a multilateral regional security arrangement. Put very briefly, the United States has unilaterally undertaken to come to the defense of the Philippines if the latter is attacked by external forces of whatever origin and to join with the Philippines and several other countries in mutual defense against external attack and, very significantly, internal subversion. These are serious commitments.

THE BILATERAL COMMITMENT

The Department of State justified the Military Bases Agreement of March 14, 1947, by reference to the wartime pledge of President Roosevelt that the freedom of the Philippines would be redeemed and its independence established and protected. It was a pledge that Japan would not again overrun the Philippines. It was in order to protect the freedom which had been redeemed and the independence which had been firmly established that the United States, according to Acting Secretary of State Dean Acheson, was given rights to the use of a small number of military bases in the Philippines. A week later the Philippines signed the Military Assistance Agreement, by which "in view of the mutual interests of the two governments in matters of common defense" the United States agreed to give military assistance to the Philippines in order to maintain its national security and to assist it in participating in such defensive military operations as the future might require. A Joint United States Military Advisory Group (JUSMAG) has been resident in the Philippines since that time to assist in the administration of military assistance, which, generously interpreted, has included the provision of weapons, training, and related economic aid. The United States Congress was informed recently that military assistance between 1948 and 1964 amounted to $312.4 million. The *Far Eastern Economic Review* gives the cumulative figure for 1946-63 as $423.3 million, as compared with $2,349.2 million for Taiwan, $2,015.0 million for Korea, and $1,031.2 million for Japan.

The negotiation of a peace treaty with Japan seemed to be an appropriate time for a more explicit reaffirmation of the United States guarantee to defend the Philippines. Hence the signing of a mutual defense treaty in Washington on August 30, 1951. By this treaty the United States and the Philippines agree to consult whenever, in the opinion of either government, the territorial integrity, political independence, or security of either is threatened by external armed attack in the Pacific. Each party recognizes that an armed attack in the Pacific area on either country is dangerous to its own peace and safety and declares that it will act to meet the common dangers "in accordance with its constitutional processes."

An armed attack on either includes an armed attack on the metropolitan territory of either country or on the island territories under its jurisdiction in the Pacific, or on its armed forces, public vessels, or aircraft in the Pacific. The reference to constitutional processes, in other words the prior consent of the United States Congress, has always been regarded in the Philippines as a modification of the assurance of automatic assistance. The United States government, however, has tended to hold the view that the guarantee is to all intents and purposes unconditional, if only because the presence of United States bases in the Philippines would make it extremely difficult for an external power to attack that country without attacking United States forces.

The commitment of the United States to come to the immediate defense of the Philippines has been reaffirmed by every American administration since the signing of the treaty. For example, Secretary of State Rusk announced on October 9, 1964, that "our own defense arrangements with the Philippines are very far reaching, are without qualifications, and that if there is an attack on the Philippines from any quarter, that is an attack on the United States. And I would think that it would be very reckless, indeed, for anyone to suppose that there is any doubt whatever about our commitment to the security of the Philippines." On November 2, 1964, President Johnson assured President Diosdado Macapagal on the occasion of the latter's state visit, "I pledge again the full and continuing support of the United States to the Philippine Republic and to other like-minded and true friends." In the subsequent joint communique, President Johnson made it clear that in accordance with existing alliances and the deployment and dispositions that they involve, "any armed attack against the Philippines would be regarded as an attack against the United States forces stationed there and against the United

States and would instantly be repelled." It would be difficult to be more explicit in words, but the credibility of a nation's intentions is likely to be judged more by its actions.

MULTILATERAL OBLIGATIONS

Eight nations—Australia, France, New Zealand, Pakistan, the Philippines, Thailand, the United Kingdom, and the United States—came together on September 8, 1954, to form the Southeast Asia Treaty Organization. On the same day they signed two documents—the Pacific Charter and the Southeast Asia Collective Defense Treaty. The Pacific Charter was perhaps the first attempt of former colonies and former imperial powers to agree on a joint statement of general principles; hence the guarded language. The parties agree to promote self-government and secure the independence of all countries whose peoples desire it and are able to undertake its responsibilities, to bring this about in an orderly manner and in accordance with their own constitutional processes, to cooperate in the promotion of economic and social well being, and to prevent efforts to subvert freedom and sovereignty in the treaty area. This novel and important effort to construct an ideological bridge between the new nations and their old masters came very largely from Philippine initiative.

In SEATO, the eight powers agree to support the United Nations and to help each other to resist armed attack and to "prevent and counter subversive activities directed from without against their territorial integrity and political stability." The widespread efforts of international communism (between 1948 and 1954) to subvert the governments of new Asian nations—in India, Burma, Malaya, Indonesia, the Philippines, and Vietnam—account for the emphasis on measures to be taken to counter subversion. It is true that none of the eight powers is obligated to take action if it does not wish to assist another member under external attack. But no alliance, however binding on paper, is ever kept unless the contracting party wishes to honor its obligations. SEATO breaks new ground in that it establishes the principle that members may assist in countering subversion at the invitation or with the consent of the government concerned. To implement the Treaty a Council of Ministers is empowered to authorize various activities—military, cultural, economic—in support of Treaty objectives. The post of Secretary-General has usually been reserved for the Asian members of SEATO, while that of Deputy Secretary-General goes to non-Asian members. On July 1, 1965, Lt. General Jesus Vargas, a retired officer of the Philippine Army, took up the post of Secretary-General of SEATO and thus became the first Filipino named to the top permanent post and the authorized spokesman of the organization. The Secretariat supports and coordinates the non-military activities of the Treaty Organization which, up to the present, have remained modest but significant.

SEATO has come in for a good deal of criticism. That from the communist side was to be expected. Others have pointed to its obvious weaknesses, to the small number of Asian states involved, to the alleged failures of SEATO to take action, and to the fact that the United States promises to act only in the event of communist aggression. Filipino critics have publicly questioned the failure of SEATO to intervene through collective military action in the Vietnamese war. Actually, half of the members of SEATO have armed units in South Vietnam which, with Laos and Cambodia, is a "protocol" state covered by SEATO security measures. The weaknesses of SEATO are quite evident, but the fact remains that the Organization entered its second decade still very much alive. The framework is there for as much or as little cooperation as the members wish to undertake. In April 1964, almost ten years after its establishment, seven SEATO members issued a strong joint declaration supporting the people of South Vietnam in their struggle for political security. Philippine Secretary of Foreign Affairs Lopez said at the time that it was better for one member (France) to abstain than to maintain the pretense of unanimity, a pretense which promised only frustration and paralysis. At this same Council of Ministers meeting, President Macapagal reaffirmed the intention of the Philippines to abide by its commitments to SEATO.

THE AMERICAN STAKE

Such are the treaty obligations of the United States in Southeast Asia, apart from its obligations to the United Nations. In the American view there are more than adequate reasons for the commitments thereby undertaken. Loss of control over the vital sea and air communications of the Far East with Europe and America would intensify beyond measure the difficulties of defending South Korea, Japan, Nationalist China, and the Philippines. It is also politically important to the future of the West that the independent countries of this vast area be protected from communist subversion and control. Communist domination of Southeast Asia would increase the prestige of the communist powers and bring under their influence 150 million people and 1.6 million square miles of territory. It would also give Peking and Moscow access to resources capable of producing large supplies of food, which would not only help them to solve a major internal problem but also change their power position in the world competition for food. The communist powers would also acquire the rich raw materials of Southeast Asia, of major strategic importance in world commerce, and be able to deny them to the West. It goes without saying that communist control of this area would give the communist powers much more influence in India, Pakistan, and Japan.

Not all Americans are persuaded that these considerations make Southeast Asia of vital interest to the United States. But if the United States wishes to persuade Hanoi, Peking, Moscow, and its own allies that it is determined to make a stand in South Vietnam or elsewhere in Southeast

Asia, then the military bases in the Philippines are absolutely essential. Denial of access to these facilities and to the cooperation of the Philippine government and people would establish a formidable constraint on the force which could be exerted in Southeast Asia by the United States. A cooperative attitude on the part of the Philippines is essential to the credibility of forceful American policies in Southeast Asia. Moreover, so long as United States relations with Communist China remain antagonistic and wars of "national liberation" are the order of the day in Southeast Asia, the importance of the bases at Clark Field and Subic Bay are likely to increase. The communist conquest of mainland China has made these bases essential to the national security interests of the United States.

Philippine Patterns of Foreign Policy

RELATIONS WITH THE UNITED STATES

Unlike some of its neighbors, the Republic of the Philippines has committed itself to an alliance with the United States and has, to all intents and purposes, placed the protection of the Republic against external attack in the hands of its powerful ally. There are good historical reasons for the Philippines' departure from the usual practice among European colonies, on acquiring independence, of severing all military connections with the former imperial power. The Filipinos did not have to fight the United States to acquire independence and, therefore, were not receptive to the Leninist image of imperialism or to communist tactics and strategy in dealing with it. They are not afraid of the West, and their distrust of communism stems directly from the Philippine value system. After World War II, therefore, as the fear of a resurgent Japan declined and the reality of an aggressive communist government in Peking became clear, Filipinos were anxious and willing to seek external security in the special relationship with the United States.

The Philippine government, indeed, has gone along with most of the major developments of American policy in Asia. It accepted both economic and military aid, refused to recognize Communist China, allowed American forces to remain on Philippine soil, sent troops to fight in Korea, sponsored the Pacific Charter, promoted SEATO, spoke up for democratic ideals and hopes at Bandung, and in general stood firmly by its former guardian and present ally. Such behavior is in sharp contrast to that of Burma and Indonesia, both of which followed the neutralist line of refusing to accept military and, on occasion, economic aid or to join in regional arrangements for collective security. The Philippines was one of the very few Asian countries to reject neutralism, a decision that made for difficulties with some of its neighbors.

THE SEARCH FOR AN ASIAN IDENTITY

At the same time, the Philippines has naturally come to feel that it should have an identifiable policy of its own toward its Asian neighbors. The Philippines has to exist in an Asian setting and to establish its own identity; it seeks, therefore, to be regarded as an ally of the United States with regional interests and responsibilities of its own. There has been a good deal of Philippine comment to the effect that existing relations between the two countries cannot endure unless the United States respects the national aspirations of the Filipinos and respects the Filipinos as equals. One Filipino commentator put the matter, as he said, in plain English—"we don't want treatment as a colony or an occupied territory. If this can't be granted to us it would be logical to hope that the Americans will pull out of the Philippines. How can they protect a people they don't respect?" Comments in this general vein have multiplied since the anti-American demonstrations in Manila in early 1965.

It is not surprising that Philippine domestic and foreign policies have shown more and more evidence of a nationalistic spirit. An independent Philippines with a strong sense of nationalism has long been considered an objective of American policy. The proper American concern is not for nationalism as such, but for its social content, as nationalism is the only force that can provide the dynamism to bring about the unification of the country and the changes necessary for economic growth and political stability. Our real interest is in the political, social, and economic objectives of those who are in a position to decide upon the nature of Philippine nationalism.

In the areas of major concern to the Philippines, relations with the United States and with the countries of Asia, a growing sense of nationhood has had a significant bearing on the problems of mutual security. The bid to establish a new relationship with the United States began with President Magsaysay. He and his successors have successfully established the image of an ally who could stand up to the United States in bilateral negotiations and force the revision of agreements. The Philippine government has insisted on the settlement of issues relating to its sovereignty and status, such as jurisdiction over American troops, the parity clause, and the participation of the Philippines in making mutual security policy. On these issues the Filipinos could plead their case in terms of promises unfulfilled, the rights of a loyal ally, or just plain equity.

The fact that the Philippines has tended to conduct the discussion more on the moral plane of comparative loyalty to the United States than to the cause of the Free World does not mean that the American position is not understood. It means that Filipinos tend to see international relations in terms far more personal than do Americans. They feel that the very special relationship they have with the United States should be expressed in concrete ways that everyone can understand. On the surface it would seem that the Philippine government, in its demands for greater economic aid, its insistence on the settlement of the war damage claims, and its persistent pressure to increase the sugar quota (unsuccessful until Castro came to power in Cuba) is interested only in money and favors. In fact, Filipinos want respect, dignity, and equality of status much more than anything else. By the same token, a concession important to them in the negotiations to revise the Laurel-Langley Agreement was American acceptance of parity for Philippine enterprise in the United States, even though it is quite clear that its economic significance was hardly comparable with that of parity for American enterprise in the Philippines.

The Philippine government has felt it necessary to demonstrate in negotiations with the United States, as well as through its position in the United Nations, that the Philippines arrives at its policies independently, even when they coincide with those of her major ally. Negotiations over jurisdictional issues relating to American bases in the Philippines were marked by a degree of acrimony that led Ambassador Bohlen to comment at the time that "any nation or any individual who would dare to say that the Government of the Philippines would be subject to pressure or any form of influence by other nations or individuals, particularly by the United States or any of its officials, has only to sit across from Secretary Felixberto Serrano at a conference table to realize that such pressure and influence are absolutely impossible." Secretary Serrano's comments on the negotiations were to the effect that Philippine-American relations had survived a crucial confrontation without impairing the means of negotiation and threshing out mutual problems. The aim of the Philippine government was to "establish a respected independence, and to help the nation find the root and soul of the national spirit." The Philippine government was clearly thinking of its national pride and of its relative standing among the friends and allies of the United States.

REALITIES AND CONSTRAINTS

As an independent country the Philippines naturally looked to the readjustment of relations with Asia. In view of the special relationship with the United States, as well as of cultural differences with Asian countries, this was no easy task. It was not made any easier by the fact that Filipinos thought of themselves as being more advanced politically and economically than other Southeast Asian countries and as potential leaders of the new nations in that part of the world. There were others who wished to lead—Mao Tse-tung and Sukarno, to mention only two. But to turn toward Asia for friends and allies was a natural impulse. Ambassador Carlos Romulo put the matter very directly when he said, "We do not want to be a pariah in Asia and no self-respecting nation wants a pariah for an ally." The Philippines obviously had to make its own contacts and arrangements with its neighbors.

As far as the most troublesome Asian neighbor, Communist China, is concerned, the Philippines has tended to take a stand even stronger than that of the United States, in fact, it stated that even if the United States were to recognize Peking it would not do so. This point of view was strongly challenged by the late Senator Claro M. Recto, who favored recognizing Communist China on the ground that this was the most realistic way of fighting communism, as contrasted with what he called a policy of evasion, indifference, retreat, and "brinkmanship." If Communist China were brought into the United Nations, he argued, its misdeeds could be challenged on legal and moral grounds. That Recto held these views continues to carry considerable weight with the intellectuals who, in the long run, create the climate of opinion in which decisions are made.

Relations with Japan have slowly improved following the signing of the peace treaty in 1951 and the negotiation of the substantial reparations agreement in 1956. Trade with Japan has increased rapidly, in part at the expense of trade with the United States. Although the Philippines has no mutual security treaty with the Republic of China, relations are satisfactory, the only serious cause of friction being the status of Chinese nationals resident in the Philippines.

INITIATIVES IN SOUTHEAST ASIA

It has been in Southeast Asia that Filipinos have felt a need to take diplomatic and political initiative. Within this region the concept of Pan Malaysia, with the Philippines, Indonesia, and Malaya at the core, has appealed to Filipino longings to renew their Asian identification. With these countries the Philippines has bonds of language, custom, and geographical proximity. After taking much of the initiative in setting up the Southeast Asia Treaty Organization and in formulating the Pacific Charter, the Philippine government sought to bring the countries of Southeast Asia into an Association of Southeast Asia (ASA), but was joined only by Malaya and Thailand. The Association of Southeast Asia was intended to provide for consultation, collaboration, and mutual assistance in economic, social, cultural, scientific, and administrative fields. The Soviet Union described it not as a regional economic bloc but rather as an auxiliary of SEATO, inspired by outsiders and designed to bring neutral Asian countries into the stream of American policy. According to Soviet propaganda, SEATO is an aggressive military bloc organized to oppose the Asian national liberation movement and ASA was intended to compensate for the shortcomings of SEATO by bringing in Indonesia, Burma, and Cambodia, all of which refused to join. Be this as it may, ASA did not flourish, although in July 1965 Thailand indicated a willingness to assist in its revival.

President Macapagal claimed that one of the main achievements of his administration in foreign affairs was the establishment of Maphilindo, a composite name given to a loose understanding between Malaysia, the Philippines, and Indonesia. In an address to the Manila Overseas Press Club in August 1963, he expressed the hope that the establishment of Maphilindo would remove the barriers that artificially divided the peoples of the Malay race. The underlying principles of Maphilindo were joint action in regional affairs and primary consideration for the interests of the peoples of the region. Although history may have been rewritten a little in order to exaggerate the degree to which the Malays were once united, there was something exciting about the idea that peoples so long divided among imperial powers should now come voluntarily together. The Filipinos saw the common bond as the threat of Communist China, counting as they do on Indonesian fear of the overseas Chinese in Southeast Asia.

In 1960, Foreign Minister Serrano said that the Filipinos can slowly win the respect of their fellow Asians and that this can be achieved only when the democratic institutions of the Philippines bear "the mark of our own national soul and native genius." It looked as if Maphilindo were a step in that direction. The foreign ministers of the three countries agreed that there should be consultative organs set up to handle their joint affairs, particularly economic matters, and that the method of discussion should be through *Musjawarah* (arriving at decisions through consensus). So far, there has been little or no consensus, mainly because Indonesian policy has antagonized both the Philippines and Malaysia.

CLAIM TO NORTH BORNEO

As part of the effort to improve relations with its Asian neighbors, the Philippines gave consistent support to Indonesia's claims in the West Irian affair. Welcome as this may have been to Indonesia at the time, it failed to lay the foundation for future cooperation in regional matters except on Indonesia's terms. This may have been due in part to Philippine initiative of another sort. On June 22, 1962, the Philippine government sent a note to the British government claiming sovereignty over North Borneo, an area of nearly 30,000 square miles and 454,000 people, one-quarter of whom are Chinese, Malays, Indians, and Europeans, and the rest indigenous people of Malay origins. Whatever the merits of the Philippine claim and the motives for making it, it ran head on into the new Federation of Malaysia and opened up the whole question of claims to this part of the world. If Malaysia and the Philippines can claim North Borneo, then so can Indonesia. The process of liquidating the spheres of influence of a retreating colonial power is hardly predictable, especially when it takes place in an area well infiltrated by communists. In 1963, the Philippine government used its claim to North Borneo to arrange for a "summit conference" between Abdul Rahman, Sukarno, and Macapagal, at which it was agreed that the birth of Malaysia should be delayed in order to give the United Nations time to conduct a survey of opinion in North Borneo to find out whether or not the people wished to join Malaysia. When the United Nations team reported that public sentiment was in favor of Malaysia, the Philippines severed diplomatic relations with the new state of Malaysia, and the power struggle for leadership in the Malay world entered a new phase.

The struggle for control of Borneo, an island of great strategic importance and of very definite concern to the mutual security of the Philippines and the United States, has already begun. If the disintegration of Malaysia should continue, it could lead to open competition for the whole of Borneo, as well as for North Borneo, which would require that the Philippine claim either be surrendered or be backed by force. Borneo, in fact, is potentially as troublesome as any other area in Southeast Asia. Since Commonwealth troops are now defending the former British colonies of North Borneo, Sarawak, and Brunei from Indonesian guerrilla infiltration, it would be possible for the United Kingdom, Australia, and New Zealand to call on their fellow members of SEATO for assistance in this task. By the same token, the Philippines may seek aid to prevent Indonesian and/or Chinese Communist subversion from succeeding in Borneo, an area in which Philippine diplomacy has ventured far.

THE PRICE OF ASIAN DIPLOMACY

The initiatives that the Philippines have taken in Asia and the greatly increased diplomatic, cultural, and economic contacts have brought unforeseen consequences, as Filipinos have discovered that diplomacy in Southeast Asia has a price. The effort to woo Indonesia brought forth a strong Indonesian propaganda effort in the Philippines to split the Philippine connection with the United States. The demonstration effect of President Sukarno's unilateral actions against Western rights and property in Indonesia has not been lost on those Filipinos who, for a combination of nationalist and economic reasons, would like to accelerate the decline of alien economic influence. The example of Pakistan, a member of SEATO, has shown that an anti-communist Asian state can have diplomatic and commercial relations with mainland China and still remain an ally of the United States. The two other members of Maphilindo —Indonesia and Malaysia—both recognize Peking. It is natural, therefore, that alternatives to the present policies of the Philippine government should be discussed and that these should include the possibility of recognition of Communist China, as well as a foreign policy based on neutralism.

The complexity of the problems of Southeast Asia and the perfectly legitimate need of the Philippines to conduct its own diplomacy in that part of the world, raise serious problems for United States-Philippine mutual security arrangements. As these problems are mainly in the political field, they call for a high degree of cooperation between the United States and the Philippines if they are to be handled successfully. Otherwise severe tensions in the alliance will be generated.

CHALLENGE TO THE UNITED STATES

The United States has the problem of supporting as carefully as possible the need of the Philippine government for a dignified and honorable role in foreign affairs, while keeping the major objectives of both countries to the fore. Such cooperation is possible only if Filipinos feel that their country is being treated as an independent ally whose own needs and interests are at stake. The other side of the coin is a willingness on the part of the Filipinos to consult with the United States on moves that may lead to serious involvement in Southeast Asia, especially those that affect the national interest of their powerful ally.

The real question is therefore one of the degree to which American and Philippine interests are really mutual. The United States proceeds on the assumption that the interests are indeed mutual. The argument runs that the Philippines cannot afford the military establishment to defend itself and therefore welcomes an American guarantee of protection. The potential enemies of the Philippines—communist powers—are also the enemies of the United States, and therefore it is to the interest of both countries to maximize their contributions to common defense against a common enemy. Since the Philippines is an Asian country, the argument continues, it is essential that it establish independent relations with the countries of Asia and persuade those countries that it is truly a sovereign, independent power. There are other countries, such as the United Kingdom and West Germany, which enjoy the protection of the American nuclear umbrella, but their independence is essentially unquestioned because they have a rich history of autonomy. The Philippines, with only two decades of independence, does not command a comparable respect for its sovereignty, and herein lies much of the problem.

An experienced American ambassador, William E. Stevenson, has suggested that one way in which the United States can help in this situation is to place special confidence in its Filipino allies. "We lose all the benefit that an Asian partner can gain for us," said Stevenson, "if we continue to call most of the shots ourselves, and make decisions at home or with others without close collaboration with our Asian ally." In his view the Philippines can play a more significant and helpful role in Asia than we are asking of it. As Asians, the Filipinos could help to bring about rapport, understanding, and cooperation with their fellow Asians that we Americans could never achieve. We would have to accept the fact that they would follow an Asian pattern and that their approaches and techniques would be different from those we would employ ourselves. He raises the question whether without more help and understanding from the United States the Philippines will be able to withstand outside pressures and stay within the ranks of the Free World. Perhaps, he suggests, we are neglecting a nation that could be very useful indeed in helping to contend with the many complex problems of Asia.

The External Threat

INTERNATIONAL COMMUNISM AND CHINESE NATIONALISM

There have been subtle changes in the influence of Communist China upon the Philippines and other parts of Southeast Asia. When the United States and the Philippines joined in SEATO, the image of Communist China was one of an aggressive power, but only one element, however important, in the international communist movement. It was assumed that the international movement, not China alone, initiated and supported communist efforts to take over Southeast Asia between 1948 and 1954. China was still "leaning to one side."

Communist China today casts its own shadow. One result of the conflict with the Soviet Union, and the struggle within the movement for domination, has been to impose upon the small nations of Asia the image of a China independent and strong enough to stand on her own feet among the great powers of the world. This view of Chinese sovereignty and power, which had been blurred in the early Fifties by the alliance with the Soviet Union and the policy of "leaning to one side," to say nothing of the automatic deference given to Stalin, has now been clarified. Communist China has come to be identified with the nation-state of China and therefore with Chinese nationalism. The demonstration effect of a large but apparently weak country defying the world's great nuclear powers has to be taken into account, as does the success of Sukarno in taking over the capital assets of the imperial powers, grabbing West Irian, and attacking Malaysia. There are certain aspects of the present posture of Communist China which are not unattractive to some Filipinos.

THE VIEW TO THE SOUTH

Another development that is of great significance for the security of the Philippines is the emphasis that both the Russian and Chinese Communists place on internal subversion with outside support. Both the Soviet and the Chinese governments have declared themselves strongly in favor of "just" wars of national liberation—wars to overthrow governments of new nations which are genuinely neutral or favorable to the West. In Southeast Asia, Communist China and the Soviet Union provide political support and direction, the training of cadres, and a certain amount of material assistance to such efforts. For countries that are contiguous to mainland China, the problems of communication are simple, and in some cases, as with Thailand and Burma, there are ethnic groups that overlap the frontiers. The Philippines presents more difficult communications problems but is far from inaccessible. The approach today is from the south, and Chinese Communist agents have been coming into the Philippines by way of the southern islands for many years. According to the Philippine government, Indonesian squatters and agents began moving into Mindanao steadily from 1963-64 onward. The Philippines, therefore, has a double interest in the techniques of internal subversion. It has an interest in cases such as South Vietnam, Borneo, and Malaya, where these techniques are used in an effort to overthrow friendly or neutral governments and to expand the area of communist influence. It is also interested in the possibility of internal subversion within the Philippines, supported by foreign agents, money, and material. The International communist movement long ago marked the Philippines as a target (the Communist Party of the Philippines was established in 1930) but has not been able to give substantial material assistance. Help has been limited to the training of cadres, ideological support, and tactical guidance.

There is possibly a very real mutual interest in finding the best techniques for dealing with subversion of the kind encountered earlier in the Philippines and Malaya, and more recently in South Vietnam. Filipinos and Americans have shared the experience of a successful application of counterinsurrection techniques. There are two reasons why it is important to recall the Hukbalahap challenge of the early 1950s. In the first place, the inspired cooperation of the American military at this time helped to restore the self-respect of the Philippine military profession which had been sorely tried in the immediate postwar years. Secondly, the successful military collaboration between our two countries was essential to Philippine survival as part of the non-communist world. The Filipino military, under the leadership of Magsaysay, provided the political dynamism necessary for reducing the Huk insurrection. They combined power, authority, and flexibility with a political approach to countering subversion. Out of this experience came major contributions to the existing body of military doctrine on the handling of armed communist insurrection in an agrarian country.

Philippine Armed Forces—Mission and Capabilities

There are probably few problems between JUSMAG and the Philippine armed forces that cannot be settled more or less amicably. This is especially true since the establishment of the Philippine-United States Mutual Defense Board in 1958 to supervise the implementation of three bilateral military treaties—the Mutual Defense Treaty, the Military Assistance Agreement, and the Bases Agreement. General Manuel F. Cabal, Chief of Staff of the Philippine Armed Forces, in 1960 assessed the advent of the Board as the first serious attempt at mutual defense planning.

The armed forces of the Philippines are not a force in national politics in the sense that armies in some of the neighboring states have become. There are few countries that are in less danger of military *coup d'état.* In very few Asian countries is the doctrine of civilian supremacy over the military more firmly established. The army has never been associated with a political party. Even President Magsaysay, who gave to the armed forces a sense of mission, a social purpose, and a new moral stature and used his prestige as the conqueror of the Huks to rise to the presidency, never looked on the army as his personal tool or source of power. There is not a deep division between politicians and military men because they share the same value system. The military is not a separate professional class with its own traditions and way of life, as in prewar Germany or Japan. The officers and men of the Philippines armed forces come from the general population, to which they return. The problem is not one of preventing the army from becoming a dominating force in politics but of preventing the Congress and local authorities from gross political inter- ference in the military profession.

POLITICS AND EFFICIENCY

The mission of the Philippine armed forces is first to guarantee in- ternal law and order, particularly against the threat of armed communist insurrection; secondly, to assist in the defense of the Philippines in cooperation with the armed forces of the United States; and, lastly, to support the international role that Philippine diplomacy has undertaken through SEATO and the United Nations. To carry out these obligations there is a total force, including the Philippine Constabulary, of less than 50,000 officers and men. The Republic of China and of South Korea each have armies of at least half a million men. Small as the Philippine force may be, there is constant criticism in the Philippine Congress and the press that the Military is too big for peacetime and too small for war, that it is top-heavy with officers and a drain on resources that should be used for economic growth. Current military appropriations amount to somewhat less than 15 per cent of national government expenditures, and 80 per cent of military expenditures goes to pay for salaries and retirement.

Filipinos criticize the structure of the armed forces. Five years ago it was revealed that the armed forces, including naval officers and ratings of equivalent grade, had more captains (2,397), majors (915), and first lieutenants (796) than "buck" privates (534). The same article, in the *Philippines Free Press* of May 28, 1960, claimed that there were more sergeants (8,895) and more corporals (12,399) than there were privates first-class (8,224). There were 5,187 officers in all, including 12 generals and 106 colonels, plus 32,531 corporals and sergeants of all grades, and only 8,758 privates out of a total of 46,476 members of the armed forces. After independence the Military Bases Agreement permitted the recruitment of Filipinos for service in the United States Navy on a voluntary basis, and by 1960 there were more Filipinos in the United States Navy, over 12,872, than there were in the Philippine Navy.

The character and structure of the Philippine military establishment is obviously of considerable significance to the United States. In order to carry out the commitments that the Philippines has made, and that involve the United States, the Philippines must have a modern military establishment satisfactory to its national self-esteem, able to assist in collective regional defense, not too great a burden on the national budget, and, above all, capable of handling domestic law and order. Yet, if the mission of the Philippine armed forces is to be judged by the way in which they are organized and the type of equipment that they demand— fast jets and sidewinder missiles, both of which have been provided—it would seem that the primary mission is that of external security.

THE PUBLIC IMAGE

The question arises whether this is a realistic estimate of the present situation. Has not the nature of communist expansion changed so much since the Korean conflict that the first duty of the Philippine armed forces must be to maintain internal law and order and counter domestic insurgency? If this is true, are the armed forces being trained and equipped in the right way? There are some Filipinos who seem to doubt this. On the demands of the army for additional appropriations to protect the country from the threat from the south, the *Philippine Free Press* argued that since the military had run out of Huks it was trying to scare the nation with Indonesians in order to get more money. It was charged that there was a systematic campaign going on to push the Philippines into a confrontation with Indonesia in order to use the Philippines "as a tool of non-Filipino interests" and "to justify appropriating 200 million pesos more for the army so that its budget would be ever more loaded than it already is—and never mind what happens to the other government services and the economic development of the country! Never mind if most of the people remain sunk in poverty, if millions continue to go jobless, or if public servants go unpaid—so long as the army gets more and more money!"

The same editorial suggested that army leaders do not understand that the perils from within are in a way just as serious as the threats from the south—"it's in a strong economy, not a strong army, wherein lies the real strength of the country." Nothing would please the communists more, it was stated, than if the Philippines were to waste its resources on a bigger army instead of a progressive economy. That would make a communist takeover in the future easier. The answer probably lies somewhere between the two extreme positions. Obviously the country has to be defended, but it is equally obvious that it would cost less for defense against internal subversion if there were more social justice, a rapidly expanding economy, and an incorruptible public administration. If taxes were properly collected there would be enough money for a larger army and a developing economy. If social progress is inadequate to meet the needs of a rapidly expanding population, the challenge to the military is likely to be domestic insurrection rather than external attack.

The argument used to justify expenditures for economic and military aid for the fiscal year 1966 was that in the Far East the communists have taken great advantage of political and social unrest and of economic frustration. The long-term security of countries threatened by Communist China and its satellites therefore depends, among other things, on the achievement of visible, broadly shared economic and social progress. In testimony before the House Committee on Foreign Affairs, however, Mr. Rutherford M. Poats, an official of the Agency for International Development, said that in the Philippines the economic horizon had darkened, that food imports were rising faster than exports, that the population growth was absorbing the bulk of the country's gains in production, that private savings and tax revenues were not keeping pace with investment needs, and that the shortage of both private and public pesos to match foreign capital was denying the country urgently needed development projects. Such a pessimistic appraisal suggests that there will be a close relationship between the economic and political future of the Philippines and the role of the Philippine defense forces.

One political fact about the armed forces is that they are the residual legatee of the Magsaysay myth. According to this myth the army and the constabulary succeeded, where the politicians had failed, in crushing the communist-led Hukbalahap movement. Then they put their Secretary of Defense, Magsaysay, into the presidency to complete the job of cleaning up graft and corruption, of bringing the government to the people, and of carrying out agrarian reform—a program of social justice for the common people and of popular participation in the responsibilities of government. Since the destruction of the military power of the Hukbalahap, the social and political program that made that destruction possible has run into serious difficulties because the sense of urgency is no longer there and the communists have changed their tactics. They are concentrating much more upon infiltration of the government, the press, the universities, the trade unions, and the professions than upon armed struggle. This change in tactics has made things difficult for the armed forces at appropriation time because they find their proud claim of having crushed the communists turned against them.

The recurrence of communist-led insurrection is always possible. Since the armed forces would be involved, there will be some who will remember the social program that helped to win the earlier struggle. Should conditions reach a crisis stage similar to that of 1949-50, the radical left might attempt to encourage idealistic younger officers to believe that it was their patriotic duty to remove those who stood in the way.

THE QUALITY OF LAW AND ORDER

To judge by the news reported in the Philippine press, the problem of maintaining law and order is more critical every day. Press reports on the growing incidence of crime and juvenile delinquency, on corrupt practices and inefficiency within the ranks of law enforcement agencies, tend to create a dismal picture of Philippine society. The intermittent press campaigns on the growing incidence of crime, particularly in the city of Manila, project an unfavorable social image, one of moral deterioration and squalid social conditions. Much of the information in the press is sensational; none of it is based on cumulative and reliable statistics. We do not know for sure whether crime and corruption are actually increasing or not. At the same time, it would be unrealistic to ignore the widespread incidence of crime or to deny the questionable practices among those charged with law enforcement. There is no question that remedial action is required to help maintain law and order and to strengthen the moral fabric in society. If this is not done there will be growing despair and frustration among young Filipinos over what seems to them to be the failure of society to safeguard public law and morality. This will encourage, on their part, a negative attitude toward the social order.

A small group of American and Filipino social scientists is making efforts to clarify the causes of crime and other social problems against the background of rapid social change taking place in the Philippine society. There is a need for careful studies of social problems and wider dissemination of the results in order to help young Filipinos understand and recognize the problems that a changing society must face. In meeting this need a closer cooperation between the United States and the Philippines could help the security of both.

THE HUKBALAHAP TODAY

The American and Philippine armed forces have shared many experiences in the field to which reference is often made in ceremonial rhetoric. But the most significant bond of all between United States and Philippine military establishments is their contributions to the doctrines of counterinsurgency. There are men in both armed forces who understand the type of warfare prevalent in Southeast Asia today, where the struggle is not for territory but for the loyalty and support of the people. They know that the Hukbalahap movement, which was the main challenge in the early 1950s, remains an organized threat to internal security that has to be taken seriously. Times have changed. Communist China is much more aggressive, and Indonesia, according to Philippine estimates, poses a threat to the "soft under-belly" of the Republic.

Estimates of the number of active Huks have been quite low, but there have been many reports of increasing Huk terrorism. It is understood that the Huk organization is active in central Luzon, where it is engaged in the liquidation of government officials, military men, and landlords who have been outspoken against the Huk movement. An avowed objective is to instill fear in Americans, especially in areas remote from the military bases. Captured documents suggest that the general strategy is to recruit cadres, procure arms, and stockpile supplies in preparation for mass uprisings within a few years. There are no exact figures available on the number of persons in and out of the government who have been liquidated by the Huks, but it is reported as being impressive. The army has sent troops to central Luzon during harvest time, the favorite period for Huk raids and tax collections, but as this happens to be a few weeks before the appropriations come up in the Congress the army is sometimes accused of magnifying the Huk danger purely for budgetary purposes.

The press has reported vengeful killings by Huk gangs at baseball games and in other open situations, and it is widely known that the Huk organization in certain areas controls communications and some commercial activities. It seems clear that the para-military organization of the Huks is strong enough to pursue with some measure of success the policy so well known in Vietnam of killing key local officials and any well known opponents of the Huk movement.

President Magsaysay refused to grant amnesty to die-hard Huks because when the amnesty technique was tried by President Quirino, Luis Taruc and other leaders returned to the hills to carry on the armed insurrection. When Taruc's successor as Huk "supremo," Jesus Lava, was captured, the general press commented that the Huk movement was not ended—witness Lava's orders to his followers to liquidate those who captured him—and that to grant another amnesty would enable the Huks to regroup and rise up in arms again later.

THE BATTLE OF IDEAS

The communist problem is not limited to the countryside. Just as serious is the infiltration of government and press, universities, labor unions, and other organizations. According to captured communist directives, party members are instructed to press the battle of ideas in these organizations at the same time as the armed struggle is being resumed. According to these directives the revolution in the Philippines is in the "national-democratic" stage, not the "bourgeois-democratic." By "national" is meant national liberation, by "democratic" is meant control of capitalism and radical agrarian changes. The correct policy for the Communist Party, therefore, is to prepare by legal and parliamentary means for the violent seizure of power. The psychological task of the party is to create the appropriate climate of opinion in this society, in other words to create in the ruling upper and intellectual classes of the Philippines as much frustration, confusion, pessimism, defeatism, and neurosis as possible. The objective of communist agitation is to raise the level of

fear and anxiety and to secure semantic domination of intellectual, emotional, and socio-political life, and of all political arguments. The communists have progressed toward this goal by taking advantage of the
need of the Filipino to re-examine his relations with the United States,
the other countries of Asia, and his own past, present, and future.

There is a tendency in the intellectual world to leave the open
skirmishing with communists to the journals, speakers, and writers of
the Roman Catholic Church. The liberal intellectuals who should be
disposing of communist ideas, whatever their disguise, tend to be anti-
clerical and to assume that the clericalism which the communists de-
nounce is the greater danger. This idea has been fortified by the considerable amount of attention that the historical revisionists have given
to the reinterpretation of the events of the Revolution of 1896. This
trend is dangerous enough, but just as dangerous is the tendency in the
political arena to put the label of communism on any movements for
social reform of which the politician in question disapproves. For if
those who want to do something about unemployment, the extremes of
poverty and wealth, social injustice, and limited educational opportunities are in any case denounced as communist, then they become potential
recruits to the movement.

The United States can hardly remain indifferent to the manner in
which the battle of ideas is being fought in the Philippines, any more
than can the Philippine government itself. The most important link in
the whole structure of mutual security is in the realm of ideas as they are
expressed in books and journals and in the schools. It is a pity that there
is so little intellectual discourse between the two countries. The study of
American history, literature, and politics has actually been decreasing in
the Philippines, and in the United States the press and the academic
world virtually ignore the Philippines. The two countries do not create
the impression that they are actually talking with each other. The intellectual relationship between them is marked by blandness and patron-
age.

There is an intellectual renaissance in the Philippines today, fed by
nationalism, which can be measured in the changing tone of the journals
and the press. This is reflected in the political sphere. Philippine students have been organized to take political action in ways that would
previously have been considered unthinkable. They have changed the
intellectual climate on the campuses and demonstrated before embassies
in Manila. A measure of the change is indicated by a comparison of the
press and public reaction to the sending of Philippine troops to Korea, at
a time when armed Huk insurrection was at its height, and the proposal
in the summer of 1965 to send 2,000 engineers to Vietnam. The level of
political discourse is rising steadily in the Philippines. As mutual security
depends in the last instance on mutual confidence, common objectives,

and mutual understanding, it is important that both countries pay attention to the nature of the discourse.

AN EXTERNAL FACTOR

The other aspect of internal subversion, which has come up particularly since 1964, is the influence of Indonesia. Both President Macapagal
and the Chief of Staff of the Armed Forces expressed alarm over the
Indonesian threat in the spring of 1965 and cited the fact of increasing
numbers of Indonesian immigrants in Balut and in the Sarangani Islands, as well as in Davao and Cotabato. The House Committee on National Defense recommended the deployment of troops to Mindanao and
the establishment of ground, naval, and air patrols for the southern
borders of the Philippines. There were proposals to increase the outlay
for the armed forces in order to train and equip some 100,000 troops in
the next five years. There were also discussions of establishing a large
military base in the south. According to the Chief of Staff, General
Alfredo M. Santos, there was need to increase the number of twenty-year-
old recruits from 4,000 a year to 20,000, and to have enough money to
keep them in the regular army for a longer period. This would provide
the basis for stepping up United States military assistance.

There seems to be no doubt about the northward movement of Indonesian immigrants. Nor is there any question that the southern
borders are not very well protected. The possibility of armed conflict
with Indonesia has to be taken into account, but the main present danger
comes from infiltration of agents, both Indonesian and Chinese, and of
immigrants who can support them. It is also well known that the Indonesian government spends large sums of money in the Philippines on
propaganda, the main purpose of which is to break up the United States-
Philippine alliance by throwing doubt upon the motives and intentions
of the United States as well as of the Philippine government. At the
same time, a responsible Philippine reaction has been to raise the question of the relative value of a quarter of a million pesos spent in increasing the armed forces as compared with using it for social and economic
improvement. This is a serious question, one of the most important to be
raised in connection with mutual security.

The Problem of Military Bases

The presence of foreign troops, even friendly ones, is usually a
source of friction under the best of conditions. In the Philippines the
presence of American military bases has been a major source of friction,
not because of the bases themselves but because of the terms on which
they are held and the reluctance of the United States to change those
terms. The most important grievance was the question of jurisdiction, for

under the original Military Bases Agreement the United States had what amounted to extraterritorial jurisdiction over American military personnel. The only conditions under which the Philippines could exercise jurisdiction were those in which the American servicemen had committed crimes against Filipino citizens when they were off base and also, by admission of the American authorities, off duty. Furthermore, many Filipinos living within the bases were under American control, and one sizable city, Olongapo, was governed by American naval authorities.

The agreements reached between the two countries in August 1965 on the revision of criminal jurisdiction arrangements came after nearly a decade of bitter negotiations, damaging to United States-Philippine relations. The United States would have been well advised to agree much earlier to what it had to accept in the end. It is worth while looking at the record of the dispute in order to understand its effect on present attitudes and the importance of the agreements of 1965 to the Philippines.

A DECADE OF FRICTION

Negotiations for the revision of the agreements did not begin until 1956, by which time a series of incidents at Clark Field, the principal American air base, had made the atmosphere tense. Over a period of ten years some twenty Filipinos had been killed by guards while scavenging for bombs dropped by United States planes on the gunnery range. The negotiations were acrimonious. The Filipinos drew attention to American agreements on bases with such countries as the United Kingdom, Japan, and Spain which were more favorable than their own, particularly in the matter of jurisdiction. It was especially irritating that the former enemy, Japan, was better treated. The American panel, composed entirely of military representatives, except for the Ambassador, called off the negotiations, and they were not taken up again until Ambassador Charles Bohlen and Secretary of Foreign Affairs Felixberto Serrano resumed negotiations in 1959.

At this time the United States agreed to several serious modifications, the more important being the delimitation of American base areas, the relinquishment by the United States of approximately 117,962 hectares of land, the reduction in the term of the lease from 99 to 25 years, surrender of the Manila Port Area reservation to the jurisdiction and control of the Philippines, and the transfer of the Olongapo community to the Philippine government. It was agreed that Filipino liaison officers would be stationed on the bases, that the United States would consult with the Philippine government before installing missile sites or using the bases for any purposes other than mutual defense, and that a Mutual Defense Board would be set up. The United States also agreed to elevate to a treaty commitment the United States responsibility to repel instantly any attack on the Philippines. President Garcia commented that, as a result of these changes, relations between the two countries had improved considerably, largely because the Filipinos felt that the United States had recognized the legitimacy of nationalism in the Philippines. The question of criminal jurisdiction was the only important matter not solved at this time. The Bohlen-Serrano talks were recessed at the time of the 1961 elections and were not taken up again until January 1965. The changes agreed on prior to 1961, however, were not to go into effect until all issues were settled and a new agreement ratified by both governments.

THE NEXT ISSUE?

In all the discussions it is clear that Filipinos were concerned less with the existence of the bases than with their own role and status. They were thinking of their national pride and of their relative standing among the friends and allies of the United States. Responsible Filipino officials have always recognized the realities of the world situation. In the summer of 1963, Vice President Emmanuel Pelaez made a particularly forthright statement on the facts of Philippine security: "In the political and military field, requirements of our national security and the imperative of our very survival as a free nation compel us to maintain existing arrangements bilateral as well as collective with the United States and other Western powers." At the same time, he frankly drew attention to the difficult problem of the disparity in power between the United States and the Philippines. For this reason the American and the Filipino peoples had to make a special effort to maintain what was meaningful in the ties that existed between them—"they must consciously try, as it were, to keep in touch." It is one thing to establish mutual respect between nations of equal power and influence, but between a great nation and a small the "feeling of consideration is needed to redress the balance and to create the condition necessary for mutual respect." Americans have not always heeded this advice. The inflexibility of the United States on the jurisdiction issue led to long drawn-out and often bitter negotiations over the bases that provided the Filipinos with a ready-made platform for the discussion of every problem, real and imaginary, that concerned the two countries. Largely as a result of this, as well as of the influence of Asian countries, more Filipinos are aware today of the case for neutralism than ever before.

Those who argue the neutralist position do not necessarily favor it for the same reasons. Some want it as a step toward an alignment with the communist bloc, others as a bargaining weapon to secure an even stronger American commitment to Philippine defense, and others as an affirmation of a truly independent Philippines. The most intellectually respectable arguments for a neutral Philippines were associated with the late Senator Claro Recto, who was in favor of this position before World War II as well as afterward. He saw neutralism as a policy that could hardly bring any greater dangers to the Philippines than an alliance with the United States, which after all had failed to protect the Philip-

pines from invasion and had destroyed a good deal of Philippine property
in driving out the Japanese. According to his view, the Philippines
should have a choice of surrender if they so wished. Alliance with the
United States, it was argued, might guarantee nuclear destruction.

Variations on these and related themes of neutralism were reflected in
certain quarters of the Philippines in 1965 when President Macapagal
first called for the dispatch of Filipino troops to South Vietnam. It was
argued that if the United States lost in South Vietnam then it would
need the Filipino bases even more than before, whereas if it succeeded
the Philippines would have been defended. Congressman Roces raised
the question of command if the Philippines sent troops, since there was
no unified command as in the Korean War. He also commented that a
Philippine force could not influence the course of the war in Vietnam or
change the attitude of the Vietnamese on the outcome of the war.
Others pointed out that to send even a small unit would be leading the
country into war, that larger and larger commitments of men would have
to be made, and that this would be done without public debate or the
constitutional requirement of a two-thirds vote for war—merely on the
basis of a Congressional appropriation to support an engineering unit of
2,000 men. In the view of Teodoro Locsin, editor of the *Free Press,* there
was nothing the Philippines could do to help the United States get out of
the "Vietnamese mess" except to help secure the American position in the
Philippines and perhaps the rest of Asia by "making democracy work" in
the Philippines and by improving relations with neighboring countries,
such as Indonesia and Malaysia. In this task, he said, American apprecia-
tion of Filipino ideals and integrity would be helpful. Others implied
that the United States had "bought" support of the Macapagal administration for cooperation in Vietnam by offering to meet the $860 million
claims against the United States government for veterans' pay and setting
up a stabilization fund to bolster the economy. There was sufficient opposition, not all of it from those who wanted to get on with reform at
home, to compel the Congress in July 1965 to postpone action on sending 2,000 engineers and combat troops to Vietnam until 1966.

Most discussion of American-Philippine problems proceeds within the
framework of agreed-upon alliances and commitments. The professors
and students who demonstrated in early 1965 in Manila did not call for
the removal of the bases but for the exercise of Philippine jurisdiction
over all offenses committed against Filipinos inside and outside the bases
by American servicemen. They were not apparently for neutrality in the
Cold War but for continued association with the United States—on
terms of mutual respect.

THE UNNECESSARY ISSUE

During 1965 the continuing debate on the bases issue produced a wide
spectrum of Filipino attitudes and claims. Senate President Ferdinand E.

Marcos, later president, stated that the Nacionalista platform, while favoring close relations with the United States, called for immediate negotiation of the Military Bases Agreement to secure full recognition of the sovereign rights of the Philippines. In the matter of jurisdiction of Philippine courts over offenses committed inside the bases by Filipinos or committed inside or outside the bases by United States military or civilian personnel, they should be punishable by Philippine laws rather than by United States military laws. President Macapagal instructed Foreign Secretary Mauro Mendez to seek the NATO-type provisions on jurisdiction in his conversations with Ambassador William McCormick Blair, Jr. on the revision of the Bases Agreement. Under a NATO-type pact the United States assumes jurisdiction only if members of her armed forces commit offenses on or off the base while on duty. Under the Bases Agreement with the Philippines the United States, since 1946, had exercised primary jurisdiction over all offenses committed by American military personnel or Filipinos on base, whether on or off duty. Senator Arturo M. Tolentino, in a privileged speech to the Senate in February 1965, argued for the revision of the Agreement in order to improve relations between the two countries, not to score any victories. He wished to see the Agreement revised so that American military authorities would have jurisdiction only over members of their armed forces who violated United States military law, without regard to the place of the commission of the offense whether inside or outside the base. On the other hand, Philippine courts should have jurisdiction over all violations of Philippine laws, wherever committed and whoever might be the offender.

Particularly thoughtful was the contribution of former Foreign Secretary Felixberto M. Serrano. He pointed out that American military bases exist with Philippine consent, to enable the United States to discharge more effectively its responsibilities of defending the Philippines against aggression. Undeniably, the subtraction from Philippine sovereign rights, to the extent that they are pre-empted in the corresponding exercise of American jurisdiction, is the price the Philippines has agreed to pay to better safeguard national security. Serrano argued that as the exercise of American jurisdiction is a derogation and subtraction *pro tanto* of Philippine sovereign rights within the Philippines, it should be limited to the unavoidable minimum; beyond this minimum, Philippine laws and sovereignty must be held supreme. In the twilight cases where both principles apply in varying degrees, suitable arrangements on concurrent exercise or reciprocal waiver of jurisdiction must be worked out with respectful regard to the interests of both countries.

Under the arrangements agreed to by both governments on August 10, 1965, each country will have exclusive jurisdiction with respect to offenses which are punishable by its own laws, but not by laws of the other country. This includes offenses relating to each country's security. The pattern is close to that of the NATO Status of Forces Agreement and in all important respects meets the conditions that Filipinos have considered essential for their national self-respect. In cases of concurrent jurisdiction, under which most cases involving United States forces fall, exercise of primary jurisdiction by the United States is confined to offenses solely against the property or security of the United States or the person or property of a member of the United States armed forces or civilian component, or dependent; and to offenses arising out of any act or omission done in performance of official duty. The primary right of the United States to exercise jurisdiction extends only to persons in the Philippines who are subject to the military law of the United States. In all other cases, including those occurring inside the United States bases, the Philippines has the primary right to exercise jurisdiction. Civilians, including dependents, were made subject to Philippine jurisdiction for on-base as well as off-base offenses.

Important for the future was the spelling out of arrangements for implementing the new provisions. On the key question of duty status it was agreed that when it was necessary to determine whether an act by a member of the United States armed forces arose from the performance of official duty, the commanding officer, on the advice of the Base Legal Officer, would issue a certificate concerning duty status which the Philippines agreed to honor. This certificate was subject to review by appropriate officials of both governments if the Philippine Secretary of Justice so required. The Philippines agreed to waive primary jurisdiction, upon request, in cases which were of no great importance, in order to assist the United States authorities in maintaining discipline over their armed forces. The agreement also included a Criminal Jurisdiction Implementation Committee of Philippine and United States government officials for mutual consultation on matters relating to criminal jurisdiction when requested by either party. There will be difficulties, but a major source of friction was removed by the exchange of notes in August 1965 and American willingness to have the new agreement go into effect immediately.

The reluctance of the United States to conclude with the Philippines a status of forces agreement as favorable as those with other allies is difficult to explain. The cost of permitting long drawn-out public discussion in the Philippine Congress and press has been high. Delay made agreement all the more difficult to achieve because national consciousness intensified in the meantime and further incidents occurred in which Filipinos were injured or killed on the bases.

THE FUTURE OF MUTUAL SECURITY

Events in Southeast Asia, among other factors, have increased the importance of the bases to the security of the United States, apart from any obligations to defend the Philippines. Military witnesses informed the

House Committee on Foreign Affairs in 1965 that the first line of defense of the United States lay in those countries which bordered on Communist China, the Soviet Union, and their Asian satellites and that a threat to the political or physical security of those countries was a threat to the security interests of the United States. Without Clark Field and Subic Bay the American security system in the Western Pacific would be seriously weakened. Because this is true the United States tends to see the bases as part of a larger security system involving the defense of areas and interests other than the Philippines. As these bases are undoubtedly enemy targets in any war in which the United States is involved, the Filipinos have a legitimate interest in being taken into account when policies are pursued that might lead to conflict or when the United States uses the bases, as it has for the South Vietnam war, to facilitate military operations in which the Philippines was not at first directly involved. As the weaker member of the alliance can, hypothetically, follow policies that might invite enemy attack under circumstances that would obligate the United States to come to its assistance, the need for understanding and consultation, however unequal, is mutual.

We live in a revolutionary world. Nothing is impervious to change, including the long-standing obligations of the United States to the Philippines and the mutual interests of the two countries. The partnership between American and Filipinos is confirmed by written commitments, but its character and effectiveness depend on the quality of human relationships. The present and prospective military arrangements between the two governments, whether open or confidential, are of little significance to the discussion of mutual security. The really important questions concern the values, attitudes, and purposes of the Philippine and American governments and people. If these change, then everything else changes. The most heavily armed bases in the world are useless if they are surrounded by a hostile population. The most powerful of allies is a liability if it cannot be trusted to fulfill its obligations. A discussion of mutual security, therefore, is really about mutual understanding and confidence. That is why it is essential to raise questions that bring to the fore the political, intellectual, and social trends of the two societies. There is no security unless there are mutual interests.

It has been the argument of this essay that the Philippines and the United States have a long-term mutuality of interest in the preservation, perhaps even the expansion, of their shared concern for politically independent and open societies in Asia. The problems of partnership stem more from the contrast in the power and obligations of the two countries than from their differences in tradition and values. It is as important for the United States, therefore, to understand the character of Philippine nationalism and the new directions of Philippine society as for the Filipinos to see the purposes and obligations of the United States in their global context. The essence of the problem of partnership is the parochialism of the Philippines, absorbed as it is in its own affairs, and the tendency of the United States, with its global commitments, to take its partners for granted. The solution is not difficult to discern. It lies in mutual understanding.

Frank H. Golay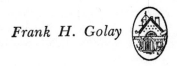

5

Economic Collaboration:
The Role of American Investment

Colonial Economic Development

The economy inherited by the independent Philippines conformed to the stereotype of the colonial-type economy. Thanks to the colonial policy of "mutual free trade," the Philippines became highly specialized in primary production for export to the industrial market in the United States. For the four years, 1937-40, shipments of coconut, sugar, and abaca products, together with gold production, accounted for 85 per cent of the value of exports. The only significant export commodity which was not a raw or processed primary product was embroideries, a handicraft product. For the same four-year period, almost three-quarters of Philippine trade was with the metropolitan country, which provided seven-tenths of Philippine imports and took four-fifths of exports.

Colonial economic development was unimpressive when assessed in terms of mid-century aspirations for modernization and welfare. Expansion was sufficient to more than keep abreast of the population growth, but did not provide Filipinos with an advanced standard of living. Agriculture, dominated by smallholders subsistence production, provided a livelihood for some two-thirds of the population but generated no more than two-fifths of aggregate income. Colonial policy denied protection to manufacturing, which experienced little development, was dominated by the processing of rice, corn, sugar, tobacco, coconuts, and logs.

Foreign investment in the Philippines, as in the colonial world generally, was attracted to the export industries which developed on the basis of the markets in the industrial world. Not surprisingly, it was dominated by American enterprise and capital, which were particularly prominent in mining. The 1933 devaluation of the dollar, which raised the price of gold from $20 to $35 per ounce, was followed by rapid expansion in gold production. By the end of the decade of the 1930s, gold mining, which provided one-quarter of foreign exchange earnings, was largely foreign owned and managed. The exploitation of the rich forestry resources of the islands was limited, but here also foreign investment was prominent.

A distinctive feature of the development of the export economy has been the relative absence of plantations. This resulted from an early triumph of Filipino nationalists who, over the opposition of the American colonial administrators, were able to impose restrictions on the amount of land that could be acquired by an individual or enterprise and limited land ownership to Filipinos and Americans. This restriction, which effectively limited such holdings to 1,024 hectares, inhibited large-scale plantation development. Western investment tended to move into export processing—sugar centrals, coconut oil mills, desiccated coconut factories, and so forth—rather than into the production of export crops. Coconut production was developed as a smallholders crop and sugar was produced on relatively small, largely Filipino-owned holdings, serviced by a Western-owned sugar mill.

Abaca production was a significant exception to this pattern, as in Davao Province a plantation-type development occurred with Japanese initiative and capital and the connivance of Filipino "dummies." Outside of this area, which accounted for half of total abaca output, production was in the hands of Filipino smallholders. Tobacco production for export was concentrated in northern Luzon and involved a mixture of Filipino smallholdings and a few medium-sized plantations with important Spanish participation.

A number of major exports, including sugar, coconut oil, desiccated coconut, minerals, logs and lumber, and pineapples were shipped directly by producers or large-scale processors. Other exports, such as copra, abaca, and minor forest products were assembled for shipment by exporting firms, both Western and Chinese. Importing was divided between Western and Chinese firms, with capital goods and large-scale imports such as petroleum products, in the hands of larger Western firms, predominantly American. Wholesaling was divided for the most part between Western and Chinese enterprises, with the latter specializing in the distribution of consumer goods. Retailing, outside of the very small "sari-sari" stores, was dominated by the Chinese.

As in the colonial world generally, an exchange reserve currency imposed by the metropolitan power rigidly tied the supply of money and credit to the state of the balance of payments. Commercial banking, with the major exception of the government-owned Philippine National Bank, was dominated by branches of foreign banks which concentrated in the finance of foreign trade, both imports and exports. Credit for market-oriented agricultural production and commercial activities, and for the real estate transactions of Filipinos, was provided, in large part, by the Philippine National Bank, which maintained branches throughout the country. Money lenders, Chinese middlemen, and landlords, provided the minimum amounts of credit required by Filipino smallholders and tenant farmers.

ORIGINS OF ECONOMIC NATIONALISM

The relatively modern, large-scale economy of export production and processing, and attendant commercial and financial functions, was poorly articulated, with the more basic economy organized to meet the minimum material needs of the population. Filipino-owned and organized, and providing a livelihood for the principal part of the population, was the tradition-bound agricultural economy providing the staple food requirements of the society. Although landlordism was endemic, the unit of production was the miserably small family farm worked by the smallholder or tenant farmer. Output was concentrated in subsistence production with the margin over subsistence, largely the share of output diverted to rentier income, moving to the urban market. Although there was considerable truck, fruit, and fisheries production centered upon Manila and the smaller cities, domestic commerce arising out of agricultural production for the local market was concentrated in rice and corn and was in the hands of the Chinese.

Colonialism found the Filipinos receptive to a relatively advanced religion, but unprepared to participate in a more sophisticated economic organization based upon individualism and specialization. As a result, they tended to remain bystanders as economic functions, outside of smallholders agriculture, were largely monopolized by aliens, Western and Chinese. Large-scale enterprises in mining, forestry, the processing of exports, manufacturing, commerce, and finance, were organized by Western entrepreneurs, with the interstices between their enterprises filled, for the most part, by smaller-scale enterprises of the Chinese. Modest expansion of this sector proved to be self-sustaining, as the favorable factor proportions maintained the returns to capital and entrepreneurship and the alien proprietors furnished the essential capitalist function by "plowing back" earnings.

Filipino nationalists, as nationalists generally, imperfectly comprehended the nature of colonial economic development and expected to transform the colonial economy once they gained control of their economic destiny. A major change in this direction occurred in the middle of the 1930s when the United States Congress drafted legislation providing for a transitional period of commonwealth status after which formal independence would be established. The Commonwealth government, established in the midst of the ferment of the "New Deal" and at a time when industrial societies were re-examining shibboleths concerning the proper economic role of the state, was given wide powers to engage in manufacturing and commercial activities. Through the effective use of these powers the political leaders expected to transform the colonial-type economy.

Progress toward this goal under the Commonwealth proved to be limited. In the first place, continuation of "mutual free trade" effectively prevented recourse to protection. Moreover, Filipino statesmen and policy makers, self-confident and oriented to the status quo by the long period of tutelage and administrative responsibility, did not aggressively intervene in the enterprise economy. Filipino nationalists believed as an article of faith that the alienization of major economic functions which had characterized colonial economic development reflected the discrimination and exploitation of colonial *laissez faire*. To believe otherwise, that alien domination of the economy had resulted from impersonal market processes, was a reflection of Filipino capabilities unthinkable to the dedicated nationalist. Filipinization was expected to result with the release of previously suppressed Filipino individualism, in conjunction with industrialization through public manufacturing enterprises. To encourage the flow of entrepreneurship, government-owned credit institutions could be created to overcome real and imagined handicaps arising out of alien domination of banking. Progress toward remolding the colonial economy, however, proved to be negligible when the Japanese invaded at the end of 1941.

The Japanese Occupation

The period of invasion, occupation, and liberation—from the end of 1941 through 1945—produced far-reaching and inadequately appreciated changes in the Philippine social environment. Such changes have been neglected because they were intangible shifts in attitudes, values, and patterns of behavior. As the occupation dragged on, and Japan's prospects waned, relations between the Filipinos and the Japanese deteriorated and subversion of order became the preoccupation of individualistic Filipinos. Access to new and varied experiences—military command, administrative and organization responsibilities, and so forth —generated Filipino aspirations as well as capabilities. As the economy ground to a halt under the impact of the submarine blockade and bombing, the problems of survival contributed to the spatial mobility of the population. Similarly, the constraints and opportunities of the occupation forced Filipinos into new patterns of economic behavior; into patterns of improvisation and innovation which deeply influenced the self-image of the Filipino. The Japanese occupation also accelerated the exodus of the Americans with economic interests in the islands. Interned at advanced ages, many major business figures did not survive the occupation. For others, the destruction of enterprises, homes, and possessions made repatriation more attractive. This change was concentrated particularly in "old timers" who had settled in the country and had created transportation, commercial, and agricultural enterprises. For many, the task of rebuilding was overwhelming and the early postwar period found them selling out to Filipinos.

War and occupation also resulted in extensive economic dislocation, capital destruction, and disinvestment. The wartime preoccupation with subversion and guerrilla activity, moreover, has been reflected in qualitative deterioration in political behavior and internal order at both the local and national level. Similarly, the confusion surrounding the issue of collaboration and the transition to civilian rule were obstacles to improvement in the political process.

Evolution of the National Economy

Following the end of World War II, with independence scheduled to materialize on July 4, 1946, the United States Congress hastily drafted two important pieces of legislation—the Philippine Trade Act of 1946 and the Philippine Rehabilitation Act of 1946. The Trade Act renewed the transitional period of "mutual free trade" of the earlier independence legislation and extended it to 1954, following which tariff duties were to be gradually imposed by the two countries until full duties would be collected beginning in 1974. The Rehabilitation Act provided for substantial payments to rehabilitate war damaged properties, both private and public.

Inauguration of the Republic found the Filipinos in a favorable position to rehabilitate their economy and to organize for further progress. The United States was committed to heavy disbursements which, combined with favorable terms of trade, enabled the Philippines to sustain imports during 1946-49 at more than double the prewar volume. Moreover, Philippine external security was guaranteed for the foreseeable future by the American military presence and, therefore, fiscal resources of the new state were not subject to heavy drain for defense.

ECONOMIC PROBLEMS OF INDEPENDENCE

Once the political arrangements for independence had been completed, the United States moved to participate liberally in the rehabilitation of the war damaged economy. Major reconstruction had been accomplished earlier by the liberation forces concerned with the development of Luzon as a staging base for the anticipated conquest of Japan. This required the restoration of basic public utilities, transportation and communication facilities, and military construction. By the end of 1949, war damage payments totaling $620 million were virtually completed. There were, in addition, large-scale United States disbursements, including military expenditures, "back pay" awards to members of the Philippine armed forces (guerillas) who had been absorbed into the United States armed forces, and Veterans Administration payments for disability pensions, hospitalization, and "G. I. Bill of Rights" benefits. Finally, the American government transferred to the Philippine government, as budgetary assistance, large sums collected as internal processing taxes on Philippine exports to the United States and a substantial budgetary loan. Other assistance took the form of surplus military stores and proceeds from the sales of Japanese assets sequestered by the United States Foreign Liquidation Commission.

During the postwar period, to the end of 1949, export earnings covered only two-fifths of import expenditures, and the cumulative import surplus of $1.4 billion was matched by net United States government expenditures. Moreover, this was a time in which the rampant inflation of the Japanese occupation was brought under control and the cost of living was reduced from an index of 100 for 1946 to 66 in 1949. By 1948, Philippine real output had fully recovered to the level of ten years earlier.

Although American assistance was liberal, rehabilitation of the war damaged economy was essentially a process of restoring the prewar primary producing export economy and contributed little to Filipino longings for industrialization and Filipinization. Frustration over the rehabilitation process was compounded by the deterioration in standards of public morality evident in the succession of well publicized scandals involving politicians and civil servants. "Anomalies" in the handling of surplus property disposal, visas for Chinese immigrants, and, following 1949, import and exchange licensing undermined public confidence in political institutions and processes. Moreover, the government, with discouraging persistence, refused to levy taxes adequate to cover expenditures and failed to collect existing taxes. The decision to restore the prewar peso exchange rate ensured that foreign exchange reserves would remain under heavy pressure, as imports continued to expand while exports made only a partial recovery to prewar levels. Overshadowing all these problems was the Huk insurrection which, by the end of 1949, had called into question the viability of the government and the economic system.

THE WATERSHED

The year and a half following the end of 1949 proved to be an eventful period in Philippine development, as far-reaching changes provided solutions to the social and economic problems which beset the country. The dramatic shift in Philippine fortunes in 1950 and 1951 had a number of major aspects. Most important was the initiation of an effective military campaign which reduced the Huk threat to minor dimensions and restored order to the countryside. Of comparable importance were the international developments which produced a firm mutual defense commitment by the United States—thereby providing the Philippine society an acceptable guarantee of external security.

Rapid movement in the economy was also forthcoming. Strong international demand conditions following the outbreak of war in Korea sustained rapid expansion in export receipts. More important, at the end of 1949 stringent import and exchange controls were imposed to manage the persistent disequilibrium in external payments. Finally, the clamorous fiscal problem of inadequate revenues was solved by tax measures imposed, following Bell Mission recommendations, as a *quid pro quo* for a permanent United States aid program to the Philippines. Congress, in 1950 and 1951, enacted a series of new revenue measures, including the productive tax on sales of foreign exchange, which virtually doubled national government revenues.

Another economic change that had taken place somewhat earlier, and which proved to be of great importance, was the abandonment of the colonial exchange reserve currency in favor of a managed currency system. At the apex of the new system was the Central Bank of the Philippines, which was established in 1949 and given wide and expandable powers to create money and credit with which to support economic development by both the public and private sectors. Reinforcing the monetary powers was an equivalent autonomy over commercial policy and protection inherent in exchange and import controls. Philippine economic sovereignty was substantially completed by these changes and postwar American efforts to prolong colonial-type constraints on Philippine freedom of action were effectively undermined.

To bring the external disequilibrium under control, the new import and exchange controls were applied with such intensity that in 1950 the volume of imports was reduced to only 58 per cent of the previous year. As might be expected, the importers charged what the market would bear for the reduced quantities of imports and prices of these goods rose rapidly.

POLICIES AND INSTITUTIONS

Initially, economic policy makers were preoccupied with maintaining equilibrium in external payments and foreign exchange was allocated to established importers. It was not long, however, before Filipino nationalists realized that the discrepancy which had been introduced between the value of the peso spent within the Philippines and the value of the peso when exchanged for foreign currency at the official exchange rate and spent abroad, provided a powerful tool for manipulating economic incentives. Very promptly they realized, that by introducing nationality as a qualification for exchange allocation, the lucrative importing activity could be Filipinized. Not surprisingly, they came to understand that the price increases resulting from restricting imports established an umbrella of protection for domestic producers. Such producers could be subsidized, moreover, by allocations of foreign exchange for imports of so-called "industrial raw materials" for local processing, and aggressive steps were taken to reserve this windfall to potential Filipino entrepreneurs. The emergence of Filipino enterprises was eased by the fact that manufacturing initially comprised packaging and minor final processing which were within Filipino capabilities. The venturesome Filipinos who responded to the new opportunities, however, received experiences which prepared them to undertake more sophisticated manufacturing processes.

THE ROLE OF PUBLIC ENTERPRISE

Meanwhile, the government continued to experiment vigorously with the public corporation as an instrument for transforming the economy. By the early 1950s, the government was operating railroads, hotels, electric power, gas, and water works as well as producing coal, cement, fertilizer, steel, textiles, yarns, and operating a shipyard and engineering shops. In addition, the government had investments in firms manufacturing incandescent bulbs and fluorescent tubes, pulp and paper, a "national" domestic and international airline, and owned three ocean-going vessels. Finally, through the government-owned National Development Company, it was, or had been engaged in the production of nails, lumber, footwear, sugar, textiles and yarns, food preserving and packaging, and warehousing.

The extensive list of manufacturing activities indicated a persistent faith in the capacity of the government to participate directly in industrialization and Filipinization. Corruption, nepotism, and bureaucratic mismanagement of government enterprises, however, produced such deep disillusionment that in the 1950s this policy was abandoned and the remaining government enterprises sold, or liquidated. In 1954, a candid self-appraisal of government entrepreneurship concluded that "the high incidence of political considerations and the 'padrino' system in the appointment, promotion and tenure of office of officials and employees . . . is the root cause of the abuses and heavy losses and waste of public funds and property and contributes to the loss of faith in government corporations."

DRIVE FOR FILIPINIZATION

The initial success with which nationalist policy makers exploited exchange and import controls to promote Filipinization and industrialization generated further efforts to extend the system of entrepreneurial incentives. Earlier, in 1946, the Philippines had established a "New and Necessary Industries" policy under which enterprises applying for and receiving such designation were exempted from specified taxes for a limited period. The initial results under the policy were not impressive but, following 1949, the designation "New and Necessary" was eagerly sought, not for the privilege of tax exemption alone but because such designation established a priority claim to foreign exchange.

Strong incentives resulted from the promotion by the government of functionally specialized money and capital market institutions, owned and controlled by Filipinos who could be depended upon to divert subsidized credit resources to fellow Filipinos. Similarly, reparations policy assigned primary importance to private initiative by allocating three-fifths of reparations to individual Filipinos and Filipino-owned enterprises. In addition, the peso counterpart funds generated by the sale of reparations were reserved for loans to the same beneficiaries. The transfer of various government manufacturing enterprises to private ownership also carried strong incentives. Although the prices at which these enterprises were transferred did not subsidize the new owners, credit terms were liberal, and continuation of high levels of protection from competing imports and a priority claim to scarce foreign exchange were assured to Filipino purchasers.

THE ECONOMY ON THE MOVE

The decade and a half following 1949 were years of sustained economic growth and industrialization. During this period real national income more than doubled, an expansion somewhat greater than twice the increase in population. Growth was broadly based, with all major industrial sectors growing at rates in excess of population growth. It was paced by manufacturing output which, as a share of national income, increased from 8 per cent in 1949 to 18.5 per cent in 1963. Although a substantial part of this dramatic expansion represented price increases resulting from high levels of protection, the index of the physical volume of manufacturing output is estimated to have increased almost three-fold over this period.

Equally remarkable has been the rapid Filipinization of all major economic sectors. Importing, other than industrial raw materials and capital equipment for direct use, was steadily diverted to Filipino enterprises by import controls. Export production, with the exceptions of mining, where foreign capital and management are still prominent, and the production and processing of pineapples and the manufacture of desiccated coconut by American-owned enterprises, today is substantially in Filipino hands. Internal commerce, with the major exceptions of the ubiquitous international oil distributing firms, is dominated by Filipino ownership and management and heavy nationalist pressures are being maintained on the remaining Chinese and Western interests. Retail trade and trade in rice and corn, long dominated by the Chinese, have been reserved by law to Filipinos and substitute Filipino marketing structures apparently have materialized with little dislocation. Similarly, public utility services, including internal transport and communications, are today essentially Filipino-owned and managed. Finally, the postwar period has seen the emergence, with government encouragement and subsidization, of a complex structure of money and capital market institutions owned and controlled by Filipinos.

The flamboyant expansion of Filipino manufacturing, commercial, and financial activity, based upon the internal market and concentrated in the Manila area, is not the whole story of postwar Philippine economic development. The basic economy of smallholders agricultural production occupies most of the population today, as it did throughout the American colonial period. The preoccupation of policy makers with industrialization and Filipinization was made possible, to a degree little understood or appreciated, by the expansion in agricultural output which proceeded throughout most of the postwar period at rates in excess of population growth. As a result, the growth in national income was widely distributed and the peasant, who continued to ignore the processes of modernization, experienced improved welfare. Agricultural expansion contributed to the improvement in stability and order in the rural areas in which the Huk insurrection had been recruited. Steady expansion in food supplies also contributed to the social stability, productivity, and discipline of the industrial proletariat, and entrepreneurial profits were subject to little encroachment from rising wage rates.

THE NATURE OF FILIPINO ENTREPRENEURSHIP

The success of the economic system evolved by the Philippine society over a quarter century of fumbling experimentation and pragmatic expediency has been dependent upon the emergence of Filipino entrepreneurship. It is a system in which discretionary allocation by the government of various economic concessions was used to ensure the viability of Filipino enterprises. The powerful tools of monetary and commercial policy with which the government managed the economy were used aggressively to minimize the competitive pressures from alien businesses. Such intervention in a competitive economy is questionable, but it is the key to understanding the peculiarly Filipino adaptation of the enterprise economy. Rapid economic growth was sustained following 1949 because adequate amounts of Filipino entrepreneurship materialized in response to overpowering incentives.

The success of the system is also understandable in terms of the political content of Filipino entrepreneurial activity. The present economic system requires a peculiar type of entrepreneurship, half economic and half political. The Filipino seeking to become an entrepreneur finds himself engaged in familiar political manipulation—to obtain foreign exchange, to obtain credit, to obtain items of reparations equipment, and so forth. Initially, he is half businessman and half political man and to the latter role he brings experience and skills. Such an adaptation of the enterprise economy made the transition from traditional patterns of economic behavior—and from political behavior—to entrepreneurship much less abrupt. It is this fact, together with the structure of arbitrary policies, which is used to prevent frustration of the expectations of Filipinos and which enables us to understand the system.

The Environment of Economic Collaboration

The objective success of Filipinos in organizing and managing their economy following 1949 contributed to a growing self-confidence which contrasts sharply with the uncertainty and doubts which made it possible for the Bell Mission to dictate major policy decisions. Price stability persisted as the monetary authorities acquired experience and developed techniques of management. Equally satisfying to Filipinos was the relative decline in the importance of the primary producing export sector, which presently contributes less than one-fifth of aggregate income. Finally, Filipinos derived confidence from the steady improvement in the political process following the low point of the corruption- and violence-ridden election of 1949. Over this period elections were held on schedule and the party in power, on occasion, has lost elections and peacefully transferred political power.

The public sector was the major exception to this success story. Bureaucratic entrepreneurship, with the exceptions of the government-owned banks and the National Power Corporation, proved uniformly disappointing. The government, moreover, repeatedly demonstrated little capacity to carry out needed social investment or to efficiently maintain minimum social services. The Philippines produced a succession of economic plans, presumably to guide the mobilization of national capabilities and to channel public investment, but they remained "paper plans" ignored, for the most part, by the Executive and Congress. Institutions to enable the government to participate in economic development proliferated—a promising system of agricultural cooperatives, institutions to regulate tenancy relations in agriculture, to promote colonization of land on the frontier, to improve budgetary and comprehensive economic planning, a community development program, and so forth. All too often, such institutions and programs were created with high hopes and assigned major responsibilities, only to lapse into ennui, burdened with staff who were neither qualified nor motivated to carry out assigned goals, but who were useful to some politician.

The major fiscal reforms of 1950 and 1951, resulting from American initiative and pressure, did not stimulate further improvement. Only minor changes have occurred since then and government revenues remain dependent upon regressive indirect taxation, particularly of import values. Although significant elements of progression are built into the tax structure, lax enforcement has prevented revenues from increasing as a ratio of expanding national income.

A succession of well publicized scandals prevented rehabilitation of the government's public image and the restoration of confidence in public enterprises. As a result, the society has insisted that the public sector remain a colonial-type, minimum government, capturing and allocating only about one-tenth of the aggregate output. Policy makers have displayed great initiative and ingenuity in devising policies and institutions for generating Filipino initiative and entrepreneurship. The failure to exercise comparable enterprise in improving the performance of the public sector is an unfortunate handicap to social and economic development.

In spite of the well publicized inadequacies of the public sector, Filipinos generally are aware that their economic development is a substantial accomplishment, that their political process is a unique success among the new states of Southeast Asia, and that they have achieved a viable political sovereignty to match their substantive economic independence. As a result, the self-confidence of the society forces itself upon the consciousness. Today there are few socialists among Filipinos and no social protest movements which seriously question the nature of the peculiarly Philippine adaptation of the enterprise economy. The vicissitudes of the early postwar period have been obscured by fifteen years of successful economic management—of the external disequilibrium, of internal price stability, of economic growth, industrialization, and Filipinization. This is not to say that there has not been continuous controversy over economic policy, but rather to suggest that the events of the past decade have instilled in the Filipino elites confidence that their system and techniques of economic management will continue to produce the national economic development to which the society aspires.

This, then, is the environment in which the United States government and the Americans as individuals seek to collaborate in economic and social development. Americans can take pride in the substantial achievements of the independent Philippines, as the tangible and intangible changes wrought during the American colonial period prepared the way for the promising postwar advances. On the other hand, both we and the Filipinos must be concerned for the future of the collaboration as the nature of the mutual adaptation required to permit effective participation by American resources is obscured by discord and confusion.

The Role of American Capital

The major institution with which the United States hopes to participate in the economic development of the less developed world is private direct foreign investment. The potential contribution of such investment is undeniable—to employment and income, to foreign exchange earned or saved, to government revenues, and to the myriad changes in the environment that economists label modernization. Private direct investment by Americans contributed solidly to the colonial development of the primary product export economy and, over the past decade and a half, direct foreign investment, motivated by the protected and growing internal market, has steadily enlarged the American economic stake in the Philippines.

THE ACCUMULATION OF DIRECT INVESTMENT

The United States Department of Commerce estimates that American direct investment in the Philippines, including American investment in corporations in which the American ownership share was at least 25 per cent, totaled $92 million in 1936, $149 million in 1950, and $415 million at the end of 1963. As might be expected, the fastest growing sector of direct investment in the postwar period has been manufacturing, which increased almost five-fold from $23 million in 1950 to $110 million. This estimate substantially understates the actual growth of American direct investment in manufacturing, however, as the Department of Commerce includes petroleum refining capacity in a separate "Petroleum" category. The Philippines today has four small petroleum refineries, whereas in 1950 none existed. The identifiable American share of the assets of these refining companies, not including Shell Refining Company, totaled some $80 million. This means that of total American direct investment in the Philippines at the end of 1963, slightly less than one-half was in manufacturing for the domestic market. Such investment had grown nine-fold from the level of $23 million recorded in 1950.

The second largest category of direct investment identified by the Department of Commerce is "trade," which increased from a level of $30 million in 1950 to $64 million at the end of 1963. Again, it is necessary to adjust these estimates since the international oil distributing firms are included in the category "Petroleum." Of the total American direct investment in "Petroleum," some $85 million can be assigned to distribution facilities, and therefore American direct investment in commercial enterprises amounted at the end of 1963 to some $150 million.

The bulk of the remaining American direct investment is accounted for by those areas in which it has been American policy to try to ensure national treatment for American enterprise—the exploitation of natural resources and the operation of public utilities. In the case of public utilities, the Department of Commerce reports that such investment declined from $47 million in 1950 to $27 million in 1963, or from one-third of total American direct investment to only 6 per cent. As is well known, the major investment in this area was the Manila Railroad and Electric Co. (Meralco), which supplies electricity to Manila and environs. Meralco was sold to Filipinos at the end of 1961 and American direct investment in public utilities declined from $104 million at the end of 1961 to $28 million at the end of 1962.

Direct investment in Philippine agriculture has remained a minor element, in spite of American efforts to maintain access to agricultural resources. The Department of Commerce estimated that such investment totaled $15 million, or one-tenth of all American direct investment, in 1950. In the ensuing seven years, a period in which American direct investment in the Philippines doubled, such investment in agriculture declined to $14 million, and at the end of 1957 amounted to less than 5 per cent of American investment. Although estimates of direct investment in Philippine agriculture have not appeared since 1957, isolated reports of transfers of American holdings suggest that investment in this category has not increased since that time and today amounts to perhaps 3 per cent of American direct investment.

The remaining area of investment which has been a persistent American policy concern is mining, which traditionally attracted American enterprise and capital. Although the Department of Commerce has not provided estimates of direct investment in mining, these can be filled in by reference to other sources. The remaining direct investment in mining is concentrated in two major mining firms, Atlas Consolidated, the major copper producer, and Benguet, the leading gold producer, with substantial but minority ownership in Philippine Iron Mines, the major producer of iron ore, and Lepanto, the second most important copper producer. Tentative estimates of American investment in these firms at the end of 1963 total $43 million, but it is not clear that the latter two would qualify as direct investments.

To summarize, direct investment expanded rapidly following 1950. Such investment was highly concentrated in manufacturing for the domestic market, including oil refineries which increased in value from $23 million in 1950 to approximately $190 million at the end of 1963, accounting for three-fifths of the total increase in direct investment over this period. The second fastest growing area of direct investment was "Trade," including oil distribution, which increased from about $50 million in 1950 to not less than $150 million at the end of 1963, and accounted for the remaining two-fifths of the increase in direct United States investment. On the other hand, direct investment in the natural resource and public utility industries experienced no aggregate growth, as the transfer of Meralco to Filipino ownership largely offset the post-1950 growth in American investment in Philippine mining and forestry industries and there was no significant movement of capital into agriculture.

FROM THE PHILIPPINE VANTAGE POINT

Equally revealing is the information on the flow of direct investment to the Philippines, which can be derived from the official Philippine balance of payments statements. Once the heavy postwar rehabilitation expenditures were completed by the end of 1949, American private investment declined to very low levels. This reflected clamorous social problems—the Huk insurrection, the alarming fiscal irresponsibility, and the balance of payments disequilibrium—which seemed beyond Philippine capacities to solve. For the three years ending with 1952, the inflow of direct investment averaged $8 million annually.

By 1953, the political and economic aspects of the investment climate had visibly improved and direct investment began to increase sharply. It will be recalled that Magsaysay campaigned for president in the summer and fall of 1953 and was elected overwhelmingly and the Nacionalistas gained control of both the Congress and the Executive. Although the Nacionalista leaders were steeped in the independence movement and could be depended upon to assert Philippine economic nationalism more aggressively than the Liberals, foreign investors, particularly Americans, were reassured by Magsaysay's vigorous leadership and amenability to American advice. Moreover, upon taking office Magsaysay cleared away the ambivalence which had arisen in the persistent experimentation with public corporations of various kinds by a firm avowal that public policy would reflect faith in and dependence upon private enterprise.

Given the tangible and intangible improvements in the investment climate, the inflow of foreign investment increased dramatically until, for the five years ending 1957, it averaged $45 million annually, five and a half times the rate of the previous three years. This "hey day" for direct foreign investment reflected the high levels of protection prevailing for manufacturing and the liberal foreign exchange allocations made for remission of earnings. Equally important, Philippine nationalist statesmen and the emerging entrepreneurs were preoccupied with taking over the lucrative import trade, retailing, and nationalist pressures impinged on Chinese rather than Western enterprise.

The situation changed quickly following the death of Magsaysay in the spring of 1957. The balance of payments situation deteriorated as reserves were drained away during the election year of 1957 when Garcia, who had succeeded to the presidency, used all the economic instruments at his disposal in his fight to retain office. The mild restraint which Magsaysay had exerted over economic nationalism was replaced by "Filipino First," which was aggressively preached within the National Economic Council, the Monetary Board, the Cabinet, and in Congress. As a result, direct foreign investment sharply declined until, for the three years ending in 1960, it averaged $28 million. The decline persisted in the 1960s and culminated in the sale of Meralco in 1961, which produced a reported net outflow of private foreign investment of $56 million for that year. In the ensuing years, moreover, earlier levels of direct foreign investment have not resumed and, for the three years ending 1963, receipts of direct investment, excluding the Meralco sale, averaged only $13 million annually.

THE MECHANICS OF FOREIGN INVESTMENT

Philippine attitudes and policies toward direct foreign investment have been influenced by growing awareness that foreign investment is created by Filipino labor and out of Philippine resources, yet the assets end up in the hands of foreign investors. They, like their nationalist counterparts elsewhere in the underdeveloped world, are aware that capital accumulation is a process in which the investor can have his cake and eat it. They are aware that such investment accumulates from a process of plowing back a portion of investment income, essentially the portion allocated to undistributed earnings.

This is readily confirmed by the Philippine balance of payments statements. During the three years ending 1952, income accruing to United States investors in the Philippines totaled $73 million, which was three times the recorded accumulation of direct investment over this period. For the ensuing five years, in which direct investment reached peak levels, recorded earnings accruing to American investors averaged $55 million annually as compared to the recorded annual accumulation of direct foreign investment of $45 million. During the next three years, earnings of United States investors reached a peak of $69 million annually, but thereafter declined sharply until, for the three years ending with 1963, they averaged $27 million. For the six years following 1957, earnings accruing to American foreign investors were in excess of twice the amount of direct foreign investment in the Philippines.

This aspect of direct investment in the Philippines is delineated more precisely by reference to Department of Commerce estimates of undistributed earnings. For the eight years following 1955, a period in which American direct investment to the Philippines, excluding the sale of Meralco, increased by approximately $223 million, the undistributed corporate earnings accruing to United States investors aggregated $168 million, or 72 per cent of the investment accumulation. The share in earnings of American owners of subsidiaries and branches totaled $393 million, of which $225 million was remitted to individuals or to parent enterprises. This latter amount was 96 per cent of the growth of direct United States investment over this period.

Deterioration in the entrepreneurial freedom of American enterprise in the Philippines occurred during a time in which American investment was accumulating rapidly, when it was our policy to preserve national treatment for American enterprise, and when we were confident that long-term private investment was an instrument uniquely suitable for outside participation in economic development. Although private, long-term foreign investment includes a number of diverse, functionally specialized forms, the American society is confident that direct investment, combining American "know-how," capital, entrepreneurial and managerial resources with Filipino skills and resources, is in the interests of both countries. Because of this confidence, we are taken aback when direct investment is not welcomed but is subjected to humiliating scrutiny, regulation, and control. The essence of direct foreign investment is control by the enterprise over decisions relating to labor costs, the use of earnings, and production decisions which determine the profitability of such investment. The ingredient of control, which the foreign investor compromises only with reluctance, tends to conflict sharply with Southeast Asian concepts of economic sovereignty.

CONFLICTING IMAGES

In the American image of foreign investment, the receiving country benefits from an increment of foreign exchange which the foreign investor brings into the recipient country to acquire or create the enterprise. This should ensure such investment a warm welcome because of persistent growth in import requirements of countries, like the Philippines, seeking to sustain rapid economic development. Filipinos, on the other hand, refer to their balance of payments and protest that during the postwar period of rapid growth in direct investment the income accruing to such investment far exceeded the growth of direct investment which, in the aggregate, accumulated through undistributed peso earnings. Filipino policy makers are aware that foreign investment is similiar to domestic investment in expanding money income and demand for foreign exchange to make import and other foreign exchange payments. Postwar direct foreign investment, attracted to manufacturing and trade supported by the internal market, produced little direct movement of foreign exchange to the Philippines but became a clamorous claimant for foreign exchange to import capital goods, industrial raw materials, and to remit earnings.

Direct investment during the colonial period, concentrated in the export sector, obviously did generate a permanent flow of foreign exchange and gave the independent Philippines a base of foreign exchange earnings which has played a crucial role in postwar industrialization and Filipinization. The discriminatory taxation of the export sector by exchange controls and currency overvaluation provided the wherewithal through which Filipino entrepreneurship was nourished by subsidization and protection. At the same time, such taxation minimized the attractiveness of investment opportunities in the export sector and since the war foreign investors have concentrated their activities elsewhere.

The American image attributes to private foreign investment an element of risk-bearing which is in short supply in the Filipino society, where savings take place at low rates and tend to flow into rural and urban real estate and construction. There is, of course, an important truth here, but in the Philippine image the risks borne by foreign investors historically have been compensated at exploitative rates. Filipinos welcome the efforts of their nationalist leaders to prevent such alleged exploitation by hampering access to economic opportunities and by restrictions on profit remission, taxation, minimum-wage laws, and diverse fringe welfare benefits.

Similarly, we tend to attribute to private foreign investment an element of "know-how" which inevitably must accompany control and which, just as inevitably, must "rub-off" on the Filipinos who work for foreign firms. Filipinos, on the other hand, have little faith in the inevitability of such a transfer and welcome a vigilant nationalism which maintains restrictions on the use of foreign personnel, prescribes schedules for upgrading and the pay of nationals, and seeks to ensure joint participation by nationals and ultimately their assumption of control.

Filipinos, as nationalists in underdeveloped countries generally, regard the terms under which private direct investment should be permitted as a problem in bilateral monopoly in which the terms will depend upon the bargaining skill and power of the opposing state and the foreign investor. Such an analogy obviously has considerable relevance. Foreign investment today is made by large-scale international corporations with great economic power and diverse interests. Such investment tends to be large scale and to involve complex questions of depreciation, depletion, levels of return, taxation, vertical integration, arbitrary pricing, and so forth, and there usually exists little basis for assessing the contributions of the parties to the "bargain."

THE SEMANTIC PROBLEM

At the level of the dialogue within the respective societies, the semantic gulf quickly becomes evident. Americans talk about the flow of foreign investment, with its connotation of a movement of productive resources from the developed to the less developed countries. In contrast, Filipinos talk about the accumulation of foreign investment, with its emphasis upon the role of foreign economic power and entrepreneurship in organizing domestic resources. Even our use of the term "foreign investor" inhibits effective communication. Implicit in the term is the image of an individual innovating with creativity and at personal sacrifice. As an individual he can carry no threat to the sovereignty or economic aspirations of the host society. Filipinos, however, are quite aware that private direct investment today results from the decisions of large, economically powerful international corporations—in oil, rubber manufacturing, pharmaceuticals, aluminum, electrical machinery—and that their goals and methods can challenge Philippine sovereignty.

It is very true that the accumulation of direct investment results from the expertise of foreign skills in organization and innovation, but it is hardly plausible to insist that it results from frugality and thrift, with their connotation of foregone consumption. Such an image was clearly relevant in the early period of colonial development when individual Americans were carving agricultural enterprises out of the jungle, building up small commercial, transportation, and manufacturing enterprises, and prospecting for minerals under adverse circumstances. Today, American direct investment in the Philippines is concentrated in large-scale branches and subsidiaries of corporations, with all the impersonality and separation of ownership and management inevitable in scale. Filipino entrepreneurs, venturesome by any previous standards of Filipino behavior, are apprehensive of confronting such corporations competitively. Nationalist statesmen and leaders, confident that they can make decisions which will sustain the national economic development which has been initiated, are little concerned with establishing conditions appropriate to an enlarged role for foreign investment.

ELEMENTS OF AMERICAN POLICY

Because of American faith in direct private foreign investment it has been United States policy in the special relationship to try to maintain and enlarge the avenues of access of Americans and their enterprises to Philippine resources and markets. Such policies have proved increasingly abrasive as economic nationalism has flourished and has generated imperative pressures to reserve resources and markets to Filipinos. The successful resolution of the obvious conflict in these divergent positions is the concern not of policy makers alone, but of the citizens of both countries hopeful that the special relationship will change and mature and continue to produce benefits shared by the two peoples.

The Philippine Constitution, drafted in the middle of the 1930s provided that the exploitation of natural resources and the operation of public utilities were reserved to Filipinos and enterprises three-fifths owned by Filipinos. Existing property rights of aliens at the time of the drafting of the Constitution were not disturbed. Immediately following World War II, American policy makers, under confused circumstances and in unseemly haste, drafted legislation which extended preferential access by Philippine exports to the United States market and provided for war damage payments. As a *quid pro quo*, Filipinos were required to amend their Constitution to provide for national treatment for Americans and their enterprises in the exploitation of Philippine natural resources and the operation of public utilities. The so-called "parity amendment" was rationalized as necessary for a massive inflow of foreign investment which would rehabilitate and develop the economy.

As the war-torn Philippine economy was rehabilitated, a substantial part of the prewar American economic presence re-emerged. The promised inflow of investment into the natural resource and public utility sectors, however, failed to materialize and a slow transfer of American assets to Filipinos took place. The American economy was expanding rapidly and opportunities at home occupied American economic interests. On the other hand, the Philippine export economy proved unattractive to new foreign investment because of the unrealistic exchange rate. Moreover, the restoration of the prewar commercial relationship precluded the development of manufacturing for the domestic market, as the economy was flooded with imports financed, for the most part, by various United States government disbursements.

Beginning in 1949, exchange and import controls initiated a process of rapid industrialization based on the internal Philippine market. Although access of United States investors to the opportunities arising in this industrialization was not guaranteed by the "parity amendment," comparable assurance arose out of Article X of the 1946 Trade Agreement which provided, among other things, that "If the President of the United States determines that the Philippine Government is in any manner discriminating against citizens of the United States or any form of United States business enterprise, then the President of the United States shall have the right to suspend the effectiveness of the whole or any portion of the agreement." Nationalist pressures on American enterprise were moderated because of this provision and also because a more immediate target of convenience was the import trade which could be diverted to Filipinos by discretionary controls.

As the eight-year transitional period of "mutual free trade" scheduled in the 1946 Agreement drew to a close, the Philippines, threatened by the loss of preferential access to the United States market, took the initiative in seeking negotiations to revise the Agreement. The resulting Laurel-Langley Agreement, which was finally ratified in 1955, includes a number of major concessions to the Philippines, although the basic principle of the scheduled elimination of the mutual trade preferences was retained.

The Laurel-Langley Agreement mutualized the "parity" provision, and in place of Article X of the earlier agreement the two countries agreed "not to discriminate in any manner, with respect to their engaging in business activities, against the citizens or any form of business owned or controlled by the citizens of the other, and that new limitations imposed by either Party upon the extent to which aliens are accorded national treatment . . . shall not be applied as against enterprises owned or controlled by citizens of the other party."

In the meantime, with Magsaysay leading the ticket, the Nacionalista Party, long identified with the independence movement, captured both the Executive and the Congress and the stage was set for more overt nationalistic measures. In the congressional session of 1954, legislation to nationalize the retail trade was enacted which, after a transition over ten years, limited this activity to Filipinos and firms wholly owned by Filipinos.

Stresses and Strains

The system of exchange and import controls which, in conjunction with peso overvaluation, was used to generate entrepreneurship and economic expansion throughout the 1950s was being eroded steadily by internal stresses and strains. Corruption became rampant and evasion of the controls, both legal and extra-legal, increased. Politics, never far removed from Filipino actions, also discredited the system as it was rumored that the foreign exchange windfall was being diverted to the campaign coffers of the party in power. As pressures on the system increased, a schedule was drawn up for dismantling the controls. Finally, in January 1962, the incoming Macapagal administration made a clean break by moving to a free market in foreign exchange and, after a period of a few months in which the peso was free to find its own level, its value was stabilized by the Central Bank at about half the official rate.

THE TRAUMA OF DEVALUATION

From the point of view of potential foreign investors, investment opportunities in the Philippines shifted drastically. The removal of exchange and import controls eliminated an element of risk which had heretofore dampened the enthusiasm of foreign investors. Moreover, the devalution dramatically improved the export prospects which traditionally had attracted foreign investors.

On the other hand, devalution, which had become inevitable, carried alarming risks and uncertainties for Filipino entrepreneurs. Although they could depend upon continued protection within the internal market, the "crutch" of peso overvaluation, through which they had been heavily subsidized, was removed. This change, welcome as it was for future development, had a number of important consequences. Entrepreneurs became preoccupied with the problem of keeping their enterprises solvent. Financial problems became severe as inventories of imported raw materials, previously the source of liquid funds in the form of the foreign exchange windfall, suddenly doubled in peso cost and required access to additional credit. In a number of cases, firms were confronted by substantial maturing debt obligations denominated in foreign exchange which had doubled in peso value. Moreover, to minimize the inflationary impact of the deflation which overnight doubled the peso prices of export commodities, the Central Bank maintained a moderately tight money policy which made more difficult the problems of the hard-pressed Filipino entrepreneurs. Although Filipino firms weathered the devaluation of the peso with virtually no failures and, after a brief interval of adjustment and rationalization, economic expansion resumed, the trauma and insecurity of the change intensified nationalist pressures on American enterprise.

THE THREATENED INVASION

Philippine business and political elites tend to verbalize their insecurity by referring to a limited number of cases since 1961 in which control of an enterprise has passed from Filipino to American hands, or in which the advent of an American enterprise has frustrated some announced Filipino plans. A case frequently cited is that of the new Esso fertilizer plant, which was projected subsequent to the announcement by two local firms of plans to go into fertilizer production on a substantial scale. Following the Esso announcement the plans of the Filipino firms were suspended or dropped. A second case involved the refinancing of the Filoil Refining Corporation, in which the participating American firm (Gulf) had to provide additional capital and in return acquired majority control. Still another recent case is that of General Electric (Philippines), Inc., which acquired control of a Filipino firm, originally established with equity participation by the government to manufacture light bulbs and fluorescent tubes. Such incidents convince the entrepreneurial elites and the nationalist statesmen that the progress toward the national economy which has been achieved since 1950 is threatened by an invasion of large and economically powerful American corporations.

Serving to communicate these apprehensions widely through the society have been the activities of the nationalist leaders in Congress. In every session of Congress since 1952, attempts have been made, with official American encouragement, to enact a foreign investment law which would specify conditions under which foreign investors would have access to Philippine resource and commodity markets. In spite of Executive initiative, Congress has not enacted such a law and continuous controversy over this issue has served to mobilize public opposition to legislation which, at least by implication, welcomes foreign investment. Over the years, the repeated failure to enact such a law has led to increasingly illiberal proposals.

Congressional apprehensions over an invasion of direct foreign investment in export production became focused in 1964 following the successful negotiation by Dole pineapple interests for the lease of sufficient land to establish a pineapple plantation and cannery in Mindanao. To get around the legal limits on the amount of land that could be leased, the required land was obtained under an agency-type of agreement from the government-owned National Development Company. Subsequently, the government, through the Program Implementation Agency, engaged in similar negotiations with the United Fruit Company, which proposed to establish a banana plantation on lands of the Davao Prison Colony. Senator Lorenzo Tañada, an influential nationalist, convened a senatorial investigating committee and in the midst of well publicized hearings the negotiations were repudiated by President Macapagal and the plans of United Fruit collapsed.

RETAIL TRADE NATIONALIZATION

Although the retail trade nationalization law presumably would little affect American economic interests, recent developments have given rise to conflict. Extension of the effect of retail trade nationalization to areas of commerce beyond any conventional definition of retail trade occurred when the Secretary of Justice in 1963 decided that "in determining whether a transaction is retail or wholesale, the criterion is the character of the purchaser or the disposition of the goods bought; if the purchaser is the ultimate user or consumer who utilizes products or goods resulting in the diminution of their utilities, the transfer is a sale at retail." In other words, direct sales—of raw cotton to a textile mill, or fuel oil to an electrical generating plant, of a tractor to an agricultural producer, of wire rope to a mine—are interpreted as retail trade.

Retail trade nationalization was extended inflexibly to a number of American enterprises by still another Justice Department opinion which held that it was necessary for a corporation to be wholly owned by American and Filipino citizens in order to engage in retail business. Inasmuch as the major remaining American firms engaged in "retailing" in the Philippines are subsidiaries of public corporations whose shares are widely traded, certification of 100 per cent American-Filipino ownership is impossible.

Directly affected by this interpretation of the retail trade nationalization law are some of the largest and longest-established American firms. The major oil firms are not only confronted by the problem of adapting their distributing activities to the formal constraints of the law, but they are precluded from directly selling petroleum products to bulk users. The same problem faces the four tire manufacturers, subsidiaries of major American producers, which have begun operations since World War II. Still another large American firm, Singer, which in the past has distributed sewing machines through branches, has been confronted by the necessity to devise new methods to comply with the retail trade nationalization law.

THE ATTRACTION OF JOINT VENTURES

In discussion of foreign investment policy by Filipinos, it is clear that joint ventures are conceptually attractive, particularly when combined with a schedule for the transfer of control and ownership to the Filipino participants. The practical significance of this instrument of foreign investment is presently unimpressive and promises to expand only slowly. Joint venture opportunities, particularly those involving collaboration with large American firms, are likely to involve capital requirements beyond the means of individual Filipinos or consortia of Filipinos. Assembling large amounts of capital immediately encounters the reluctance of Filipinos, steeped in the familialism of their society, to extend economic cooperation beyond trusted family members.

Filipino commercial and manufacturing entrepreneurship has flourished since 1949 because ready access to subsidized credit has permitted the creation of enterprises with minimum equity capital and maximum borrowings. This state of affairs enabled entrepreneurs to maintain and enlarge their traditional and prestigeful holdings of urban and rural real estate at the same time they were accumulating manufacturing and commercial assets. For the past five years, the Philippines, and particularly Manila, has experienced a construction boom which has sustained an insatiable demand for credit resources. So long as urban construction remains an irresistible investment alternative, joint ventures will languish. The practical significance of this obstacle was brought home to potential foreign investors in the summer of 1964 when the Esso fertilizer subsidiary, after careful planning and preparation was able to raise only a minor portion of a $5 million equity issue marketed in the Philippines.

THE ROLE OF LOAN CAPITAL

Philippine consideration of foreign investment policy has also been diverted by the prospect that the real and imagined drawbacks of direct investment could be avoided by obtaining foreign capital in the form of loans. Beginning in the late 1950s, substantial amounts were obtained in loans from United States banks to Philippine commercial banks and in intermediate and long-term loans by foreign financial institutions to Philippine enterprises. Loans in the former category, the repayment of which was guaranteed by the Central Bank of the Philippines, reached a maximum of $53 million at the end of 1956 and were subsequently liquidated. Net borrowings in the latter category, which averaged about $1 million annually for the four years prior to 1959, jumped to $27 million annually during 1959-61, but since that time the amount outstanding has undergone little change.

Such borrowings were particularly attractive to Filipino businessmen because of the windfall to be realized by borrowing dollars and repaying pesos converted to dollars at the official exchange rate. This opportunity ceased to exist with devaluation of the peso at the beginning of 1962, but even prior to that time the chronic balance of payments difficulties had caused the Central Bank to curtail such borrowing. Foreign loan capital obviously has a role to play in Philippine economic development, but it promises to substitute for direct investment only to a limited extent.

THE "NEW" FOREIGN POLICY

The intensification of Philippine economic nationalism and its focus on the American economic presence in the Philippines was also encouraged by the venturesome foreign policy of the Macapagal administration, associated with the North Borneo claim and the flirtation with Indonesia in Southeast Asian regionalism.

Philippine nationalism, subverted by paternalism and autonomy during the colonial period, has been pragmatic and rational to a degree which has made it unrecognizable to Asian nationalists generally. Ideological nationalists motivated to reduce the American presence and influence in the Philippines are growing in number, however, and are to be found in the Congress, among journalists, in a few universities, and in the labor movement. They exercise a growing influence on Philippine foreign policy and can be expected to move it toward a position more consistent with norms of independence and sovereignty associated with ex-colonial societies.

The new entrepreneurial elements, economically conservative and normally apolitical with respect to foreign policy, coalesced with the ideological nationalists once their insecurities and fears of American foreign investment were aroused. Among the results of this coalition were the well publicized demonstrations before the American Embassy in late 1964 and early 1965. Ultimately, the basic antipathy of the two elements must lead to friction as ideological nationalism in the Philippines, over the longer haul, is incompatible with entrepreneurial leadership, and vice versa.

In the meantime, nationalist pressures on the American economic presence were intensified as the coalition focused on "parity" as a slogan. The success of "parity" as a slogan is undeniable and measures the cost to the United States of the failure to appreciate the humiliation imposed on the Philippine society twenty years ago, and to rectify the error once it became clear that "parity" was economically insignificant. "Parity" has persisted as an effective slogan with which the economic nationalists and their junior collaborators—the ideological nationalists and "fellow travelers"—have inflamed the incipient anti-Americanism. Fortunately, its usefulness for this purpose promises to be short lived, as Assistant Secretary of State, William Bundy, in a press conference in Manila on March 8, 1965, announced that the United States had no plans to seek the extension of "parity" beyond the termination of the Laurel-Langley Agreement in 1974.

A SPURIOUS ISSUE

The potential effectiveness of the Bundy announcement, which was at least a decade and a half overdue, was undermined by a final and gratuitous comment that Americans "assume, of course, that rights acquired prior to 1974 will be protected in accordance with the Philippine Constitution." Anyone familiar with Filipino sensitivity could not have been surprised at the sharp reaction to the Bundy statement which, by implication, questioned Filipino trustworthiness. The vigorous Filipino reaction was climaxed three days after the Undersecretary's statement when a resolution of the National Economic Council, rather suspiciously dated February 18, was announced, which provides that property rights acquired by American citizens and enterprises under the parity amendment will not extend beyond 1974.

The belated American decision to unilaterally abrogate "parity," which embodied a clear potential for improving relations between our two countries, was not only handled ineptly, but it promises to create a new spurious issue to replace that of "parity." The issue of property rights established under the parity amendment is spurious for the simple reason that such rights are economically insignificant. Postwar American investment has moved into manufacturing and trade for reasons which have been explained above, and investment in the exploitation of natural resources and in public utilities has increased little, if at all. In addition, many prominent firms engaged in activities covered by "parity" are within striking distance of 60 per cent Filipino ownership originally specified in the Constitution.

The Outlook for American Participation

The problems of establishing arrangements under which United States enterprise can participate effectively in Philippine economic development have become formidable. The period of the 1950s, in which direct investment accumulated in unprecedented amounts, was a deceptive lull before the storm. Today the frictions are open and the accumulation of private direct investment has declined to a fraction of earlier levels. Philippine nationalists are vigilant in resisting change in policy which would enlarge access by American corporations to Philippine resource and product markets. Although United States investors are guaranteed "parity" rights until 1974, the United Fruit Company episode suggests that "parity" has little practical significance. Repeated efforts on the part of the Philippine Executive to induce Congress to enact a foreign investment law have been futile and the proposals presently receiving consideration are, in terms of their avowed purpose, cynical parodies.

INTERNAL CHANGES

The situation, bleak as it may seem to potential American investors, is not without hope as rapid change is likely in the Philippine society. The decision to devalue the peso is a number of years past and convincing evidence has accumulated that few Filipino enterprises failed to survive this drastic change. Devaluation has eliminated the major opportunities for graft and corruption and the introduction of greater economic rationality into the peculiarly Philippine enterprise economy will moderate the incentives to dispossess alien entrepreneurs. Equally important, the transition to a more rational economy ultimately will be reflected in a more mature self-confidence on the part of Filipino businessmen and their assimilation to a more appropriate functional role.

Pressures for change in this direction are also likely to develop within the Philippine society generally. Filipino entrepreneurs have been unusually favored in the past by windfalls and concessions of various kinds. The subsidization of Filipino entrepreneurship has involved "costs" to the Philippine society in high prices of imports and domestically produced import substitutes of inferior quality. Although the threshold of economic discrimination is high, the stoicism and economic naïveté of the society are not unlimited. The unrelieved pursuit of self-interest by the new Filipino entrepreneurial elites has benefited from the longing of the society for industrialization and Filipinization. Progress toward these goals ultimately will weaken their priority, and concern for egalitarian and welfare objectives will generate pressures for changes. This is not to predict a reversion to colonial *laissez faire,* but to suggest that the "dog in the manger" drives of the Filipino entrepreneurial elites may be moderated as Filipinos generally recognize that the narrow interests of this favored group do not always coincide with the national interest.

SOURCES OF AMERICAN LEVERAGE

There is also the fact that the United States is not without leverage which can be applied to moderate the impact of Philippine economic nationalism. Philippine exports to the United States, which enjoy substantially greater rates of preference under the Laurel-Langley Agreement than do counterpart United States exports to the Philippines, far exceed Philippine exports to any other country. The importance of this preferential position in the United States market is unmistakable and Philippine initiative to renegotiate to extend the preferences was evident during the Macapagal administration.

The United States is challenged by the diplomatic problem of using its economic leverage effectively. The problem is challenging for the simple reason that using the leverage, as in the past, to insist doctrinairely upon some minimum access to Philippine resource and commodity markets is not promising. The experience with "parity," both as symbol and substance, should prevent our making a similar mistake. Moreover, the past history of formal negotiations between our countries suggests that in formal agreements the American adaptation tends to be permanent, while the Philippine accommodation will be reconsidered when the circumstances are assessed as propitious by Philippine policy makers.

We can be sure that economic interests will exert pressures on the State and Commerce Departments and on the Congress "to do something." American interests should consider the possibility that more would result from doing nothing and letting the scheduled economic transition of the Laurel-Langley Agreement run its course. American enterprise in the Philippines derived security in the Philippines under the 1946 trade agreement, not by reason of "parity," which proved to be economically insignificant, but because of the discretionary authority of the President of the United States to retaliate to nationalist pressures by withdrawing American concessions. An approximation of this state of affairs is scheduled to materialize with the expiration of Laurel-Langley in 1974.

It is unlikely, however, that pressures for renegotiation and extension of Laurel-Langley preferences, arising both from Filipino and American economic interests, will be resisted by American policy makers. It is also difficult to be deeply concerned over this approaching issue. The economic magnitudes are not of major significance and paternalism in our relationship with the Philippines has paid off handsomely in the past and may continue to do so in the future, although this should not be assumed lightly. The essential argument for letting Laurel-Langley run its course is the case for forcing the Philippines to undertake an aspect of economic independence which up to the present she has feared and resisted. The United States, by insisting on severing the remaining economic umbilical cord, may hasten the maturation of Philippine nationalism to the benefit of both countries. The potential gains from making the special relationship less special represent a calculated risk which should not be obscured by the cacophony of special pleading by narrow economic interests, American and Filipino.

THE NEED FOR UNDERSTANDING

For the most part, the rapid changes in the Philippine social environment has not been matched by comparable changes in the understanding of Americans of that environment. As a result, major differences and misunderstandings have resulted, and some have persisted to stimulate changes in the special relationship to accommodate Philippine aspirations. For Americans, this process of adaptation is always one-sided and frustrating because it is poorly understood. For example, Philippine insistence upon periodic revision of formal agreements, such as the trade agreement and the bases agreement is interpreted, at best, as irresponsible and frequently as bad faith. In fact, such behavior represents the groping of Filipinos for a sovereignty to match their formal political independence. Americans may not like it, but the effective time span of agreements with the Philippines will be short at this juncture because that society is undergoing rapid change, as is the surrounding, potentially hostile, world. It is announced American policy to encourage Philippine independence and we need to understand that the constant one-sided adaptation which has characterized the special relationship over the postwar period is no more than recognition on our part of the emerging requirements of Philippine sovereignty.

Adaptation is also difficult for the simple reason that our advice, tendered in good faith, is treated with increasing skepticism bordering on hostility as Filipinos have discovered that they are capable of managing their own economic affairs. Not only are they less dependent upon the special relationship, but they are confident that only they are capable of recognizing the national interest and, therefore, that only they can make decisions in that interest. It is little consolation for Americans to realize that Filipinos insist on making their own decisions—and mistakes —because the objective success with which they have made decisions over the past decade and a half convinces them that what they choose to do will not be a mistake. They insist on making their own decisions, moreover, because they are convinced that in the flux of social and economic change mistakes can be undone and will not carry permanent consequences.

We should also recognize that the continuous process of American adaptation to Philippine aspirations is not entirely satisfying to Filipinos. Philippine foreign policy in the area of the special economic relationship with the United States has been an almost unrelieved success story. Within four years of independence, the Philippines managed to escape from the residual colonial constraints on monetary and commercial policy which the United States attempted to impose as the price of war damage payments. They have been completely successful in minimizing the consequences of "parity" and they have been able to maintain intact the preferential access of Philippine exports in the United States market.

Filipinos are sensitive and proud and in spite of this record they articulate dissatisfaction with the special relationship by protesting that they "are taken for granted." It is clear that they are restless with their junior role in the relationship and tormented by the knowledge that the relationship can never carry for Americans the same relative importance that it does for the Philippine society. They are frustrated by the suspicion that their success in demanding steady revision in the special relationship may have resulted from paternalistic indulgence on the part of the United States rather than from aggressive diplomacy on their part.

The Diplomatic Challenge

Two decades of Philippine independence have seen far reaching changes in the special economic relationship between our two countries. Over this period the United States has bargained away or acquiesed in unilateral Philippine termination of all the economically significant concessions which in the initial treaty relationship of 1946 established a clear net advantage in favor of the United States. At the present juncture, the elimination of the remaining trade concessions scheduled in the Laurel-Langley Agreement arouses Filipino apprehensions and has prompted Philippine initiative to prolong and expand the preferences enjoyed by Philippine exports in the United States market. Such initiative is encouraged by the history of the special relationship since 1946. Moreover, it is not unlikely that the growing pressures on the American presence in

Southeast Asia contribute to the conviction, shared widely by Filipino elites, that the importance to the United States of the military bases in the Philippines ensures the Philippines' economic advantage can be maintained and enlarged.

The Laurel-Langley Agreement provides that the two countries shall "consult with each other as to joint problems which may arise as a result or in anticipation of the termination of the Agreement" not later than July 1, 1971. The forthcoming negotiations challenge the United States to use the Philippine concern to maintain trade preferences to restore a meaningful mutuality within which the special relationship can mature and be adapted to serve common interests. Clearly there is little American interest in, and obvious hazards in seeking to roll back the commercial relationship to some economically meaningful variant of "mutual free trade." The postwar decline in the concentration of Philippine trade with the United States has been just as welcome to Americans generally as it has to Filipinos. Rapid industrialization and Filipinization resulted once the Filipinos acquired autonomy over their commercial policy and they would strenuously oppose attempts to encroach on their hard won economic sovereignty.

Alternatively, the American bargaining strength might be used to negotiate conditions under which American investors can participate in Philippine economic development. Defined in this way, this goal is a legitimate one, attractive to Americans. But this is not to say that it will be acceptable to Filipinos, who presently recognize little need for direct foreign investment. Philippine nationalism has been nourished by the past decade and a half of successful economic management, a success achieved to a considerable degree in circumvention of constraints on Philippine autonomy which the United States unwisely sought to impose in 1946. This is not to say that future Philippine economic development can be taken for granted, but it is clear that a promising start has been made.

For these reasons, as well as those elaborated earlier, the forthcoming reconsideration of the Laurel-Langley Agreement carries obvious diplomatic hazards for the United States. Americans generally recognize an important stake in the social, economic, and political progress of the Philippines and we are anxious that our policies contribute constructively to this goal. On the other hand, our understanding of the evolving avenues of participation is confused by our ethnocentric image of the special relationship, and history abundantly confirms that our adaptation to the Philippine need to contract the American presence—political, military, and economic—has been awkward and reluctant. Reconsideration of Laurel-Langley challenges our representatives to assess the lessons of history and define a policy which will contribute to the evolution of a responsible Philippine nationalism. Such a policy is clearly in the interests of both societies.

Benito Legarda, Jr. and Roberto Y. Garcia

6

Economic Collaboration:
The Trading Relationship

Prior to the independence of the Philippines, the basic fabric of Philippine-American trade relations was essentially of American design. The United States, as the colonial power, was able to subordinate Philippine interests to her own. It is not surprising, therefore, that Philippine-American economic relationships before the Second World War were characterized, on the surface at least, by harmony and amity. The Philippines maintained the characteristic passivity of the dominated.

This picture, beginning with Philippine independence, has taken a different hue. The Philippines, feeling the growing self-confidence of a young nation, has begun to regard as unreasonable certain conditions which she had taken for granted as the inevitable lot of a "colonial." Looming large are the mounting differences between our two countries over the Military Bases Agreement and the existing trade pact.

Fortunately, there seems to be manifested on both sides a willingness to meet and resolve these differences. Americans realize today that rising

BENITO LEGARDA, JR., *Director, Department of Economic Research, Central Bank of the Philippines, received his Ph.D. (Economics) from Harvard University. Dr. Legarda was the founder and first editor of* The Philippine Economic Journal *and has contributed articles to numerous publications. He has frequently represented his country in major international conferences and has served on various international commissions and committees.*

ROBERTO Y. GARCIA, *Assistant Director, Department of Economic Research, Central Bank of the Philippines, was educated in the Philippines and the United States and is a member of the faculty of Far Eastern University. He has represented his country in various meetings of the Economic Commission for Asia and the Far East and was recently a member of the Philippine delegation to the United Nations Trade and Development Board.*

Philippine nationalism will not be contained and will not allow anything less than equal and non-discriminatory treatment. For his part, the Filipino negotiator has learned, often to his discomfort, that sentiment and emotionalism have no place at the bargaining table in dealing with his American counterpart.

Because of these new convictions on both sides, present American economic policy appears to be responding to the changing economic conditions in the Philippines and the temper of the Filipino people. This responsiveness augurs well for the solution of problems which may arise in the future. As an economic tract, this essay hopes to contribute toward better communication and greater understanding between two traditionally friendly countries whose national interests may lie in divergent but not necessarily irreconcilable paths.

THE NINETEENTH CENTURY PATTERN

Throughout the nineteenth century, there was a significant amount of trade between the Philippines and the United States. This dated back to the activities of Yankee merchants from Boston and Salem in the late eighteenth and early nineteenth centuries, which led to the establishment of American business houses in Manila. In the second half of the century the American share of Philippine export trade, with the exception of the Civil War years and certain other isolated periods, was typically between 30 and 40 per cent, which exceeded that of any other country. On the import side, however, after an initially strong start, the American share sank to very low levels, fluctuating between 2 and 6 per cent in the last two decades of the century. Thus, during most of this period, Philippine trade with the United States characteristically resulted in a large export surplus.

The Treaty of Paris of 1898, which ended the Spanish-American War, marked the formal acquisition of the Philippines by the United States and the implementation of American sovereignty in the islands. From that time and even after the independence of the Philippines on July 4, 1946, American commercial policy dominated the structure and growth of the Philippine economy through variants of mutual free trade, from the Tariff Act of 1901 to the Bell Trade Act of 1946. Since Philippine independence, American commercial policy influence has been continued in bilateral trade agreements, although with waning strength.

Preferential Trade: Variations on a Theme

American commercial policy toward the Philippines since 1898 followed a distinct pattern. The basic objective moved from qualified to unlimited mutual free trade during the first three and a half decades of the American regime and thereafter drifted to gradually diminishing trade preferences. Thus, American policy before 1935 favored mutual specialization and greater interdependence, while after the establishment of the Commonwealth it sought to reduce interdependence and to normalize economic relations.

1898-1909: PREFERENTIAL TRADE

During the first decade of the American occupation, commercial policy was one of cautious liberalization of mutual trade through preferential tariffs. The relaxation of trade barriers to imports of American goods during the early occupation years was deferred mainly because of provisions of the Treaty of Paris, which extended to Spanish goods (and also other European goods if shipped in Spanish bottoms) any concession granted American goods. The first customs tariff enacted by the Philippine Commission in 1901, which superseded the Spanish customs tariff, however, initiated preferential trade and greater Philippine dependence on United States imports by providing for reduced duties on goods which Spain did not produce, such as certain types of canned foods, gasoline, paper, and beer.

Meanwhile, the United States Supreme Court, in a series of decisions on the so-called "Insular Cases," established the constitutional status of the Philippines. According to the Court's ruling, the Philippines was not a foreign country within the meaning of American tariff legislation and therefore the United States tariff was not applicable to Philippine exports. It was also decided that the constitutional proviso that all duties and imports must be uniform within American territory did not apply to the Philippines. The United States Congress thereby was vested with the power to establish commercial policy governing trade with the Philippines.

These legal decisions, defining the constitutional status of the Philippines, permitted what Professor Amado Castro, in his Harvard doctoral dissertation, *The Philippines: A Study in Economic Dependence,* called a "reconciliation of the protectionist and imperialist aims of the United States." Thus, the expansion of American exports into the colonial market was pursued at the same time that goods produced in America were protected from the competing products of the insular possessions. In the conduct of commercial policy during the American regime, changes were concentrated mostly on the export side, that is, on establishing or changing trade preferences granted Philippine exports in the American market, while the free and unlimited entry of American goods into the Philippines was assured practically throughout the American rule.

United States tariff legislation in 1902 and 1905 conceded preferential rates of 25 per cent and 75 per cent of American duties, respectively, on Philippine products. On the other hand, in 1906 existing schedules on cotton imports into the Philippines were altered to favor American interests. Philippine exports to the United States continued to exceed imports in mutual trade throughout the first decade of the American regime, being typically double or more than the value of imports. The rate of growth of United States imports into the Philippines, however, exceeded the rate of growth of Philippine exports, reflecting the low level from which growth started as well as the increasing impact of the preferential trading practices.

Over the next decade, two developments sharply raised the level of Philippine trade with the United States: American tariff legislation in 1909 on the import side, and World War I on the export side.

1909-13: QUALIFIED FREE TRADE

After the expiration of the equality provision of the Treaty of Paris, the Payne-Aldrich Tariff Act of 1909, and a corresponding act called the Philippine Tariff Act of 1909, ushered in an era of qualified free trade. Under these two laws, American goods shipped directly were permitted to enter the Philippines duty free without limitations as to volume and foreign material content. Philippine products, with the exception of sugar and tobacco products which were subject to fixed annual quotas, were permitted to enter the United States duty free provided the value of the foreign material content of the product concerned did not exceed 20 per cent of the value of the finished product.

Philippine-American trade flourished under the 1909 Tariff Act, as the United States strengthened its premier position in Philippine foreign trade. Philippine exports increased significantly and imports from America rose even more sharply until, in 1913, they accounted for half of Philippine imports as compared to one-sixth in 1908.

During this period, investment flowed into the agricultural sector, particularly the export industries. Commerce and certain manufacturing activities, largely involving the processing of exports, also expanded along with the general economy. These trends not only underscored the growing dependence of the Philippines on the American market, but also the effectiveness of the American commercial policy in directing the course of colonial economic development. A transient change, reflecting in part the asymmetrical features of the colonial commercial policy, was the appearance of a persistent import surplus in Philippine trade.

1913-35: MUTUAL FREE TRADE

The next phase of Philippine-American commercial relations started with the Underwood-Simmons Tariff Act of 1913, which provided for reciprocal free trade relations, the removal of quota limitations, and the removal of export duties on Philippine products exported to the United States.

Except for a few very insignificant amendments to the tariff law, Philippine-American commercial relations remained virtually unchanged thereafter until 1934. The Jones Law of 1916, which represented the first tangible measure by the American Congress, albeit tentatively, toward the future declaration of Philippine independence, also gave the Philippine Legislature the power to legislate its own tariffs subject, however, to the approval of the President of the United States. Notwithstanding this provision, Philippine import duties retained their 1909 structure. Stability in Philippine tariff rates may have reflected the fact that upward revisions in tariff rates would have widened the margin of preference for American goods, thereby reducing imports from other countries as well as revenues collected therefrom.

With mutual free trade, the principle of comparative advantage operated fully between the two countries, although not with the rest of the world. As specialization tightened economic ties with the United States, the Philippine economy continued to respond to colonial commercial policy. World War I stimulated further the rapid rise in Philippine exports to the United States, which more than doubled in value between 1914 and 1918 and doubled again by 1920.

During the Twenties, major Philippine export crops enjoyed unprecedented prosperity, with sugar exports to the United States increasing in value by 450 per cent and coconut products by 223 per cent, although abaca remained stationary. The balance in mutual trade, a consistent surplus of Philippine imports during the previous decade, was reversed. The tariff preference enjoyed by principal Philippine exports in American markets, and the war boom in Philippine industries, generated unprecedented material prosperity, particularly in agriculture. Consequently, the Philippine economy became extremely export-oriented, with production concentrated in the few primary export products which had dominated Philippine export trade since the early days of the American regime.

With productive resources concentrated in producing for the export market, the promotion of home consumption industries was neglected. Basic necessities, such as textiles and even many food products, formed a substantial portion of Philippine imports. The free entry of American mass-produced products discouraged domestic manufacture of these and other consumer products. Although production and income rose appreciably, the foreign exchange surpluses and domestic savings realized were not directed toward the long-term expansion and diversification of the country's productive capacity. Without protection for domestic industries and adequate incentives for new industries built into the policy structure, diversification and industrialization could not be realized. Thus, the Philippines inevitably continued to grow along the narrow and lopsided confines of the colonial pattern.

THE DEPRESSION, THE COMMONWEALTH, AND INDEPENDENCE

The coming of the depression produced a partial reversal of the upward trend of Philippine trade which had been experienced since the beginning of the century. There was a precipitous drop in the value of exports from 1929 to 1932 of about 40 per cent, and only the gold boom resulting from the devaluation of the dollar in 1933 saved the Philippines from a worse plight than that into which it was to be plunged by the restrictive legislation accompanying the grant of independence. The depression, however, did finally give the Filipinos that for which they had long clamored, namely, a definite date for their independence.

At the insistence of Filipino nationalists, as well as American farm and Cuban sugar lobbies, several bills for Philippine independence were filed in the incoming Congress of 1933, dominated by the Democratic Party which historically had been receptive to Philippine autonomy and independence. The most important of these were the Hare-Hawes-Cutting proposals, which became the basis of subsequent legislation providing for Philippine independence. Certain objectionable features of the bill, however, led to controversy and factional differences among Filipino leaders, resulting in its rejection by the Philippine Legislature in 1933. The substitute Tydings-McDuffie Act, with provisions almost identical with those of the Hare-Hawes-Cutting Act, was accepted by the Philippine Legislature in 1934, and became the organic act for Philippine independence.

1935-46: PLANNED DISMANTLING OF MUTUAL FREE TRADE

With the establishment of the semi-autonomous Commonwealth government on November 15, 1935, the third phase of Philippine-American commercial relations began. Aside from its political provisions, the Independence Act provided for continued mutual free trade from 1935 to 1940, with certain major Philippine exports to the United States remaining duty free, but subject to quotas with exports in excess of quota paying full United States duties. Such exports included: sugar, limited to 850,000 long tons; coconut oil, 200,000 tons; and cordage, 3 million pounds. American products, however, were to continue to enter the Philippines in unlimited quantities. Between 1941 and 1946, Philippine products exported to the United States duty free were to be subject to a Philippine export tax, progressively rising at the rate of 5 per cent a year to 25 per cent in 1946, the proceeds of which were to be used to liquidate Philippine bonded indebtedness. Immediately after the grant of independence, scheduled to take place on July 4, 1946, full tariffs were to be paid on Philippine products entering the United States, and vice versa.

As a result of pressure from American protectionist groups, the Agricultural Adjustment Act of 1934 replaced the duty-free quota for Philippine sugar in the American market with an absolute quota. Set at a level below those attained by Philippine sugar exports in years preceding 1934 and made retroactive to the beginning of the year, the Philippine sugar producers suffered considerable losses as adjustments in production could not be carried out in time. The situation worsened when the quota was reduced further in 1935.

With the passage of the Cordage Act in 1935, the duty-free quota of 3 million pounds of Philippine cordage exported to the United States was replaced by an absolute quota of 6 million pounds a year for three years. In like fashion, domestic American producers of fats and oils, through the Revenue Act of 1934, managed to cut the incentive for Philippine exports of copra and coconut oil to the American market by imposing a 3-cent processing tax on coconut oil entering the United States or extracted from Philippine copra. The proceeds of the tax, however, were to be returned to the Philippine government.

Realizing that the abrupt termination of trade preferences after independence could lead to serious dislocations, as the development of new sources of income, the diversification of industry, and the establishment of new markets would take time, the Filipino leaders requested a re-study of the trade relations of the two countries. A Joint Preparatory Committee on Philippine Affairs composed of Filipinos and Americans was created to make such a study and propose changes to strengthen the country's economic structure. Subsequently, a number of recommendations of the Committee were incorporated in the Tydings-Kocialkowski Act of 1939, although the basic timetable of the scheduled transition was retained.

The state of the Philippine economy just before the outbreak of World War II was little changed from a decade earlier except that the islands had become more dependent on the American market as the war in Europe and unsettled conditions in East Asia further diverted Philippine trade to the United States. The country's trade balance during the decade of the Thirties displayed the persistent export surplus which had appeared in the 1920s as the gold-mining boom filled part of the economic vacuum left by the precipitous cut in sugar exports.

The prewar Philippine economy was dominated by the primary and extractive industries. While trade expanded rapidly, industrialization lagged. Some three-quarters of the country's labor force was employed in primary industries, preponderantly in agriculture. Only 10 per cent were employed in secondary industries, including manufacturing, and two-thirds of those so employed were engaged in handicrafts. Of the estimated gross national product in 1938, primary industries accounted for 56 per cent. In 1940, trade with the United States accounted for 83 per cent of the islands' exports as compared to 70 per cent in 1920. Moreover, two-thirds of export earnings were heavily dependent on American trade preferences. Likewise, America's share in the country's imports jumped from 62 per cent in 1920 to 77 per cent in 1940. Thus, America's share of total Philippine trade expanded from 66 per cent to 81 per cent over this period.

1946-55: RENEWAL OF THE PLANNED TRANSITION

The outbreak of World War II not only isolated the economy for more than three years but also interrupted the scheduled ten-year transition in commercial relations. Worse still, the war brought death and destruction and drastically impaired productive capacity, thus wiping out many of the limited economic gains of the past. It was in this sorry setting that the long promised Philippine independence was finally granted.

On the date of Philippine independence, an executive trade agreement, embodying the terms of the Philippine Trade Act passed by the American Congress, was concluded between the two governments. The Trade Act, a controversial piece of legislation, provided for preferential trade relations between the two countries for twenty-eight years while a companion law, the Philippine Rehabilitation Act, provided for American war damage payments to assist in the economic rehabilitation of the Philippines. The two laws were in a sense complementary since acceptance of the Trade Act by the Philippines was the price for war damage payments. In view of the prevailing economic circumstances, Filipinos had no alternative but to accept, after considerable controversy and with obvious reluctance, the Philippine Trade Act.

In general, this Act provided for eight years of free trade between the two countries beginning July 4, 1946, and for gradually increasing tariffs (or declining duty-free quotas in the case of certain specified Philippine exports) for the following twenty years. It also provided for certain special preferences to American investors, with respect to immigration, utilization and exploitation of Philippine natural resources and the operation of public utilities, as well as restriction of the Philippines' monetary autonomy.

From the Philippine standpoint, the Trade Act represented a compromise in which the immediate advantage of prompt rehabilitation of the export industries was offset by the disadvantage that the Philippine economy would continue for a limited period to be tied closely to the American economy, together with the possibility that the Philippine government might not be able to exercise complete freedom to choose its economic policies.

On the American side, it represented a compromise between American traders and investors who had interests in the Philippines and American agricultural producers who feared Philippine competition. To satisfy these factions, the Trade Act established privileges which favored American investors and traders, such as national treatment for American enterprise, the full convertibility of the peso to the American dollar, and twenty-eight years of gradually diminishing preferences for American imports. For the American farmers, the Act continued absolute quotas on Philippine products and included a clause that gave the American president the power to curtail the entry of any Philippine product likely to imperil a domestic industry.

On the part of Filipino producers, the trade advantages were substantially a continuation of those of the Tydings-McDuffie Act, as amended. From July 4, 1946, to July 3, 1954, the following products could enter the United States duty-free, up to the amount of their respective quotas: sugar, 850,000 long tons; cordage, 6,000,000 pounds; rice, 1,040,000 pounds; cigars, 200,000,000 pieces; scrap tobacco, 6,500,000 pounds; coconut oil, 200,000 long tons; and buttons of pearl or shell, 850,000 gross.

Beginning on July 4, 1954, imports into each country from the other would be subject to a gradually increasing proportion of the basic tariff rates until, beginning on January 1, 1973, and presumably thereafter, full duties would be paid. In addition, the duty-free quotas, other than those for sugar and cordage, were scheduled to be gradually eliminated over the twenty-year period beginning July 4, 1954. As before, no quota was fixed on American products entering the Philippines during the life of the agreement. Thus, as far as the tariff provisions were concerned, the agreement was literally and technically reciprocal; but in the imposition of quotas there was no reciprocity.

The so-called parity clause of the Trade Act, which required the amendment of the Philippine Constitution to establish national treatment for Americans in the exploitation of Philippine natural resources and the operation of public utilities, provided for no reciprocity as the power to extend similar rights to Filipinos belongs, under the American Constitution, to the individual states and not to the federal government. Defenders of this clause argued, however, that it was designed to stimulate investment necessary to rehabilitate a war-torn economy. Moreover, it was alleged that restrictions on foreigners doing business or owning property in the Philippines were more severe in the Philippines than in the United States.

Another one-sided provision of the Trade Act restricted the power of the Philippine government to control and administer its own currency; a restriction incompatible with independence. The Philippine government, even for balance of payments reasons, could not impose exchange controls or restrict capital movements without the approval of the president of the United States.

The primary aim of the Trade Act, particularly the provisions on free trade for a period of eight years, was to give the Philippines ample opportunity to rehabilitate its war-torn economy. In spite, however, of the ostensibly exalted intentions behind the Act, results achieved were not altogether satisfactory. Although the concessions encouraged investment in the export industries to the extent that, by 1951, the Philippine economy once again assumed the unbalanced prewar pattern, the slow process of rehabilitation prevented the principal beneficiaries of the agreement from utilizing fully the concessions granted. Except for copra, desiccated coconut, lumber, and chromite, production for export after six years of the agreement was still below the 1940 level. In the case of cordage, although it exceeded its quota in the United States in 1951, its production was still below prewar levels.

The free trade provisions of the agreement, together with the pent-up demand released by the ending of the war, stimulated heavy imports. At the same time, higher internal costs, and prices caused by supply shortages retarded the expansion of domestic production. As a result, the millions of dollars of war damage payments made under the Rehabilitation Act and various expenditures of the United States government in the Philippines under military and non-military programs, which helped cushion the huge deficit in the country's balance of payments, in effect, went back to the United States in the form of payments for imports, to the benefit of American industry and labor.

The heavy influx of American goods, particularly luxuries and nonessential items, led to a continuous drain on the country's foreign exchange reserves and eventually compelled the Philippine government, in January 1949, to impose partial import controls in order to minimize the outward flow of dollars. Less than a year later foreign exchange controls were also introduced as a complementary measure to correct the country's balance of payments position.

The continuing balance of payments difficulties merely mirrored the fundamental maladjustments in the economy. The level of imports which constituted 20 per cent of national expenditures during the entire period of free trade in the postwar era betrayed the inadequacy of the country's productive structure. More serious for the long run, this state of affairs measured the shortcomings of Philippine industrial efforts, especially in the manufacture of consumer goods.

Thus, in the end, the technically reciprocal free trade provisions of the agreement did tend to favor the United States more than the Philippines as American goods, particularly during the first four years of the agreement, flooded the domestic market to the prejudice of the local industries. It could therefore be said that the conditions obtaining during the early postwar period were such that the disadvantages to the Philippines of tariff-free imports from the United States far outweighed the benefits derived from tariff-free exports.

1955-PRESENT: THE LAUREL-LANGLEY AGREEMENT

On December 15, 1954, after three months of negotiations, the governments of the Philippines and the United States concluded an agreement, now known as the Laurel-Langley Agreement, to replace the 1946 trade agreement.

The Laurel-Langley Agreement, compared to its predecessor, was a definite improvement as it not only eliminated the one-sided infringements on Philippine monetary autonomy of the earlier agreement and mutualized the provision on parity, but it also established a forward-looking trade arrangement designed specifically to make the Philippines less dependent on the American market. But more significant was the fact that the Filipinos, as *The Economist* stated at the time, "gain(ed) more than the Americans from an agreement which has aroused practically no controversy."

Actually, the Agreement did not really grant new rights to the Filipinos but merely restored those denied to them under the 1946 agreement which were theirs to begin with. Moreover, the tariff preferences merely served to equalize the obvious economic advantage of the American industrial economy over the developing Philippine agricultural economy.

In general, the Laurel-Langley Agreement maintains the scheduled gradual elimination of mutual preferences in trade between the Philippines and the United States. Customs duties are to be applied gradually over the period beginning January 1, 1956, and ending on July 4, 1974, with preferences diminishing more rapidly for American than for Philippine products.

The absolute quotas for sugar and cordage were preserved, but the Agreement provides that the quotas shall not constitute an impediment to any increase which the United States Congress may grant to the Philippines in the future. It is on the basis of this provision that, following the Castro take-over in Cuba, the Philippines was allocated approximately 8 per cent of the quota previously granted to Cuba.

Exports of Philippine cigars, scrap and filler tobacco, coconut oil, and buttons of pearl or shell, as in the earlier agreement, are subject to gradually diminishing duty-free quotas so that by 1974 such quotas will be eliminated. On the other hand, these export commodities are released from the absolute quota provisions of the 1946 agreement, and can be exported in excess of the duty-free quotas, with the excess subject to full duty.

Aside from these trade concessions, the Agreement also recognizes the right of the Philippine government to manage its own currency system and to determine its own monetary and exchange policies. It also recognizes the right of the Philippines to impose quantitative import restrictions on a non-discriminatory basis. Moreover, for the purpose of protecting domestic industries or for reasons of balance of payments, discriminatory import quotas may be imposed, subject to prior notification and consultation.

On the question of taxes, the Agreement affirms the right to the Philippines, as provided for in its Constitution, to impose export taxes. It prohibits the imposition of internal taxes (including processing taxes) by both countries on articles imported for the exclusive use of their respective governments. The United States is prohibited from imposing any internal taxes (including processing taxes) on both manufactured and un-manufactured abaca fiber. Lastly, the United States is required to preserve the existing processing tax preference of 2 cents per pound accorded Philippine coconut oil. The Philippines, on the other hand, agrees to replace the 17 per cent tax on sales of foreign exchange which tended to discourage the flow of foreign capital, particularly American capital, with a special import tax beginning at 17 per cent ad valorem for 1956 and declining gradually at the rate of 1/10 each year for the next ten years.

For the protection of Filipino and American business enterprises, the Agreement prohibits discrimination by either government against the citizens and enterprises of the other with respect to the right to engage in business activities. This provision, in which national treatment is explicitly extended to the citizens and enterprises of either country, may have been sought by the American negotiators as a hedge against the rising tide of Philippine legislation restricting the economic activities of foreigners. However, if a state of the United States restricts the freedom of Philippine citizens to engage in business activities, the Philippines may similarly limit the freedom of citizens of that state to engage in business activities in the Philippines.

Likewise, under the parity provision of the 1955 Agreement, the right to engage in the development of natural resources and operation of public utilities were made reciprocal for the citizens of the two countries. If a state of the United States denies these rights to Filipino citizens, the Philippines may also withhold such rights from the citizens of that state. The condition does not apply, however, to rights previously acquired in the Philippines by American enterprises.

Lastly, the two countries also agree to consult with each other not later than July 1, 1971, on the joint problems that may arise as a result of, or in anticipation of the termination of the Agreement. Thus, the two countries are given ample time and opportunity to review and negotiate appropriate changes in the Agreement.

Summing up, the Laurel-Langley has gone far to redress the imbalance of the 1946 agreement. More importantly, it allows the Philippines greater leeway to develop a more balanced economy than was possible under the 1946 agreement. Specifically, the new schedule of declining tariff preferences affords Philippine export industries time to adjust their operations in the American market and develop other markets as well. At the same time, Philippine domestic industries are provided with a built-in control mechanism against competition from mass-produced American products. Moreover, the objectionable provisions constituting an infringement upon the Philippines' right to manage her own economic affairs are rectified. Thus unshackled, vigorous internal development policies contributed substantially to the industrial expansion of the Philippines from the mid-1950s to the early 1960s.

The Commodity Pattern of Philippine Trade

The rapid development of manufacturing industries, beginning in the Fifties, which was encouraged by nationalistically oriented economic controls, produced significant changes in the commodity composition of Philippine imports. On the other hand, the pattern of export trade, which had been characterized by excessive dependence on a few primary commodities and markets throughout the American regime, underwent little qualitative change. Exports—the country's principal source of foreign exchange—still consist mainly of raw materials, namely: copra, sugar, logs and lumber, abaca, tobacco, copper concentrates, iron ore, and chromite. Such exports in 1963-64 accounted for 75 per cent of total exports; with the leading exports, copra and logs and lumber, accounting for 22 per cent and 21 per cent, respectively.

EXPORT TRADE

The so-called mutual free trade relationship with the United States and the onerous tariff structures of the leading trading partners of the Philippines, contributed to the increasing share of Philippine exports of primary products between 1927-29 and 1963-64. Over this period the share of primary products increased from 67 per cent to 75 per cent, whereas that of manufactured products, including processed agricultural products, declined from 20 per cent to 16 per cent. The shares of sugar and abaca, the leading exports in 1927-29, declined between then and 1963-64 by 12 percentage points and 14 percentage points, respectively. These changes reflected, in part, the regulated premium sugar market of the United States and the development of synthetic fibers. Exports of copra and logs and lumber, which experienced rapid increase between the periods under consideration, largely accounted for the rise in the share of primary products in total exports. The share of coconut oil in Philippine exports declined from 16 per cent to 7 per cent as the processing tax and the quota imposed by the United States hampered expansion. This shift was mainly responsible for the decline in the share of manufactures, a decline moderated by the increase in the exports of plywood and molasses in recent years.

IMPORT TRADE

In contrast to the concentration of exports, Philippine imports are composed of a wide range of foodstuffs, fuels, raw materials, and manufactures. Strong import demand, in general, reflecting factors similar to those found in other primary exporting countries, namely, population growth, urbanization, increased government consumption, and inequalities in income and wealth enhanced by inflationary forces. Since part of the growth in demand could not be fully absorbed by imports, especially during the period of exchange controls, it provided a stimulus to domestic industrialization.

In the pursuit of industrialization following independence, the Philippines could not rely on tariffs to protect domestic production because of the duty free privileges accorded to American products under the 1946 trade agreement. Local industries, beginning in 1950, were afforded protection, however, through exchange and import controls which were imposed initially as exchange conservation measures. These directly protective measures were replaced by tariffs in 1962, following the elimination of import controls and the *de facto* devaluation of the peso. In the meantime, the development of manufacturing reduced imports of such manufactures as textiles, tobacco, and rubber products and to increases in imports of a number of industrial raw materials.

The demand for both luxury consumption goods and producer goods increased owing to the unequal distribution of income resulting from wartime and postwar inflation, from the difficulty of enforcing progressive income taxation, and from the addition of the *nouveau riche* to the established affluent families. Imports of producer goods, however, were stimulated while luxury imports and construction expenditures were discouraged by government policies. Accordingly, imports of producer goods have expanded considerably, particularly non-electrical machinery, which increased as a share in total imports from some 6 per cent in 1927-29 to 18 per cent in 1963-64. Import groups, in which it is difficult to separate goods used for consumption and productive purposes, and which, therefore, reflect the mixed effects of repressed consumer demand and encouraged investment demand, include mineral fuels, up from 7 per cent in 1927-29 to 18 per cent in 1963-64, transport equipment, up from 5 per cent to 11 per cent, and electrical machinery, apparatus, and appliances, up from 2 per cent to 5 per cent. Largely because of the government's policy of supporting consumption appropriate to established nutrition and health levels, imports of foodstuffs and of chemicals, drugs, dyes, and medicines have remained fairly substantial and in the past decade averaged more than one-fifth of Philippine imports.

On the whole, the pattern of Philippine imports changed little between 1929 and 1949, but by 1955-57, substantial changes were evident which reflected policies for promoting economic development and industrialization, the Filipinization of commerce, and the maintenance of nutrition and health levels. While more than one-third of Philippine imports in 1949 were consumer goods, in 1964 their share had dropped to less than one-sixth, with a corresponding increase in the share of producer goods.

The Geographic Pattern of Philippine Trade

Changes in commercial relations since independence are reflected in the growing geographic diversification of Philippine foreign trade. The extent to which a country's foreign trade is concentrated or dispersed may be measured by means of an index of concentration devised by Albert O. Hirschman, which ranges from a theoretical high of 100 for a country with only one trading partner down to lower levels as a country's trade is more widely distributed. Applied to the Philippine data, the indices for both exports and imports clearly show a downward trend, confirming that the concentration of Philippine foreign trade, which was built up during the era of mutual free trade under the American regime, has declined markedly in recent years.

DESTINATIONS FOR EXPORTS

The index of concentration computed for Philippine exports stood at 74 in 1945, slid to 62 in 1955, and on down to 55 in 1964. The basic explanation of the decline in concentration was the decline in the share of the United States in the Philippine export trade from an average of 72 per cent in 1949-50, to 57 per cent in 1955-56, and to 47 per cent for 1963-64. This explanation, however, does not tell the whole story, as this was a period in which the Philippine export trade experienced continual expansion from the low levels that prevailed immediately after World War II. As compared with 1950, the Central Bank of the Philippines reports that the volume of exports increased to an index of 142 for 1955 and to 236 in 1964. As a result, the decline in the share of the United States in Philippine export trade took place over a period in which Philippine exports to the United States increased in value from an average of $208 million for 1949-50, to $342 million for 1963-64. At the same time, the volume of such exports necessarily increased even more rapidly since this was a period over which the prices of Philippine exports declined from the high levels prevailing during the Korean War boom in primary commodities. The index of the volume of exports to the United States in 1964 stood at 182, as compared with 100 in 1950.

Inasmuch as the contraction in the share of the United States in the Philippine export trade occurred over a period in which Philippine exports to the United States increased steadily, the decline in the index of export concentration reflected an even more rapid expansion of Philippine exports to other areas—principally Japan and Western Europe. The value of exports to Japan increased eleven-fold between 1949-50 and 1963-64, from an average of $17 million to $193 million and, for the reason explained above, the increase in the volume of such exports was still more rapid. The share of Japan in the Philippine export trade jumped from an average of 6 per cent in 1949-50 to 26 per cent in 1963-

64. Somewhat less rapid was the growth of Philippine exports to the industrialized countries of Northwestern Europe—Belgium, Denmark, France, Germany, the Netherlands, Norway, Sweden, Switzerland, and the United Kingdom. The value of Philippine exports to these countries increased from an average of $33 million for 1949-50 to $148 million for 1963-64, with over four-fifths of the exports in the latter period shipped to the Netherlands and Germany. The share of industrial Northwestern Europe in the Philippine export trade increased from an average of 11 per cent in 1949-50 to 20 per cent in 1963-64. Although there has been a dramatic redirection of the Philippine export trade over the last decade and a half, the share of exports to the United States, Japan, and Northwestern Europe has increased from 89 per cent of total exports in 1949-50 to 93 per cent in 1963-64.

EXPORTS TO THE UNITED STATES

Corollary to the redirection of Philippine export trade has been the shifting portions of specific commodity exports. Whereas in 1949-50 over half of Philippine exports of copra, chromite ore, canned pineapple, and copra meal were shipped to the United States, by 1963-64 the United States' share had declined below half in each case. Today these exports, together with abaca fiber and cordage, are shipped to diversified markets. In the case of logs, copper concentrates, iron ore, and molasses, the United States' share was never substantial and by 1964 Japan was absorbing virtually all Philippine exports of these commodities. On the other hand, practically all shipments of sugar, plywood and veneer, embroideries, copper and silver concentrates, and scrap tobacco went to the United States in 1963-64, and the United States accounted for over four-fifths of Philippine exports of coconut oil and desiccated coconut, and seven-tenths of lumber exports.

According to figures published by the United States Department of Commerce, the Philippines is still the principal, if not the only supplier to the United States of copra, unmanufactured abaca, desiccated coconut, and coconut oil. In 1962, the Philippines provided around 23 per cent of the sugar and 13 per cent of the plywood import requirements of the United States. The concentration of Philippine export shipments to the United States, as well as examination of the structure of American tariff rates, supports the view that the effects of the remaining preferences extended to Philippine exports in the United States market, including the quotas on sugar and coconut oil, are concentrated on sugar, plywood and veneer, embroideries, desiccated coconut, and coconut oil. It is clear that the elimination of mutual preferences scheduled in the Laurel-Langley Agreement will confront Philippine producers of these commodities with difficult problems. It is not clear, moreover, that alternative markets exist or can be developed which will permit these industries to be maintained at current levels of output.

NEW EXPORTS

The growth of Philippine exports, and their geographic diversification, has also been accompanied by the development of new exports and their expansion to positions of major importance. Most rapid has been the growth in exports of logs and timber, which in 1963-64 accounted for 21 per cent of Philippine exports as compared with 2 per cent in 1949-50. Of comparable importance has been the expansion in exports of iron ore, copper, and chromite which have more than made up for the stagnation in gold production, handicapped by the unchanged price of gold since 1933. During 1963-64, the value of exports of ores (and minor amounts of scrap metal) averaged 9 per cent of total exports as compared with only 4 per cent in 1949-50. Even more encouraging has been the growth in exports of plywood and veneer, and lumber, which did not appear in the export list in any significant quantity in 1949-50. In 1963-64, these exports averaged $31 million, or 5.4 per cent of total exports. Similarly, exports of molasses, largely to Japan, which were valued at $12.4 million in 1964, are encouraging.

SOURCES OF IMPORTS

With regard to Philippine imports, the index of concentration declined even more precipitously than that for exports, falling from 88 in 1945, to 61 in 1956, and 46 in 1964. This is only to say that the United States' dominance as a supplier of imported products has weakened faster than has its importance as a customer for Philippine export products. This reflects, in part, the fact that preferences for American goods in the Philippine market diminished faster than did those for Philippine products in the American market, as provided in the Laurel-Langley Agreement. The Philippine demand for imports of American goods, industrial manufactures for the most part, proved to be relatively responsive as the collection of Philippine tariffs raised the peso prices of such goods and narrowed the advantages they enjoyed over those from alternative sources of supply.

The significance of the changes produced by the Laurel-Langley Agreement is illustrated by the balance of trade between the two countries which in 1959, for the first time since World War II, resulted in a surplus of Philippine exports over imports. Moreover, this Philippine export surplus was maintained in five out of the six years following 1959; convincing evidence that the changes resulting from Philippine postwar economic development are not transient. It is interesting to note that the index of concentration of the Philippine import trade in 1964 of 46 is even lower than the comparable index for 1894, before the beginning of American rule, when it was 48.

Although the United States is still the principal supplier of Philippine imports, its position is being challenged by Japan, Germany, and other countries. The United States' share in the Philippine import market decreased from an annual average of 76 per cent over the decade 1946-55 to 47 per cent over the ensuing nine years. Moreover, by 1964 the ratio had declined to 40 per cent. On the other hand, the share of Japan rose from an average of 3 per cent in 1949-50 to 19 per cent in 1963-64, while over this same period the share of imports from the industrial countries of Northwestern Europe increased from 4 per cent to 16 per cent. During 1949-50, the United States, Japan, and Northwestern Europe provided 85 per cent of Philippine imports, whereas for 1963-64, their share declined to 75 per cent. The Philippines' import trade, in contrast to its export trade, was diverted to a greater degree to countries other than those of the three major trading areas. Imports from Canada and Australia, principally cereals and other food products, and petroleum from the Middle East and Indonesia increased sharply, to account for 8 per cent of imports. The remaining major sources of imports in 1963-64 included Taiwan, Hong Kong, Malaysia, and Thailand.

The decline in Philippine dependence upon imports from the United States, in contrast to the geographic dispersion of Philippine exports over the past decade and a half, has involved a moderate contraction in volume as the index for 1963-64 stood at 88 as compared with 100 in 1950. On the other hand, the average annual value of imports from the United States increased moderately and in 1963-64 amounted to $283 million as compared with $255 million in 1950. Viewed against the rapid expansion in Philippine exports, which made it possible for exports to the United States to increase in both volume and value at the same time the Philippine export trade was experiencing a healthy geographical diversification, Philippine imports experienced little growth as policies of industrialization stimulated domestic production of substitutes. During 1963-64, imports averaged $699 million as compared with $586 million in 1949, prior to the imposition of import controls to manage the external disequilibrium. Inasmuch as the dollar prices of Philippine imports rose over this period by some 25 per cent, it is clear that the volume of imports in the mid-1960s has not changed significantly from the level of 1949.

IMPORTS FROM THE UNITED STATES

On a commodity by commodity basis, the United States' share in the market for each of the fifteen leading imports of the Philippines declined between 1956 and 1964. While in 1956 the United States supplied from 57 per cent to 95 per cent of Philippine import requirements in eleven out of fifteen leading categories, by 1964 the United States supplied only 51 per cent to 59 per cent of only seven out of the fifteen leading categories. The contraction in America's percentage share was greatest in the following categories: professional, scientific and controlling instruments, dairy products, electrical machinery, non-electrical machinery, transport equipment, base metals, explosives, chemicals, paper products, and other manufactures. By 1964, substantial proportions of imports of base metals, non-electrical machinery, transport equipment, and electrical machinery were supplied by Japan and Common Market countries, while the Netherlands and Australia shipped increasing amounts of dairy products. The industrialization effort and the rising import requirements of a developing economy made the Philippines an attractive expanding market for producer goods, particularly machinery and equipment and raw and semi-processed materials, as well as consumer goods.

The composition of Philippine imports from the United States reflects this assessment of the market. Over the three years 1962-64, imports from the United States in the three categories: electrical machinery, non-electrical machinery, and transport equipment, which exceeded those in all other categories, totaled $114 million. Such imports accounted for 42 per cent of imports from the United States and were equal to 63 per cent of Philippine imports in these categories. A further 16 per cent of Philippine imports from the United States in these years were foods and agricultural raw materials, primarily raw cotton. The remainder of such imports are spread widely over diverse categories of industrial raw materials and miscellaneous manufactures.

Commercial Policy and Investment Patterns

The influence of commercial policy was felt not only in the growth, pattern, and direction of Philippine foreign trade, but also in the flow of investment into the country. Before the war, American capital in the Philippines, invested mostly in power, transportation, and communication systems; extractive, agricultural, and other export industries, was considerably larger than that in any other country in the Far East. Although such investments comprise an insignificant proportion of total American investments abroad, American capital has figured prominently in the structural formation of the Philippine economy.

In the postwar years, despite the operation of the parity clause in the Laurel-Langley Agreement, the inflow of American capital into the Philippines has not gained momentum. On the contrary, the Philippines has steadily been losing her share of the American capital outflow to the Far East to nationalistic Japan. Whereas the Philippines accounted for 40 per cent of total American investments in the Far East in 1953, this share was down to 27 per cent in 1963. In 1957 the Philippines' share of American direct investment exceeded Japan's share by $121 million, but by 1963 Japan's share surpassed that of the Philippines by $60 million.

INVESTMENT INCENTIVES

While American capital has not reacted perceptibly to the much-resented concessions granted under the parity clause, it has been more responsive to the inducements created by the protective and incentive effects of Philippine policies. The response, however, has been more discernible in the pattern of investment than in the magnitude of the investment inflow. This observation is borne out by the shift in American direct investments from public utilities and agriculture before the war to manufacturing in the postwar years, particularly beginning in the mid-1950s. The shift is attributable, in part, to the effects of changes in commercial policies, particularly in trade and exchange controls.

During this period, domestic manufactures were afforded protection from imported goods through the imposition of quantitative exchange and import restrictions. Furthermore, the allocation of foreign exchange at official rates for producer goods or profit remittances also assured manufacturing firms of built-in profits as a result of exchange rate disparities and the then prevailing structure of prices. These conditions contrasted with the prewar situation when the free entry of American goods discouraged investment in manufacturing industries, which were provided with neither protection nor incentives. Moreover, whereas prewar commercial policy favored export industries, the exchange control system brought about a rechannelling of income streams, thus encouraging capital to shift to manufacture of import substitutes.

Another effect of exchange controls on American investment movements is seen in the fact that the accumulation of American capital in the Philippines in the past decade has resulted not so much from the entry of capital as to retained earnings, mostly in blocked accounts, which account for two-thirds of the postwar increase in such investment. Thus, if the entry of American capital is to be encouraged, stronger measures, such as the provision of economic protection and incentives for priority investments, would appear to be more effective than the mere extension of parity rights beyond 1974.

THE YOUNG ECONOMY ON THE MOVE

The Philippine experience following 1950, striking for its success in promoting industrialization and boosting the development process while maintaining a reasonable degree of stability, demonstrates the need for autonomy in economic policy and the effectiveness of protection. The favorable revision of the 1946 Trade Agreement and the imposition of trade and exchange controls, as well as other economic measures, channeled resources to industrial and other development projects. In addition to tax concessions for new and necessary industries, credit policy measures were also tailored to encourage such projects. An important milestone in the Philippines' progress toward autonomy in economic policy was the adoption in 1949 of the managed currency system in place of the dollar exchange standard, which enabled the economy to minimize the disturbing effects of adverse external and internal developments. Moreover, with the establishment of the Central Bank, the agency responsible for the administration of monetary policy, credit policy became an important instrument for maintaining stability and at the same time promoting economic development goals.

The tangible result of these measures is the remarkable transformation in the economic structure, as manufacturing and import-substitute production outpaced agriculture and primary industries. Less progress was made in export diversification, perhaps precisely because of the keen interest in import substitution. The pattern of imports reflected the industrialization as imports of producer goods and industrial raw materials came to displace consumer imports.

The Future of Philippine-American Commercial Relations

It can be seen, in retrospect, that the early postwar attempts to rehabilitate the Philippine economy were an ill-advised attempt to restore the structure of the prewar economy, which at its best proved inadequate for the country's needs. Subsequent moves in Philippine-American trade relations have modified this erroneous approach and given it a different orientation.

With the approaching expiration of the Laurel-Langley Agreement, the future of Philippine-American trade relations lies in any one of three directions. The special relations between the two countries could be terminated sooner than 1974 through the abrogation of the Agreement after five years notice. Another alternative would be to effect no changes in the Agreement and to let it run its full course. The third alternative would be to extend the special trade relations between the two countries beyond 1974 on a selective basis.

THE ALTERNATIVES

The first two alternatives have basically similar implications, the only difference being the time element. The immediate termination of the special relations shortens the adjustment period and could therefore magnify or intensify both the advantages and disadvantages of the normalization of trade. The cessation of special relations would leave each country free to pursue the expansion of trade relations with other countries, particularly with logical partners such as those of the Philippines in Southeast Asia. Since the full duty rates would apply on the dutiable products traded, protectionist policies could be pursued more vigorously. Furthermore, to the extent that the volume of trade does not contract as a result of increased tariffs, government revenue collections of both countries would be likely to increase. For example, it has been estimated that the Laurel-Langley Agreement deprived the Philippine government of revenues equivalent to almost one-fourth of the total public investment outlay projected under the Five-Year Socio-Economic Development Program of 1962.

The untimely cessation of special trade relations, however, could cause dislocations and disturbances contrary to the national interests of both countries, particularly in the short run. The United States, for instance, would lose a growing market which for over sixty years she has dominated, a loss which could contribute to her current balance of payments problems. For the Philippines, the effects could be even more serious, since the initial impact would reduce export earnings and gravely threaten stability and the economic development effort. While both countries could compensate for their respective losses by seeking markets elsewhere, their efforts could be seriously hindered by trading blocs in Europe, Latin America, and Africa. Moreover, the prospects of the Philippines' competitiveness in world markets are limited, in particular by the nature of her products and resources, and, more generally, by her present stage of development, which in the short run restricts the variety and volume of new exports within her capabilities.

Under the third alternative—the revision of the Agreement to extend special relations beyond 1974—the recent trend toward diminishing trade relations between the two countries is likely to be arrested or at least slowed down. To the Philippines, it would mean assurance of continued foreign exchange earnings necessary to finance economic development projects. To the United States, the extension of special trade relations would at least forestall the probable loss of an expanding market which has already developed a taste for American products.

The danger exists that free trade arrangements would adversely affect the industrialization efforts of the Philippines due to the free entry of certain American manufactures. This danger could be minimized if the revision of the Agreement were based on a selectivity which recognized the shifting pattern of demand induced by the development aspirations and changing structural formations of developing countries, technological advances, and even international political re-alignments. On this basis, the special relations between the two countries, for instance, could be arranged to allow the duty-free entry of selected American goods—particularly producer goods such as machinery, equipment, semi-processed and raw materials, and selected consumer goods. It will be recalled that it is in the machinery and equipment categories that the United States' share of Philippine imports has declined significantly these past few years. In return, concessions similar to those currently granted Philippine export products could be continued. Thus, if the revision of the Agreement were done on a selective basis which gave due consideration to the economic resources and national goals of each country, a trade agreement acceptable to both could be found.

NEW INTERESTS AND PROTAGONISTS

The changes in economic structure have been accompanied by changes in economic protagonists. The more influential American interests in the Philippines are no longer the individual oldtimers but are more likely to be impersonal international corporations with worldwide connections. On the Philippine side, a new generation of domestic entrepreneurs has grown up eager to take part in business and with a drive to industrialize that was absent before the 1950s. New arrangements would have to be worked out to reconcile possible areas of conflict. One such area arises in the fear of domestic entrepreneurs of being overwhelmed by giant international companies. Yet, properly channelled, the activities of such companies can be beneficial to the economy, inasmuch as they are more likely to take a long-range view in assessing alternatives. While their size may give pause to Filipino policy makers, their ability to mobilize investment and their relatively long-time horizons are something that the economy badly needs and is not likely to get from other quarters in amounts sufficient to propel rapid economic growth.

The indices of concentration show that much progress has been made in diversifying Philippine foreign trade geographically. In fact, the deconcentration of imports may have been extended about as far as possible by general policy measures. Henceforth, if further diversification is to be achieved it will probably require specific policy measures which impinge on products rather than countries. The same will increasingly hold true for the export side, although with different relative emphasis in the choice of policies.

COMMERCIAL POLICY FOR DEVELOPMENT

This leads to consideration of the opening of new markets for Philippine products. Realistically speaking, the most promising markets are still the developed countries with high incomes and advanced economies. It is perhaps over-optimistic for the Philippines to depend, in the short run, on regional arrangements for a significant increase in foreign exchange earnings. Perhaps there is more to be gained by measures to facilitate access to the markets of the developed countries. In this connection, the moves being made under the aegis of the United Nations Conference on Trade and Development (UNCTAD) bear close watching.

For some time now the United States has been embarked on a policy of assisting developing countries to attain their economic development objectives through various financial, technical, and material assistance programs. Although the United States has spent billions in foreign aid, it is generally observed that foreign aid, as such, has not gone very far in improving the economic strength of these nations. To accelerate development, it has been suggested at the UNCTAD that economic assistance must be supplemented by one-way trade concessions extended to developing countries by advanced nations. On this basis, the Philippines could hope to maximize the benefits of American assistance in the pursuance of economic development objectives through a revision of the Laurel-Langley Agreement along lines which are frankly designed to favor the

Philippines. In historical perspective, this would merely make up for the long decades during which the balance of advantage in Philippine-American economic relations lay with the United States. In terms of the future, it would be a concrete realization of ideas which have begun to secure increasingly general acceptance at the UNCTAD, and without which the growth of developing countries will be a more protracted and more costly process than it need be. In the struggle for her economic progress and well being, the Philippines is motivated by the conviction that only a strong and economically progressive nation can contribute effectively to the attainment of global prosperity and stability upon which the maintenance of world order, balance, and lasting peace can be founded.

David Wurfel

7

Problems of Decolonization

The Special Relationship

The Philippines was America's only colony in Asia. This historical fact makes the tie between the two countries inevitably unique. But the relationship, so often characterized as "special" by each party, is special for different reasons and in differing intensity when viewed by Washington and by Manila. There are even differential perceptions of the history of the connection. It is the purpose of this writer, admittedly with an American bias, to try to understand and compare these differences and then to examine the changing character of the relationship since Philippine independence in the light of the differing assessments. Special emphasis will be placed on aid giving and receiving, since it seems to highlight broader problems. Finally, consideration will be given to factors which, on both sides, have affected changes in attitudes or angles of vision; for only if Americans and Filipinos understand better how they look at each other, and why, is there a basis for friendly and mutually beneficial relations in the future.

Some have suggested that the Philippines is of special significance because it provides the most secure American military base in Southeast Asia. This is not the source of the Philippines greatest importance to the United States, however. Not just in Southeast Asia, but

DAVID WURFEL, *Professor of Political Science and Chairman, Committee on Asian Studies, University of Missouri, received his Ph.D. (Government) from Cornell University. From 1960 to 1962, he was visiting professor at International Christian University, Tokyo, and in 1964-65 at the University of Singapore. Professor Wurfel first went to the Philippines as an undergraduate student in 1947-48. He returned in 1955-56 as a Ford Foundation scholar and in 1961 on a Social Science Research Council fellowship. He is the author of "The Philippines" in* Government and Politics of Southeast Asia *(ed., George M. Kahin).*

throughout the "third world" of late developing societies, the Philippines is the only nation into which the ideas and institutions of American democracy have been so deeply transplanted. Even after necessary grafts and trimming, the gardener is not fully satisfied with the new plant, but whatever the imperfections of Philippine democracy—some of which are the gardener's responsibility—this system stands as one of the most stable, representative and progressive among the new nations today. It is supremely important for the United States that Philippine democracy continue to prosper and to mature within its own constitutional framework.

For the Philippines, the importance of America is not hard to explain. The United States is her main trading partner, major source of foreign investment, strongest military ally, origin of a large part of her political tradition, and cultural model for many of her people. Clearly, every kind of American influence is greater in the Philippines than anywhere else in Asia. But precisely because of this fact the American presence is at the same time the greatest obstacle to mature nationhood, to the successful quest for national identity. The weight of history impels the Filipino to think of the relationship with the United States as a very special one, but his yearning for recognition as Asian among Asians presses him to try to alter the historical legacy.

THE LEGACY OF 1946

The search for an Asian identity is partly responsible for the coloring of the recent re-evaluation of the Philippine revolution, the Japanese occupation, and the 1946 transfer of power, a process in which historian Teodoro Agoncillo figures prominently. But even before this trend there were distinct differences between the general Filipino view of the events of 1946, when power was transferred, and the American perception. And, as Professor George Taylor has said, "Many of the problems that dominate United States-Philippine relations today owe their origin . . . to the arrangements made in 1946."

After Japan's surrender the United States saw the need of substantial assistance for economic rehabilitation from wartime destruction if Philippine sovereignty was to be meaningful. Several hundred million dollars was appropriated by the United States Congress for this purpose, largely due to the persistence of Senator Millard Tydings. The Philippine Rehabilitation Act, authorizing an outlay of $620 million, was the largest installment. Out of this sum, $400 million was to go to private claimants for reimbursement of war damage, which amounted to only a little over half the amount of claims—based on 1941 replacement prices—filed with the United States War Damage Commission. Enacted at the same time was the Bell Trade Act establishing an eight-year period of free trade between the two countries before the gradual application of tariffs. Its ostensible purpose was to revive Philippine export industries by maintaining access to a protected American market. The first draft which, according to David Bernstein's account in *The Philippine Story,* reflected the wishes of President Osmeña, provided for twenty years of free trade. Both the State Department and Senator Tydings were opposed to such an extended period. The Senator charged that most Americans who favored such a bill were "fundamentally opposed to Philippine independence. . . ." The legislation also reflected hard bargaining among various Philippine and American economic interests and, under the circumstances prevailing at the time, the views of the latter strongly colored the final draft. There was at least one American Congressman in 1946 who expressed the feeling, widespread among Filipinos, that "the people of the United States, in all fairness, stand a far greater chance . . . to benefit under this legislation than do the people of the Philippines."

Most official Washington statements, however, interpreted these enactments as a magnanimous American gesture to a people in need. Said President Truman as he signed the bills, "I am happy to approve these two measures, which give notice to the entire world that we are redeeming our promises to the heroic Philippine people." This view is sometimes still reflected in such accounts as that found in Robert Aura Smith's *Philippine Freedom.*

Through Filipino eyes the gesture was less magnanimous. President Roosevelt's promise, made in the dark days before Bataan fell, that Filipinos would be "assisted in the full repair of the ravages caused by the war," and reiterated later by President Truman, was well remembered. The damage was conservatively estimated at more than one billion dollars, so that the compensation appropriated for losses was not "full." And however a lawyer may interpret the promise, full restitution had become the general Filipino expectation. But the bitterest resentment was stirred by the provision in the Rehabilitation Act which prohibited payment of large war damage claims until after the Philippine government had accepted the terms of the Trade Act. Apparently there was some doubt in Washington as to whether the great "boon" which the Bell Trade Act bestowed on the war-weakened Philippine economy would be recognized as such in Manila. Acceptance of the Bell Act was doubly galling to Filipinos because it necessitated an amendment of their Constitution to permit Americans to enjoy the same rights as Filipinos in the exploitation of Philippine natural resources and in the allocation of public utility franchises. Inclusion of such a provision in the law was opposed unsuccessfully by Carlos Romulo—and the State Department—in Washington; in Manila, President Roxas, when faced with an all or nothing proposition, was willing and able to "sell" the unpalatable necessity. To do so, the use of both carrot and stick proved helpful; the constitutional amendment was just barely approved by the Philippine Congress, but only after several prospective opponents had been denied their seats on grounds of "election fraud." Ratification by plebiscite followed. In retrospect, we can add that these special rights for Americans did not attract the great flow of investment which the devastated economy so urgently needed.

There were other Filipino grievances which can be traced to the first year of independence, such as the unsatisfactory provisions on jurisdiction which resulted from the hard bargaining on military bases, and the requirement that the peso be pegged to the dollar and revalued only with the approval of the American president. No further history need be recounted to show that there were fundamental differences between the views of Americans and Filipinos on the significance of the arrangements which accompanied the transfer of sovereignty. Of course, there were also differences among Filipinos and among Americans, depending on ideology and interest, but intranational differences tended to be blurred in time, while international disagreements festered. This is so for several reasons, all springing from the clear distinctions between Filipino and American cultural values.

In the first place, the tragic experience of war, occupation, and liberation had intensified the Filipino's emotional tie with Americans. There was a strong feeling among Filipinos that their struggle against the Japanese had proven their loyalty to and friendship for America. When Senator Tydings went to the Philippines in June 1945, he was greatly impressed by the "reservoir of good will and respect" for the United States. Because Filipinos, like Americans, tend to project to the international scene their conceptions about the proper relationships of individuals, it was assumed that the small, devastated nation, having displayed its loyalty to a great and prosperous friend, should be treated in turn with undemanding generosity. Truman had reinforced this perception of the relationship by broadcasting to the Philippines before the war had ended, that the "heroic and loyal stand [of the Philippine people] . . . has won the affection" of Americans. It was the expectation of affectionate friendship which caused the Filipinos to be so startled by sharp demands from Americans in 1946.

UTANG NA LOOB

The nature of the Filipino perception of loyalty and friendly assistance has been perceptively analyzed by the Filipina sociologist Mary Hollnsteiner. She points out that in the traditional Filipino patron-client relationship the poor and weak give loyalty to the rich and powerful with the expectation that they will receive help from their benefactor whenever needed. Each side owes to the other a debt of gratitude, or *utang na loob,* although the subordinate in this hierarchical relationship is not expected to repay the debt in equivalent amounts. For many Filipinos, the Filipino-American tie in 1941 approximated some type of subordinate-superordinate bond. In that context the Filipino, having bravely expressed his loyalty during the war, should have been able to expect, in his desperate need after liberation, unstinting assistance from America. As already noted, Roosevelt and Truman had underscored that expectation. Then for the United States to offer aid which seemed insufficient for full rehabilitation and at the same time demand a *quid pro quo,* as if there had not already been an adequate expression of loyalty, would, in Filipino interpersonal interaction, have been termed "shameless." In fact, many Filipinos regarded the American government's behavior in just that light.

On the other hand, if Filipinos had regarded their relationship with the United States as essentially coordinate, they could have viewed the pattern of *utang na loob* rather differently. To receive services from a friend in a crisis is a typical way of acquiring a debt of gratitude. For those Filipinos who saw the war with Japan as essentially an American war—and there were many—Filipino heroism on Bataan, the taking of great risks to aid American guerrillas, serving in the intelligence network, or guiding the liberation forces were sacrifices *for America,* which America could never fully repay. American oratory which praised those sacrifices reinforced this perception of the situation. But payment of the American "debt" was, in fact, accompanied by that rude jolt to Filipino national pride, the parity amendment.

The Westernized Manila elite, which makes most of the political decisions in the Philippines, seldom articulates the traditional values explained here; nevertheless, such values mold their behavior to a far greater extent than is usually realized. In fact, the failure of American officials and businessmen to be aware of the values implicit in the actions of so many "Americanized" Filipinos is one of the most fundamental causes of tension today.

SMOOTH INTERPERSONAL RELATIONS

Americans, at the same time, are often unaware of the implicit values in their own behavior, and can hardly expect Filipinos to be more so. For Americans, every relationship between groups, and therefore nations, is a matter of hard bargaining. We tend to come to the bargaining table with only a hazy idea of the historical context of foreign policy issues, and thus of the limits which history places on the outcome. We also come with the expectation—usually correct if he is an American—that our counterpart too is prepared for hard bargaining and thus are often insensitive to his pride and self-esteem, so important among Filipinos. Filipinos are by no means inexperienced in bargaining. Jean Grossholtz has, in fact, maintained that it is the foundation of the democratic process in the Philippines. But Filipino bargaining is circumscribed by the need to maintain smooth interpersonal relations and by the network of existing personal ties. One does not bargain, for instance, about repayment of a debt of gratitude. Nor does one make demands which would require one's counterpart to swallow his pride.

Under conditions of stress, many Filipinos are sufficiently pragmatic to see the advantages to be gained by swallowing their pride. Such a man was President Manuel Roxas in 1946. But the humiliation continues to fester. The farther away one is from the exigencies by which he was forced into humiliation, the greater the resentment tends to become toward those held responsible. Thus, some Filipinos who accepted parity in 1946 as an unfortunate necessity now recall it as a national disgrace for which the United States is blamed.

It has been said by Filipino journalist Max Soliven that "the Filipino is a creature of emotion." This is an effective hyperbole, just as it would be to say that the typical American is a calculating "economic man." But the two characterizations have meaning if thought of simply as tendencies in the dominant behavior patterns of the two cultures.

EQUALITY AMONG UNEQUALS

Thus, in a bargaining situation the American is exasperated when the Filipino seems unimpressed by rational arguments designed to prove, for example, a mutuality of interests, and is instead much perturbed by a careless phrase used by the American which seems to imply disrespect for Filipinos. But the oft-mentioned emotional sensitivity of the Filipino is, in part, a function of the unequal status of the two powers in world politics, which so often mocks the formal diplomatic equality of sovereign states. The attempt to maintain the fiction of equality in dealings which inevitably must reveal the basic inequality increases the psychological strain on the representatives of the weaker power, who are liable to be termed "emotional."

It is also easier for the American to be rational about issues in Philippine-American relations because they so seldom involve what diplomats call "vital national interests." For Filipinos, on the other hand, these issues are usually very vital, indeed, "gut issues," which by their very nature invite emotional reaction. Or, to describe the same phenomena in a somewhat different fashion, the intensity of the relationship is uneven. For the Philippines, relations with America are paramount, as we have noted earlier, and United States policy can be crucial for her future development. For the United States, however, trade with the Philippines is a minor fraction of total trade, the military alliance is one of dozens, and cultural ties seldom touch the American awareness. Only a handful of Americans have a large stake, either economic or emotional, in the Philippines. United States government representatives, seldom resident in the Philippines for long, can speak of Philippine problems with a detachment not possible for their Filipino counterparts. Too few official Americans acquire a constructive concern. In sum, Filipino "emotionalism," which springs, in part, from basic cultural values—and which has been ably defended by some Filipinos as evidence of a greater sensitivity to personality, a greater humanity—must be explained also in terms of the unavoidable inequalities between the Philippines and the United States. For the Philippines, the relationship is more "special" than for the United States.

Having traced some historical and cultural causes for tensions, let us summarize the relationship of donor to recipient of economic and technical assistance. In this facet of United States-Philippine relations the problems of cross-cultural communication became most apparent.

Aid Giving and Receiving

REHABILITATION

From 1945 through 1949, total United States government disbursements in the Philippines amounted to $1.4 billion. More than half of this was in the form of cash payments to individuals. Besides the $400 million for private war damages, which only permitted payment of 52.5 per cent of the approved amount of claims over $500, more than $450 million in back pay was distributed to members of officially recognized wartime guerrilla units. But these amounts did not buy political harmony. The unpaid portion of large war-damage claims became the basis of further demands on the United States, while political discrimination in the recognition of guerrilla units helped fan the fires of unrest in Luzon. The Rehabilitation Act of 1946 authorized the transfer of not more than $100 million worth of surplus military equipment—excluding weapons and ammunition—to the Philippine government. The equipment transferred was estimated to have a "fair valuation" of ₱274,000,000, whereas the Philippine government only received ₱73.5 million from its sale. Part of the loss represented deterioration; the rest went to politicians and their friends in one of the most flamboyant scandals in Philippine history. Fortunately, direct assistance from United States government operating agencies to their Philippine counterparts was more efficiently used.

Although American assistance for rehabilitation from the ravages of war was not as consequential as it should have been, or even as much as originally intended in Washington, it undoubtedly contributed to the rapid economic expansion. From 1946 to 1949, the physical volume of production more than doubled, reaching prewar levels.

Economic recovery was not matched in the political and administrative realms. In fact, it is likely that the flood of American money into an administrative system demoralized by the Japanese occupation, with its galloping inflation, simply served to increase the temptations to corruption when officials were least prepared to resist them. Lack of public probity had long been a problem, but rampant corruption tarnished the reputation of the party in power. Furthermore, the overwhelming financial backing of the United States made the elite less sensitive than they might otherwise have been to the demands of new political interests, including an aroused peasantry in Central Luzon. An alliance between peasant leadership and nationalist intellectuals—both infiltrated by communists —highly critical of the United States, made it easier for an American-supported government to neglect the causes of peasant unrest. Minor reforms on paper were unenforced.

As a result, in November 1949 the Liberal Party had to engage in massive election fraud in order to stay in power. And the questionable morality of electoral techniques was reflected in the post-election administration. In central Luzon the Hukbalahap, a communist-led, anti-Japanese guerrilla force which after the war espoused radical reform, had so gained in political and military strength that in February 1950 they felt emboldened to call themselves a "People's Liberation Army." Their forces launched daring attacks on *poblaciones* near Manila, which was itself surrounded by check-points manned by government forces.

THE BELL REPORT AND AFTER

In that same month of February 1950 President Quirino was in the United States for medical and other reasons. Aware that American assistance for rehabilitation was on the decline—1948 was the peak year—that foreign exchange reserves had dropped to less than half what they were in 1945, and that the government treasury was so bare that school teachers often were unpaid, Quirino asked for a new American aid commitment. After consultation the two governments decided— apparently on prompting of Ambassador Cowen in Manila—that a careful study of the Philippine economy was necessary, so that aid might be designed more appropriately to cure the Philippines' economic ills. Quirino appointed an Economic Survey Mission headed by Secretary of Finance, José Yulo, and Truman sent a similiar group to Manila headed by former Under Secretary of the Treasury, Daniel Bell.

The Bell Mission, which conducted its survey independently of the counterpart Philippine mission, surveyed more than economic problems, concerning itself also with social unrest and administrative disorganization and venality. The Report which it produced contained such straightforward criticism of the Philippine government and its policies that there was an abortive effort in Malacañang to prevent release of the Report's full text. This event highlights the problems corollary to the philosophy of American aid which the Bell Report embodied, a philosophy which did not have wide acceptance in American foreign aid policy until the launching of the Alliance for Progress by President Kennedy.

REFORM AND ECONOMIC DEVELOPMENT

This philosophy holds first that aid is intervention, so that inadequate aid programs cannot be defended by the doctrine of non-intervention; intervention must be used wisely. Secondly, it reflects the belief that, while economic development is the primary goal of aid, social and administrative reform may be necessary prerequisities to the fullest economic progress and to that just distribution of the fruits of progress which is essential to political stability. Finally, this approach insists upon a firm commitment from the recipient government to both development and reform *before* the aid program begins. Although exponents of this view are usually firmly anti-colonialist, it implies a broad concern for the social, political, and economic growth of an underdeveloped society which is not entirely unlike the concept of tutelage for the enlightened colonialist. It was precisely because United States tutelage in the Philippines before 1941 had not pushed for social reform—and thus was partly responsible for the agrarian unrest in Central Luzon—that liberal American opinion could espouse such an approach to an independent Philippines. American pressure for social reform in the 1950s could be considered unfinished business.

The full Report of the Bell Mission was released in October and almost immediately William C. Foster, head of the Economic Cooperation Administration, flew to the Philippines to negotiate an agreement to implement its recommendations. The Quirino-Foster Agreement of November 4, 1950, assured American aid of $250 million over "several consecutive years," but only "in consideration of the determination of the Philippine Government to act boldly and promptly on a major program designed to fulfill the aspirations of the Filipino people." Highest priority was assigned to "tax legislation of an equitable measure" to bring total revenues up to ₱565 million and "a minimum wage law for all agricultural workers [sic] as a first step towards labor and rural legislation." In effect, tax and minimum wage laws—along with a Congressional resolution of intent to enact further reform—became prerequisites for the release of American aid. Much political wrangling in the Congress delayed, until April 1951, passage of the last required measure, the minimum wage law covering industrial as well as agricultural workers. Agricultural employers had been a major stumbling block. American business interests, unhappy about a rise in corporate taxes and the imposition of a new tax on foreign exchange transactions, also appeared to contribute to the delay. Caught between the pressures of American policy and of special economic interests, some members of the Philippine Congress raised a familiar cry. The Chairman of the House Ways and Means Committee maintained that the United States government should "show more understanding and sympathy," especially considering that the "economic maladjustment was brought about due to our political affiliation with the United States during the war." "The imposition of a condition *sine qua non* requiring the Philippine government to increase the tax burden by 60 per cent as a condition for ECA aid nullifies the beneficent spirit of that aid," he added.

But American administrators continued to be more interested in a bold program to fulfill popular aspirations than in showing a "beneficent spirit." Vincent Checchi, who became the first Economic Cooperation Administration mission chief in the Philippines, was perhaps one of the most forceful exponents of the new concept of aid for development and reform. Although the handicap of wartime destruction was still in the forefront of Filipino thinking, American policy makers became concerned with economic and social development and tended to assume that "rehabilitation" was no longer a useful approach. Strict adherence to the philosophy of the Bell Report and the Quirino-Foster Agreement continued to guide United States aid policy to mid-1953. Such major reform measures as the Industrial Peace Act and the Agricultural Credit and Cooperative Financing Act were adopted on American advice during this period. Only the far-reaching agrarian reform proposals of Bob Hardie, land tenure specialist in the aid mission, were not translated into official American recommendations to the Philippine government.

During this period opponents of United States-backed policies, and of the fact of American backing, were vocal. The vehemence of the attacks of House Speaker Eugenio Perez on Hardie and his proposals was largely responsible for the failure of the latter to receive official American endorsement. But at the same time there were both bureaucratic and political interests—including many critics of the Quirino administration—sufficiently enthusiastic about the substance of the proposed reforms that they were willing either to ignore or to justify United States intervention in the policy process.

IMPETUS LOST

By 1954, the attitudes of the American and Filipino governments had become inverted. A Republican administration in Washington made substantial changes in the personnel of the aid program. Social or administrative reform dropped to a low point on the scale of operational priorities. The Magsaysay administration, on the other hand, was enthusiastic for reform—although not as effective in its implementation as some would have liked. Thus, despite reduced American pressure, important measures, such as the Agricultural Tenancy Act of 1954 and the creation of the Agrarian Court, were adopted. But, in seeming paradox, criticism of American involvement in policy making grew. For instance, Senator Claro Recto attacked the Land Reform Act of 1955 as being American-inspired when, in fact, such inspiration was less than it had been for any major reform measure in four years.

What appeared paradoxical could be explained in part by the fact that beginning in 1954 Filipinos, having greater faith in their own leaders, found less justification for American intervention. This was particularly true of the question of United States supervision of aid-financed projects. In November 1950 the *Manila Chronicle* could say in an editorial: "The plain fact is that the administration can no longer be expected to further the interests of the people. Any affront to it as the proposed (United States) supervision is interpreted to mean cannot be taken as an affront to the Filipino people. . . . Experience has shown how previous American loans and aids have been dissipated by ranking government officials." Magsaysay had, however, maintained the highest level of official probity of any president since independence, and the conditions that warranted the *Chronicle* editorial had ceased to exist early in his administration. And, by 1956, there arose a chorus of Congressional criticism of "meddling" by the aid mission. Furthermore, the Recto blast, directed at alleged intervention in the legislative, not the administrative, process, revealed a rise in nationalist sentiment. Finally, an improvement in the level of technical training of Filipino administrators decreased both the need for and the willingness to accept American advice.

Implementation of the Bell Report had been envisaged by its drafters to be a five-year process. Shortly after the end of that period Magsaysay met his tragic death. Many of the Report's recommendations had been buried, either by the Philippine Congress or the bureaucracy. But neither had American aid fulfilled the widespread unofficial expectation of $250 million over five years. It was not until 1959 that the $250 million mark was reached.

THE DECLINE OF AMERICAN AID

1959 marked the maximum flow of American aid following 1950, nearly $50 million. Since then the program has dropped to less than half that. The drop would have been even more precipitous if it had not been for the substantial transfers to the Philippines of agricultural surpluses under Public Law 480.

By 1961, although the philosophy of the Bell Report had returned to Washington with the Kennedy administration, the Manila aid mission was faced with a declining budget. It did not have the wherewithal to exert pressure on the Philippine government if it had wanted to; nor did that government have as much interest in development and reform as its predecessor. The atmosphere was one of politics more "usual" than ever before—and of rising nationalism.

At the same time, access to other major sources of foreign assistance had opened. The greatest of these was Japanese reparations. The Reparations Agreement, signed in May 1956, committed the Japanese government to provide $550 million in capital goods, cash, and services over a twenty-year period. Deliveries have averaged about $25 million per year since then. Thus, by 1964 it was of approximately the same magnitude as the United States aid program. However, unlike aid, over half of reparations consignments were made to individuals and private firms. In addition, United Nations and Colombo Plan technical assistance transfers to the Philippines have grown to the extent that in 1964 they were nearly equivalent to United States technical assistance of $3.45 million.

Besides these governments funds, increasing amounts are becoming available as private loans, especially from Japan and Germany. When Japan signed the Reparations Agreement with the Philippines, she promised to "facilitate" the extension of private loans to finance Japanese equipment exports of up to $250 million. By 1964, only $3.8 million of such loans had been authorized, but applications for nearly $50 million were pending. German loans for almost as much were also under negotiation. Still, when placed beside a total of more than $200 million of credits from the United States Export-Import Bank since 1956—a mixture of public and private loans—these amounts are not large.

While United States aid was declining, both absolutely and relative to other programs, the number of American technicians declined also. From 207 in 1957 the total dropped to less than one-third of that in 1962, rising only slightly in the succeeding two years. This meant, of course, that fewer Philippine government agencies had American advisors. For those few who did still work closely with their Filipino counterparts, there were increasing obstacles to effectiveness. The case of the advisor to the Bureau of Customs whose minor disagreement with a high Filipino official was sensationalized by the Manila press is perhaps not typical, but nevertheless instructive. The willingness to receive American advice, which had contributed to the implementation of the Bell Report, eroded as Philippine nationalism flourished.

WAR DAMAGE FIASCO

In 1962 a further installment in payment of America's "moral obligation" to the Philippines created neither leverage nor good will, but stimulated the restless nationalism. As indicated above, approved war-damage claims over $500 could not be fully paid out of the 1946 appropriations. As early as 1955 the Philippine government had pressed the United States to complete the promised payment. But not until May 1962 did the matter reach a vote in the House of Representatives. In a poorly attended division the House, by 201 to 171, defeated the war damage bill, much to the consternation of the White House. In an immediate statement designed to mollify Filipinos, President Kennedy said the House action showed "a lack of appreciation of the moral obligation the United States owes to the people of the Philippines." In fact, many House members were displeased with a measure which they thought would benefit only wealthy individuals and corporations. Others were just tired of "hand outs" to the Philippines, and made the mistake of saying so. Tempers flared in Manila. The Philippine Congress demanded that President Macapagal cancel his scheduled visit to the United States. When he announced an "indefinite postponement" the next day, the President accused the United States of negating its "legal and moral commitments to our country." The Kennedy oil had not quieted the troubled waters. Anti-American waves splashed into print for weeks. The celebration of Independence Day was moved from July 4th to June 12, although it was officially explained that "this had been under consideration for some time."

Later in the year the American Congress passed an authorization bill for $73 million to complete payments due to 86,000 claimants. But actual appropriation was delayed until the 1963 session. In the meantime, revelation of improper lobbying caused Senator Fulbright to push for a lump sum payment to the Philippine government, rather than to individuals. In the bill's final version, a Fulbright compromise, only claims up to $25,000 were to be fully reimbursed while the remainder, amounting to more than $30 million, was put into an "educational exchange" fund to be administered jointly by the two governments. In Manila, even those who were passionate exponents of education and who held no brief for the wealthy, were affronted that the United States should attempt to retain joint administration over a sum which she was paying to the Philippines as a "moral obligation." Seldom was it more evident that men of good will on both sides of the Pacific could not see mutual problems in the same light.

NEW DEPARTURES

After the advent of the Johnson administration, one could sense some fundamental rethinking of aid policy in Manila. Some key figures in the aid mission recognized that techniques of aid administration developed in the early 1950s were no longer appropriate for the Philippines. United States foreign assistance programs for economic development had been launched on a wave of enthusiasm for the "Point Four" concept that the United States could participate in social and economic development most effectively and most cheaply by providing technicians and technical training. In this respect, the United Nations and the Colombo Plan followed in our footsteps. Since 1951 the Philippines has received more than 2,000 man-years of technical advice from all donor agencies and 5,000 man-years of training for Filipino technicians abroad. There are now few Philippine government agencies which are without staff members trained in the special technology of the agency's functions, although this has not made the administration appreciably more efficient. In a few cases efficiency was improved by the aid-financed introduction of office machines, but by 1965 those machines frequently stood idle. Administration is more likely to be improved by training for administration, and by bolstering the political position of administrators.

If lack of trained technicians is no longer a serious problem, a rethinking of aid policy might lead to the conclusion that the Manila aid staff, although reduced to only 80 technicians by 1964, is largely superfluous. Certainly few American technicians have contributed anything more than their professional skill—acquired in meeting American problems—to the task of reform and development in the Philippines. The aid specialist who has studied Philippine conditions carefully and adapted himself well to the Filipino pattern of decision making has been rare, and his contribution great. There are even some advantages which a sophisticated outsider has in helping to improve the quality of public administration. But the number of Americans who are sensitive, cross-cultural innovators—and that is the kind of person really needed—appears to be severely limited. Nor have personnel policies of the successive aid administrations always been well designed to recruit them. The Philippine government has tired of supporting the all too frequently superannuated extension workers—and the financial burden does fall partly on the Philippines. Inasmuch as the leverage which United States aid might be able to exert on the Philippine government has diminished, technician-advisors must rely increasingly on their abilities in human relations if they are to accomplish anything.

Current plans to decentralize aid administration promise to prove beneficial. Decentralization is no administrative panacea, but hopefully a workable formula has been found in which a portion of aid funds are being channeled to province-size projects. This not only allows greater flexibility of programming to meet the needs of different agricultural regions, permitting greater experimentation because projects are on a small scale, but it bypasses much of the bureaucratic red tape between Manila and the people. Furthermore, such a procedure energizes provincial government, long a goal of American technical assistance in public administration.

For a time such projects were stymied because President Macapagal considered direct links between the aid mission and the provincial governments a violation of Philippine sovereignty. But what is politically possible is also legally possible. Thanks to the ingenious maneuvers of dynamic Governor Benigno Aquino, Jr., of Tarlac Province, both the President and the National Economic Council, the Philippine government agency which administers United States aid, agreed to "channel aid more directly to the people." Aquino and hard-working young Governor San Luis of Laguna Province, president of the Liberal Party Governor's Association, were the first two governors to receive assistance for irrigation and road building under the new arrangement. After these pilot projects were underway, machinery was established by the NEC to screen applications from other governors. If early expectations are fulfilled, the allocation of Public Law 480 funds to provincial projects could be usefully increased to as much as $50 million per year. The reduced need for technicians should not be confused with a diminished need for production-increasing capital projects.

Rapid growth in agricultural productivity in Taiwan was one of the major reasons for the American decision to terminate aid to that country. Some have suggested that similarly strict economic indices might be used to evaluate the Philippine aid program. If they were, it is apparent that in the agricultural sector aid would be needed for some time to come— and thus the justification for expanding provincial projects. But if the importance of the Philippines to the United States is the success of a political system into which so much of our own tradition has been poured, then economic indices will be inadequate to measure the need for aid. Progress, or its lack, in education, in public administration, or in fulfillment of the aspirations for social justice will be at least as important as production figures.

THE PEACE CORPS

This consideration was probably one among the several which motivated policy makers to introduce a large contingent of Peace Corps Volunteers into the Philippine educational system. Of course, the most important reason that the Philippines received the first large Peace Corps program was simply that Washington found the Philippines easiest to work in and most likely to produce success stories—which were badly needed on Capitol Hill. And produce success stories they did.

The Peace Corps has constituted the most important new dimension of American involvement in the Philippines since the dispatch of the Bell Mission. Beginning in 1962, nearly one thousand volunteers have gone to villages and towns to teach in elementary and secondary schools, and more recently in teachers colleges. An average of about 325 PCVs have been kept in the field at a cost of little more than $1 million per year. Nearly half the volunteers have been assigned to English teaching, a decision based on a growing recognition that declining levels of language proficiency have become a major cause of instructional problems in Philippine high schools and colleges, where all teaching is in English. The rest of the volunteers are about evenly divided between math and science teachings, subjects which are receiving more and more emphasis in the curriculum planning of the Department of Education in Manila.

Until December 1964 the PCVs were officially designated "educational aides," but little effort was made by either side to define their role. Thus, both the Filipino teachers and the volunteers assigned to them were uneasy about their relationship. For the most self-confident and activist volunteers the tendency was to do too much; for the least self-confident Filipino teacher, the fear was precisely that the volunteer would do too much. In most cases adjustments by both sides led to workable arrangements, but volunteers complained that the Peace Corps staff in Manila could offer no more helpful advice than "Be creative!" Finally the Peace Corps and the Bureau of Public Schools prepared a joint memorandum providing "guidelines for the utilization of volunteers" and rechristening them "co-teachers." This document helped to clear the air by spelling out the American co-teachers' proper functions, and at the same time expanded the volunteers' role. While some of the

previous misunderstandings have been avoided, and some of the volunteers' frustation at not being fully utilized has abated, there are, of
course, still frictions, particularly since young rural Filipinos, accustomed
to putting the foreigner on a pedestal, are being asked to treat Americans
as equals. Moreover, the very fact that Americans offered assistance implied for many Filipino teachers an assumption of their own inferiority.
Thus, eager PCVs were occasionally greeted by their counterparts with
quiet resentment.

On the whole, however, volunteers were met by such overwhelming
hospitality from the communities to which they were sent that they
found it difficult to get to work. It would have undoubtedly "turned
their heads" more often than it did had it not been for the intensive
cultural orientation which they received before arriving in the Philippines. Peace Corps Volunteers are more deeply immersed in Filipino
society than any other Americans working there today, except for some
missionaries. In part, they have been more cordially received than most
other Americans precisely because they do not live in American com-
pounds or move in American social circles. Their commitment to service
has, in most cases, been obvious. But their immersion would certainly
have produced greater friction and frustration without the carefully
planned training in Philippine language and culture which they were
given.

THE TRAINING PROCESS

Professor George Guthrie of Pennsylvania State University, who organized and guided the program, and David Szanton, a trainee, have
provided excellent critiques of the first training program for a book on
the Peace Corps edited by Professor Robert Textor. Volunteers were
prepared intensively to perceive and appreciate cultural differences. They
were told, for example, that while Americans valued the achievement of
concrete objectives very highly, Filipinos were more concerned with
smooth interpersonal relations; that for Americans personal friendships
were often functionally specific, while Filipinos tended to have long-term
personal alliances for diffuse purposes; or that whereas Americans considered frankness and directness great virtues, Filipinos felt pleasantness
was much more important. The trainees were warned not to be deceived
by the American veneer on Filipino behavior, and advised to spend considerable time learning about their new situation before attempting to
teach or serve. Instructors reminded them that because of cultural differences they should not expect to be able to accomplish too much.
Volunteers, with a few exceptions, were also given initial training in the
dialect of the region to which they were to be sent. Such thorough and
appropriate training has seldom been provided to Americans going to
the Philippines and the volunteers benefited greatly.

Upon arrival in the field they were disappointed to find, however, that none of the staff members in the Manila Peace Corps office had either had the advantage of the volunteers' training or of previous experience in the Philippines. Thus, they were plied with such redblooded American advice as "be perfectly frank," or take the initiative to "get results," and usually found such advice counterproductive. Other volunteers, even without staff advice, remained blind to culture differences and thus never understood Filipino behavior. They suffered over time from what Professor Guthrie calls "culture fatigue." One volunteer described it as "hitting his head against a sponge rubber wall."

ACHIEVEMENTS

On the whole the carefully selected volunteers were able to adjust, were able to appreciate Filipino differences, and were not frustrated by small, yet sometimes significant accomplishment. For most, their own superficial training for teaching duties helped them climb off the "American pedestal." In the final analysis, the most perceptive volunteers discovered that they were effective co-teachers only after they had established warm personal ties with their counterparts—some eventually leading to the altar. They found, in effect, that Filipinos were eager to learn in a Filipino cultural milieu, and could be reached only on those terms. Would that more foreign technicians in other times and places might have learned that lesson!

Despite justified criticisms, then, it is probably accurate to say that the Peace Corps has so far been a success, at least if one takes some of its stated objectives with a grain of salt. Certainly it has marked the highpoint of Philippine-American relations in a period of growing tensions between the two peoples.

Growing Tensions: Some Explanations

War damage has heretofore been included, in the broadest sense, in the category of "aid," although such use of the term would not occur to Filipinos. This facet of the aid relationship has continued to produce tension. Certainly the breakdown of cordiality after the 1962 rejection of the war damage bill was serious, and not just temporary. But the ongoing economic and technical assistance program, declining since 1959, has not and could not have been an important cause of tension in recent years—even though the administrative relations necessary for its implementation inevitably have produced friction. Underlying causes of tension must be found elsewhere.

Relations had warmed again sufficiently by October 1964 for Macapagal to reschedule his state visit, although it was preceded by an announcement that the Philippines would no longer rely upon the United States to look after Philippine interests wherever there were no Philippine diplomatic or consular representatives. But the October attempt to respark the warmth of the "special relationship" was thoroughly negated by the course of events in the succeeding two months.

INCIDENTS ON THE BASES

During November and December there were two separate incidents in which Filipinos were killed by American guards while scavenging in outlying areas of United States bases. The more celebrated was that of Larry Cole, an air force enlisted man, who was so vigilant that even when off duty at Clark Field he shot at trespassers. In this instance he killed a Negrito boy. Under the terms of the bases agreement, which Filipinos had repeatedly sought to change through negotiation, the United States had jurisdiction. There was immediate Filipino anger and agitation. Previous cases were recalled, and some new ones discovered, where American servicemen had been quickly transferred back to the States rather than being tried for the shooting of Filipinos. Apparently in an attempt to relieve the pressure of criticism, Ambassador Blair held a meeting with newsmen in which he described the magnitude of the provocation which pilferage and trespassing posed on the military bases. By way of example, he cited the report of a Filipino guard that a "bomb" had been thrown into a school yard in the Subic Bay Naval Base. The incident was headlined abroad; "Filipinos fail in attempt to bomb school for servicemen's children." Some Filipino newsmen cried "hoax" and claimed the guard lied. In any case, most Filipinos considered the statement a national insult. Before the month was over, Filipinos demonstrating in front of the American Embassy, almost unheard of in Manila, were demanding the withdrawal of United States bases. Although Philippine-American negotiations on the bases jurisdiction question resumed in early January, an even larger anti-American demonstration later that month was extravagantly lauded by the Peking press.

Filipino opinion was mollified somewhat by the meticulous fairness of Cole's courts martial, open to Filipino observers, and his conviction in February for "unpremeditated murder." Some critics complained about the light sentence—three years and dishonorable discharge. Others complained more bitterly about the acquittal of two marines the following month who had been accused of shooting two Filipino fishermen. *The Washington Post* echoed Filipino sentiment: "The U. S. has taken Filipino goodwill too much for granted."

THE JURISDICTION ISSUE

In August 1956 Emmanuel Pelaez, then Senator and head of the Philippine panel negotiating revision of the Military Bases Agreement, had said: "We are all aware there exists a special and unique relationship between the Philippines and the United States. This . . . should result in greater deference to our just claim as a sovereign nation to exercise fully our authority over every inch of our territory [and in] . . . added trust and confidence in our institutions. . . . There should be no fear, for instance, that American servicemen, if brought within the jurisdiction of our courts in appropriate cases, would get something less than complete justice and fairness." Although recognition of just claims should not require a special relationship, it was not until nine years later, in mid-1965, that an exchange of notes revised the jurisdiction provisions of the Military Bases Agreement to give the Philippines, with appropriate exceptions, primary jurisdiction over offenses within the bases. There are indications that such a move had long been advocated by the American Embassy, but opposed by United States military commanders. After more than a decade of rising bitterness the issue had been resolved, giving the Philippines jurisdictional rights comparable to those retained by Japan and NATO nations.

THE NEW NATIONALISM

Although it is now popular to refer to the Philippine variety of nationalism as "late blooming," Filipino nationalism was the first to take root in the soil of Southeast Asia. That it achieved its proximate goal of self-government, for the most part, by 1916 and its ultimate goal, sovereign independence, by 1946—in both cases before other Southeast Asian colonies—naturally produced a nationalism of almost relaxed moderation by Asian standards. Since 1955, however, it has flowered anew.

That year marks a turning point because, from the opening of the Bandung Conference, Filipinos began to have more regular contact with other Asian peoples. Filipino journalists and scholars began to tour Asia. In Operation Brotherhood Filipinos, in a private capacity, became actively concerned with the course of events in Vietnam. In the Southeast Asia Treaty Organization the government also showed a continuing concern. The exchange of state visits in Asia multiplied. Completion of the reparations negotiations was followed by Philippine ratification of the Japanese Peace Treaty, which facilitated greater contact with Japan. In these and other ways, Filipinos began to have a clearer understanding of their own image in Asia. The educational process was jolting. Whereas Filipinos had been billing themselves as the bridge between East and West, they discovered to their chagrin that most other Asians did not consider the Filipino to have even one foot on Eastern shores! Filipinos were accused of being so Western they did not understand Asia!

QUEST FOR A NEW IDENTITY

The self-image of the Filipino elites, if not shattered, was at least badly damaged. Such a traumatic experience caused those who were aware of what had happened to search frantically for a new sense of identity. Among writers and artists this often took the form of looking for new, distinctively Filipino, themes. There was new enthusiasm for the official national language, which was rechristened "Pilipino." Some politicians talked about "Asia for the Asians." Clearly the new identity sought was to be an Asian identity, or an image for Asia. Some historians suggested that wartime ridicule of Western cultural influences in the Philippines may have had a deeper impact than was recognized in the early postwar period when anti-Japanese feeling was intense.

The quest for a new identity, however, could not be complete in positive expressions alone. By its nature, such a quest must negate those elements of tradition which threaten the confidence of the Filipino in his new self-image. And the traditional Filipino ambivalence toward the United States—a combination of respect, even awe, for American accomplishments, and resentment because the Philippines cannot expect to equal them, or perhaps because Filipino values taught other goals—was such a threat. Thus, as the Asian identity of Filipinos was reasserted, American accomplishments and intentions had also to be denigrated.

The assertion of an Asian identity in foreign policy took several forms. In 1961, for instance, the Philippines took the lead in the creation of the Association of Southeast Asia, ASA, composed of Malaya, Thailand, and the Philippines. In 1963 an even bolder step was the attempt to move toward confederation with Indonesia and Malaya in "Maphilindo." Rejection of American advice on the North Borneo claim, changing the date of Independence Day, terminating the special services of the United States foreign service, postponing the President's visit to the United States, and increasing the pressures on American businessmen, all these were the negative aspects of assertion which reflected underlying resentments. Reducing the American connection was an essential prerequisite for creating an Asian image.

If "nationalism" is explained in these terms, it is easy to understand why it has not become a more widespread phenomenon in the countryside. *Provincianos* are not aware of the Philippines' image in Asia; neither are they so affected by the American way of life as to transform the question of cultural identity into a personal psychological problem. Nor does the peasant, like the Manila elite, see Americans as competitors in their political, economic, and social life. Since all political leadership generally participates in the quest for identity, and since there is equal unconcern among the major parties' mass following, this cannot become an important domestic political issue. But the fact that Filipino nationalism is today essentially an elite phenomenon does not mean that it should be of any less importance for the American policy maker. The search for national identity is an inevitable part of the process of decolonialization in the Philippines. The United States cannot positively assist the search, but neither would it be profitable to attempt to frustrate it.

RISE OF THE FILIPINO ENTREPRENEUR

Growing Philippine-American tension is not to be explained solely in terms of ideology or psychology. Solid conflicts of interest are also present. When Ambasador Leon Ma. Guerrero says "July 3, 1974 is the new date we have set for our liberation," he voices not only nationalist sentiment, but the interests of the rising middle class. In 1946, the major interests of Filipino capital were complementary to those of American business. Agricultural exporters were glad to allow "parity" for American investors in exchange for tariff free quotas in the American market. But after a decade and a half of import and exchange controls, subsidized credit, tax moratoria, and increased tariffs designed to stimulate and protect Filipino entrepreneurship, it is not surprising that American and Filipino interests have become sharply competitive. That they are is a tribute to the progress of Philippine economic development. The end of the Laurel-Langley Agreement and of constitutional parity in 1974 is not really a "new date for liberation," but promises to mark the culmination of the process of gaining economic sovereignty, which began at least as far back as 1949. The course of economic nationalism has been closely connected with the steady increase in size and diversity of Filipino firms. When they were smaller and concentrated in importing and retail trade, their main competitors were Chinese. Thus, Professor Remigio Agpalo, in his careful chronicle of the Retail Trade Nationalization Act, concludes that the target of the Act when passed in 1954 was simply the Chinese. Not until it was to be fully implemented in 1964 did Americans also become the target, by means of an unusual definition of "retailing."

Filipinos, whether motivated by patriotism or profit—and often both, are understandably determined to be masters of their own economy. They are wary of the great power of large agglomerations of American capital, and have been willing on occasion to forego foreign investment and development in some fields rather than face the threat of intrenched and extensive foreign control which they feel such development implies. Although they comprise only one-twentieth of Philippine commercial banks and operate only 1 per cent of banking offices, the branches of United States banks which are believed to have liberal access to capital mobilized abroad and to favor credit lines to American firms are increasing objects of dissatisfaction for credit-short Filipino industrialists. The latter are also determined that there shall be no extension of the Laurel-Langley Agreement to enlarge the access of foreign capital to Philippine markets and resources, although the once powerful, but now enfeebled voice of the "sugar bloc" argues for renegotiation of the Agreement. While the State Department has expressed willingness to see the parity provisions lapse, there are some American business figures who are not willing to surrender without a fight.

In the swirl of argumentation which now surrounds the future of

Philippine-American economic relations, a clear understanding of political processes and of cultural differences is essential. First must be the recognition that economic interests are frequently reflected in emotional slogans, as well as in rational arguments. The nationalism of nineteenth century America was occasionally so inspired. One need not find a plot, therefore, to explain how the cry of "economic imperialism," once monopolized by leftist ideologues, has now been taken up by some tycoons. Even *ad hoc* alliances between the two groups are to be expected. But this does not mean that either has abandoned its ultimate goals. Profit, the goal of the tycoon, can be inextricably mixed with patriotism. And this patriotism, by definition emotion, protects him from being pushed too far by cold rationality. When added to these factors are the cultural differences explained above, it should be apparent that Americans who expect Filipino businessmen to speak and act on the basis of the same kind of calculations that would move their American counterparts will be disappointed. They may even be frustrated.

But the attitudes of Americans, with irrational as well as rational foundations, are as significant causes of tensions in the special relationships as are the interests—or the emotions—of Filipinos.

AMERICAN ATTITUDES

Former Vice President Emmanuel Pelaez laid down some excellent ground rules for the conduct of Philippine-American relations when he said: "We must treat each other as equals, not as guardian and ward. Each must refrain from taking the other for granted." He referred obliquely to one of the most common, most justified, and least understood of Filipino complaints. "Taking the Philippines for granted" is a phenomenon with several causes and several manifestations, only a few of which can be noted. Basically, however, they all stem from ignorance of things Filipino.

One form of "taking for granted" is the assumption that "Filipinos love us, they need us, and will always be our friends." Filipino hospitality, which demands the concealment of any hostile feelings toward a guest, has fooled many Americans, including some policy makers. The Filipino was not being insincere by his standards, but merely courteous. For Americans to assume that Filipinos "need us" may be objectively valid, but ignores the fact that a feeling of need is in essence subjective. And it is hard for Americans to empathize with Filipino subjectivity. This attitude leads Americans to repress their irritation with nationalist criticism and to grossly underestimate the political significance of the nationalist movement. "It is not strong enough to be the basis of a winning political campaign, and is therefore not a serious threat to our relations," may be the comment. The policy implication of such an assessment is a tendency to deflate the urgency of Filipino complaints and entreaties.

Ignorance of things Filipino is an even more direct cause for the confusion between the superficialities and the depths of Philippine life. "But, you know, basically Filipinos are just like Americans" is the way a former head of USIS in Manila put it to visiting American journalists. "Little brown American," the derisive phrase reserved by some Filipino news-paper columnists for their worst enemies, is not too far from the image many Americans have of Filipinos. One might say, as some Filipinos do, that the Filipino is at fault for acting this way. Yet Filipino culture *is* an amalgam of Malay, Spanish, and American strains, and the Filipino can only be himself. But it is the responsibility of Americans who must deal with Filipinos, and particularly those in American government agencies, to try to understand this amalgam and to communicate with all levels of Filipino personality, the most important of which is probably the Malay.

Yet no American agency besides the Peace Corps has even begun to construct a training program adequate for the task. Little effort is made to introduce American officials or business executives to the implicit values in Filipino culture or patterns of behavior in any systematic fashion. Moreover, if a foreign service officer should take the initiative to educate himself in these matters, he could only expect to be transferred to another post in compliance with the State Department policy of rota-tion. It will be hard for American diplomats and economic advisors to persuade Filipinos that they are not being taken for granted until more time is spent in the study of Philippine history and culture.

PACE OF DECOLONIALIZATION

Despite an almost tautological ring, it is nevertheless correct to say that one of the most basic causes of tension in the process of decoloniali-zation is the delay in the process itself. The United States was the first colonial power in Asia to give independence to colonial peoples. The easy American abandonment of sovereignty helped to create an atmosphere in which vestiges of the colonial era were tolerated. In the other colonies in Southeast Asia, except for Malaysia, the pace of events was quite different. The colonial desire to hang on generated virulently anti-colonialist revo-lutions. Even after independence the legacy of revolution was a determina-tion to destroy every reminder of the colonial regime. Thus by the late 1950s, when Filipinos were beginning to be exposed to the political currents of the region, they found themselves behind, rather than ahead, in the march of decolonialization. Filipinos could hardly be held re-sponsible for having had a colonial mentor who gave independence "too easily," but many Filipino commentators blamed the state of affairs on the Filipinos' own "colonial mentality." In any case, whatever lethargy may have existed in Philippine government circles in times past, the push for decolonialization is now evident.

American military and economic interests can hardly be blamed, either, for clinging to privileges to which they have become accustomed, and for which they have seldom, until recently, been challenged. Even aid administrators demand a degree of supervision over aid planning and use—first introduced in the early 1950s—which is now inappropriate to the level of Filipino sensibilities. But rights and privileges for American government agencies and private interests in the Philippines can only be justified if they are consistent with the highest goals of worldwide United States policy. The long-range purpose in preserving a democratic Philippines allied to the United States must take precedence over all other American purposes in this nation of islands. Unfortunately, however, this test has yet to be consistently applied.

A Brighter Future

If the explanations here presented are valid, there are grounds for optimism about the future. Almost all of the phenomena identified as causes of tension are either moving in and of themselves toward long-range solution, or are subject to alteration by well intentioned policy makers. The Filipino search for national cultural identity promises to begin to bear fruit. The more successful artists and writers and historians and anthropologists are in discovering distinctively Filipino elements in their own tradition—and in informing the contemporary Filipino about his past—the more secure the Filipino personality will become. A declining dependence on the United States, accompanied by a great variety of contacts with other nations, will contribute to the same end. As Filipinos consciously cultivate an Asian identity it will be easier for Americans to avoid the confusion that "they are just like us." Likewise, the more secure the Filipino entrepreneur becomes the more he can contribute to democratic politics, and the less sensitive he will be to the threat of foreign competition.

Decolonialization does indeed proceed at an increasingly rapid pace. If the Laurel-Langley Agreement is allowed to expire quietly in 1974 and if renegotiation of the Bases Agreement is completed soon, reduced tension in relations between our countries can be expected over the next decade. But a greater American effort to understand Philippine culture and tradition remains to be made if the United States is to gain the potential benefit in good will from any substantive concessions. Before 1955 the consequences of taking the Philippines for granted were minimal. But since the rise of the new nationalism Americans can no longer afford to regard either Filipino interests or Filipino values lightly.

Whatever the advantages that one may discern from future trends, it is hard to find a prescription more appropriate for a relationship which is inevitably special but not necessarily smooth, than that provided by former Vice President Pelaez:

> Only the deliberate cultivation of the interests common to both peoples can keep Philippine-American friendship alive and strong. The condition for

the cultivation of such common interests is the determination of both peoples to observe the rule of mutual respect . . . in their relations with each other. It is easy to establish mutual respect between nations equal in power and influence; between a great nation and a small one a feeling of consideration is needed to redress the balance and to create the condition necessary for mutual respect.

Greater consideration is the requisite duty of the greater power.

Statistical Appendix

Table 1

Selected Comparative Social Statistics
for the United States and the Philippines
(1963, unless indicated)

	United States	Philippines	Ratio U.S./Philippines
Population, mid-year	189,375,000	30,241,000	6.3
Area (sq. km.)	9,363,389	300,000	31.2
Gross National Product ($ billions)	585.1	4.4	134.7
Manufacturing employment (1958)	16,209,000	249,000	65.1
National government expenditure ($ millions)	113,751	475	239.5
Defense expenditure ($ millions)	53,429	70	763.3
Total trade ($ millions)	40,071	1,345	29.8
Trade, per capita ($)	211.6	44.5	4.8
U.S.-Philippines trade, per capita ($)	3.1	19.3	.16
Students in school, all levels (1960, as per cent of population)	22.8	5.3	4.3

Source: Unted Nations, *Statistical Yearbook, 1964.* Philippine pesos converted to dollars at rate of 3.9 pesos per dollar.

Table 2

Population of the Philippines, 1896-1965

Census year	Total population (millions)	Intercensal annual rate of increase (%)	
1896 (estimated)	6.6		
1903	7.6		
		(1903-18)	1.9
1918	10.3		
		(1918-39)	2.2
1939	16.0		
		(1939-48)	1.9
1948	19.2		
		(1948-60)	3.1
1960	27.1		
		(1958-63 estimated)	3.2
1963 (estimated)	30.2		

Source: United Nations, *Demographic Yearbook.*

Table 3

Philippine Real National Income by Industrial Origin (₱ *millions, constant 1955 prices, per cent of total*)

Industrial classification	1949		1955		1960		1964	
Agriculture	2033	(39.8)	3161	(41.4)	3342	(34.3)	3504	(31.0)
Mining	57	(1.1)	121	(1.6)	153	(1.6)	178	(1.5)
Manufacturing	469	(9.2)	1001	(13.1)	1503	(15.4)	1972	(17.5)
Construction	251	(4.9)	230	(3.0)	260	(2.7)	379	(3.4)
Trade	646	(12.7)	861	(11.3)	1081	(11.1)	1408	(12.5)
Transportation and communications	176	(3.5)	250	(3.3)	345	(3.5)	357	(3.2)
Government services	371	(7.3)	648	(8.5)	862	(8.9)	1027	(9.1)
Other services	1103	(21.6)	1352	(17.7)	2183	(22.4)	2476	(21.9)
Total: national income	5106	(100.0)	7624	(100.0)	9729	(100.0)	11301	(100.0)

Source: Republic of the Philippines, National Economic Council, *Statistical Reporter.*

Table 4

Data on the Accumulation of Foreign Investment in the Philippines ($millions)

	As reported by the Central Bank of the Philippines		As reported by the United States Department of Commerce		
	Investment Income due U.S. Investors[a]	Total Direct Foreign Investment in the Philippines[a]	Value of Direct U.S. Investment in the Philippines[b]	U.S. Investors' Share of Undistributed Corporation Earnings[b]	Total of U.S. Investors' Share of Corporation Earnings and Branch Profits[b]
1950	22	13.5	149	11	39
1951	35	5.0	163	9	36
1952	18	5.5	178	6	36
1953	35	29.5	198	5	31
1954	37	37.5	216	8	34
1955	66	56.5	229	15	38
1956	69	54.6	267	22	45
1957	69	47.2	306	21	42
1958	57	20.6	341	29	55
1959	68	36.5	385	22	58
1960	81	28.3	414	21	52
1961	34	—55.6[c]	440	24	63
1962	25	—3.3[c]	375	14	40
1963	22	—2.8[c]	415	16	38

[a] International Monetary Fund, *Balance of Payments Yearbook.*
[b] United States Department of Commerce, *Survey of Current Business.*
[c] Excluding the share accruing to foreign investors of retained earnings of Philippine corporations.

Table 5

Scheduled Collection of Normal Tariff Duties under the Laurel-Langley Agreement

Beginning year	Per cent of Philippine duty collected on imports from the United States	Per cent of United States duty collected on imports from the Philippines.
1956	25	5
1959	50	10
1962	75	20
1965	90	40
1968	90	60
1971	90	80
1974	100	100

Source: Revised United States-Philippine Trade Agreement, September 6, 1965, Article I.

Table 6

United States-Philippine Trade under the Laurel-Langley Agreement ($millions, f.o.b. value, per cent of total)

Period	Total Philippine Imports	Imports into Philippines from the United States		Total Philippine Exports	Exports from Philippines to the U.S.	
		Value	Per Cent of total		Value	Per cent of total
Average 1949-50	464	362	78	289	208	72
Average 1951-54	460	332	72	393	255	65
1955	547	356	65	401	240	60
1956	506	300	59	453	244	54
1957	613	336	55	431	226	53
1958	559	289	52	493	275	56
1959	524	232	44	529	293	55
1960	604	255	42	560	284	51
1961	611	289	47	500	269	54
1962	587	253	43	556	281	51
1963	618	253	41	726	331	46
1964	780	312	40	737	352	48

Source: Central Bank of the Philippines, *Statistical Bulletin*, Volume 16, December 1964.

Table 7

Philippine Exports to the United States and Applicable United States Tariff Rates

($millions, average annual value, f.o.b., for 1963-64)

Commodity	United States Tariff Rate	Philippine Exports United States	World
Sugar	0.428 ¢/lb.	156.7	156.7
Copra	free list	47.2	155.4
Coconut oil	1.0 ¢/lb.	41.7	53.8
Embroideries	40-45 ad valorem most categories	24.3	25.0
Plywood	20% ad valorem	23.3	24.3
Desiccated coconut	1.75 ¢/lb.	15.7	18.6
Concentrates of gold, silver, and copper	free list	11.0	11.3
Abaca fiber	free list	8.7	30.5
Veneer	10 % ad valorem	8.4	8.5
Canned pinapple, juice, and concentrates	0.55 ¢/lb. (canned pineapple)	5.4	9.4
Lumber	1.20 $/1000 bd. ft.	4.8	6.8
Scrap tobacco	12.6 ¢/lb.	4.5	4.8
Chromite ore	free list	4.3	9.9
Copra meal	0.3 ¢/lb.	1.6	10.7
Cordage	2.0 ¢/lb.	.9	2.7
Logs	free list	.8	136.1
Pearl buttons	1.25 ¢/gross plus 25%	.4	.4
Glycerine	0.4 ¢/lb.	.3	1.1
Cigars	1.91 $/lb. plus 10.5%	.3	.5
Shells and mfrs.	free list	.1	.2

Source: Republic of the Philippines, Bureau of Census and Statistics, *Foreign Trade and Navigation of the Philippines.*

Table 8

Philippine Imports from the United States
($millions, average annual value, f.o.b., 1962-64)

Commodity category	Philippine Imports United States	World
Machinery and parts, other than electric	62.4	120.0
Transport equipment	33.3	73.9
Electrical machinery and apparatus	17.0	30.8
Cereals and cereal preparations	16.5	51.1
Textile fibers not manufactured into yarn and thread	16.3	26.0
Base metals, shapes and forms	11.9	59.3
Textile yarns, fabrics, and made-up articles	11.7	18.6
Paper, paperboard, and manufactures	10.7	18.6
Dairy products, eggs, and honey	9.9	24.6
Explosives and miscellaneous chemical materials	9.9	19.8
Mineral fuels, lubricants, and related materials	7.1	67.2
Chemical elements and compounds	7.0	15.9
Manufactures of metals	6.8	17.3
Professional and scientific instruments	3.8	6.8
All other imports	48.5	111.8
Total imports	272.8	661.7

Source: Central Bank of the Philippines, *Statistical Bulletin,* Volume 16 (December 1964), part IV, External Trade.

The American Assembly

The American Assembly holds meetings of national leaders and publishes books to illuminate issues of United States policy. The Assembly is a national, nonpartisan educational institution, incorporated in the State of New York.

The Trustees of the Assembly approve a topic for presentation in a background book, authoritatively designed and written to aid deliberations at national Assembly sessions at Arden House, the Harriman Campus of Columbia University. These books are also used to support discussion at regional Assembly sessions and to evoke consideration by the general public.

All meetings of the Assembly, whether international, national, or local, issue and publicize independent reports of conclusions and recommendations on the topic at hand. Participants in these sessions constitute a wide range of experience and competence.

American Assembly books are purchased and put to use by individuals, libraries, businesses, public agencies, nongovernmental organizations, educational institutions, discussion meetings, and service groups.

The subjects of Assembly studies to date are:

1951——United States—Western Europe Relationships
1952——Inflation
1953——Economic Security for Americans
1954——The United States' Stake in the United Nations
——The Federal Government Service
1955——United States Agriculture
——The Forty-Eight States
1956——The Representation of the United States Abroad
——The United States and the Far East
1957——International Stability and Progress
——Atoms for Power
1958——The United States and Africa
——United States Monetary Policy
1959——Wages, Prices, Profits and Productivity
——The United States and Latin America
1960——The Federal Government and Higher Education
——The Secretary of State
——Goals for Americans
1961——Arms Control: Issues for the Public
——Outer Space: Prospects for Man and Society
1962——Automation and Technological Change
——Cultural Affairs and Foreign Relations
1963——The Population Dilemma
——The United States and the Middle East
1964——The United States and Canada
——The Congress and America's Future
1965——The Courts, the Public, and the Law Explosion
——The United States and Japan
1966——The United States and the Philippines
——State Legislatures in American Politics
——A World of Nuclear Powers?
——Population Dilemma in Latin America
——Collective Bargaining